The Chickenhawk Syndrome

The Chickenhawk Syndrome

War, Sacrifice, and Personal Responsibility

Cheyney Ryan

ROWMAN & LITTLEFIELD PUBLISHERS, INC.
Lanham • Boulder • New York • Toronto • Plymouth, UK

ROWMAN & LITTLEFIELD PUBLISHERS, INC.

Published in the United States of America
by Rowman & Littlefield Publishers, Inc.
A wholly owned subsidiary of The Rowman & Littlefield Publishing Group, Inc.
4501 Forbes Boulevard, Suite 200, Lanham, Maryland 20706
www.rowmanlittlefield.com

Estover Road
Plymouth PL6 7PY
United Kingdom

British Library Cataloguing in Publication Information Available

Library of Congress Cataloging-in-Publication Data:

Ryan, Cheyney, 1948.
  The Chickenhawk syndrome : war, sacrifice, and personal responsibility /
Cheyney Ryan.
    p. cm.
  Includes bibliographical references and index.
  ISBN 978-0-7425-6503-6 (cloth : alk. paper) — ISBN 978-0-7425-6505-0
(electronic)
  1. War and society—United States. 2. Sacrifice—United States. 3.
Responsibility—Social aspects—United States. I. Title.
  HM554.R93 2009
  303.6'6—dc22   2008048467

Printed in the United States of America

⊗™ The paper used in this publication meets the minimum requirements of
American National Standard for Information Sciences—Permanence of Paper
for Printed Library Materials, ANSI/NISO Z39.48-1992.

The kind of war which we are conducting is an enterprise that the American government does not have to carry on with the hearty cooperation of the American people but only with their acquiescence. And that acquiescence seems sufficient to float an indefinitely protracted war for vague or even largely uncomprehended and unaccepted purposes. Our resources in men and materials are vast enough to organize the war-technique without enlisting more than a fraction of the people's conscious energy.

—Randolph Bourne, "A War Diary"

Some of you may die, but that is a sacrifice I am willing to make.

—Shrek

Contents

Preface

This book was written in the shadow of the Iraq War and America's broader War on Terror. It embodies the conviction that war remains the most pressing problem of our time. The Iraq conflict is unique in many ways. I can think of no historical precedent for a nation's responding to an attack on its shores (9/11) by invading a country that had absolutely nothing to do with it (Iraq). Next to this, the Vietnam War looks like the cube of good sense. The Vietnam War was allegedly about stopping communism. However one judges that war, at least "communism" existed. The same cannot be said for Iraq's "weapons of mass destruction." The Iraq conflict will soon be the second most expensive war America has fought. We may never know the number of lives it has cost. We may never grasp the ruin it has inflicted on that nation and its region. Mindful of such facts, this book seeks to be logical but not dispassionate. I do not try to hide my distress at these events or my fears for the soul of our country. Political philosophy analyzes arguments and assesses facts; it is also a form of bearing witness to its time—for us, a time of war.

The Iraq War has brought to light a striking fact about our nation. Americans are fond of war but have little interest in its sacrifices. The vast majority of Americans have zero interest in fighting it themselves. This is the heart of the *chickenhawk syndrome* addressed in these pages. A chickenhawk is someone who champions war but avoids its costs. George W. Bush is the most celebrated chickenhawk. But a central claim of this book is that the chickenhawk syndrome is a central feature of our time that will not disappear with Bush. Rather, Bush symbolizes a fact about Americans generally: we have become detached from the conflicts that are waged in our name. We no longer approach war as a matter of personal responsibility but assume that its costs will be born by others. We live in a time of what I call *alienated war*. The chickenhawk stands as the symbol of this.

Does the solution lie in *un*alienated war? The chickenhawk syndrome marks a dramatic departure from the citizen-soldier ideal that informed America's thinking about war and military service until recently. The demise of that ideal is explored in this book. Proponents of that ideal believed that sharing the sacrifices of war would make us more prudent in our decisions. They hoped that a more responsible approach to war would mean less war. The Iraq War has shown that we certainly need more responsibility in these matters. But what we need, most of all, is a stronger commitment to seeking nonviolent solutions to our problems. The solution to alienated war is a world in which war is no longer considered a responsible option.

What follows is a recent product. But I have been thinking about these issues for a long time. Like others of my generation, I was first confronted with the issue of war and personal responsibility by the Vietnam War. The possibility of fighting, even dying, in a pointless criminal war can focus one's thoughts. The views in these pages on war and responsibility were foreshadowed by a letter I wrote to my draft board many years ago explaining why I regarded its system of deferments as unjust and hence was refusing their student deferment. My draft board did not think it necessary to respond to my views on war and responsibility. They did oblige me by immediately reclassifying me 1-A (draft eligible). I now regard my actions as rather impetuous (young men have delusions of invincibility, as the military knows). But the sentiment was right. For me, as for others, the issue of war and personal responsibility faded with the end of the Vietnam War and the end of the draft. But the issues posed by Vietnam were never resolved, just ignored. We of the Vietnam generation have a special obligation to rectify this fact now that members of our generation have led the nation into the most pointless war in its history.

My parents were the source of my thinking about war. My mother, Jessica Cadwalader Ryan, was a Quaker who regarded all war as immoral. My father, Robert Ryan, believed that people should fight their own fights; hence, if you believed in a war, you should be ready to fight it yourself. This prompted him to enlist in the Marine Corps in World War II, though he was well beyond draft age. A Quaker and a Marine may seem an odd fit. But they agreed in matters of personal responsibility. For my mother, war's immorality was in part a matter of the irresponsibility with which it was fought—the fact that those who championed war rarely bore its consequences. For her, war was not a story of people fighting their own fights. It was one of the privileged sending others to pay the costs while they reaped the benefits and attacked the patriotism of others along the way. For reasons I wish I knew (they both passed away long ago), Dad's experience in the Marine Corps convinced him that Mom was right about all this. He returned from war a pacifist. Together they taught me that promoting peace was also a matter of personal responsibility. I was blessed by their love and wisdom.

ACKNOWLEDGMENTS

This book began as an article—"War without Sacrifice? The Loss of Personal Responsibility," published in the journal *The Responsive Community* in the winter of 2003. As I note in the introduction, it was the response to that article that inspired me to develop its claims further. Conversations with James O'Fallon and Hans Christopherson were important in the early stages. Henry Shue and David Rodin helped clarify my thinking about military service and shared sacrifice in the later stages of this project. This book was completed while I was a visitor at Oxford University in 2007–2008. I am indebted to Merton College and its Warden, Professor Dame Jessica Rawson, for their great hospitality, and the Oxford Leverhulme Program on the Changing Character of War and its director, Professor Hew Strachan, for their support. Lectures based on this material were given at Oxford University, Vanderbilt University, the University of Maryland, the North American Society for Social Philosophy, Linfield College (as the Powell Lectures), Gettysburg College, and Oregon State University. I am especially indebted to the comments of Ken Pendleton, Steve Stern, Bill Uzgalis, and Teresa Amott. Material from chapter 4 was presented as a symposium paper at the American Philosophical Association, Pacific Division. I am indebted to Rahul Kumar and George Klosko for their comments. Jim Sterba was key in helping this book see the light of day. Rob Gould and Howard Zinn read the manuscript and provided valuable comments. Ross Miller, Melissa McNitt, and the editors at Rowman & Littlefield have been a great help. I have also benefited from discussions with students in my undergraduate political philosophy class, some of whom were headed to Afghanistan or Iraq or had just returned. I am especially indebted to my former student Michael Brown. Tamsen Morgan, Carolynn Langston, and Aimee Clott assisted me with the manuscript.

Sandy Ryan has been a source of insight and support from the start of this project. My greatest debt is to the late Henry Alexander, my colleague at the University of Oregon and a Marine Corps veteran of World War II's Pacific theater. Henry and I discussed issues of war and responsibility and many other things in our weekly luncheons over many years. His

great good humor and love of life were grounded in a profound serious-
ness about our mission on this earth. He was a constant source of good
advice and sound moral judgment and an unwavering supporter of my
attempts to wed academic life and social activism. I will always miss him.
I dedicate this book to his memory.

Introduction: Bowling Alone, Bombing Together

There should be a law, I thought. If you support a war, if you think it's worth the price, that's fine, but you have to put your own precious fluids on the line. You have to head for the front and hook up with an infantry unit and help spill the blood. And you have to bring along your wife, or your kids, or your lover. A *law*, I thought.

—Tim O'Brien, *The Things They Carried*

"Chickenhawk" (definition): Someone who vigorously endorses a war and its sacrifices while diligently *avoiding* such sacrifices himself.

THE AIMS OF THIS BOOK

It may be laid down as a primary position, and the basis of our system, that every Citizen who enjoys the protection of a free Government, owes not only a proportion of his property, but even his personal service to the defense of it.

—George Washington[1]

The "chickenhawk" issue first surfaced in the 1980s in relation to bellicose supporters of Ronald Reagan who had avoided military service in Vietnam or, in some cases, Korea.[2] It arose later that decade with the vice-presidential nomination of Dan Quayle. Dormant in the 1990s, it reemerged with George W. Bush, Dick Cheney, and their hawkish neoconservative allies, most of whom had histories of avoiding combat

1

service.[3] Since 9/11, the issue has expanded to include the children and close family members of prowar political leaders. These leaders call for a global War on Terror in Iraq, Afghanistan, and elsewhere. They celebrate the virtues of sacrifice with policies that impose great burdens on those who fight these wars. Yet their own children do not serve, nor do they encourage their children to serve. The sacrifices of war are something to be born by others.

The chickenhawk charge is a recurring one, especially in the popular media.[4] It is also a controversial one—one that conservatives and some liberals reject as foul play. They insist that it is no real argument at all, only name-calling. Not untypical are dismissals of it as "the substitution of reaction for thinking."[5] Columnist Jeff Jacoby writes, "It isn't an argument. It is a slur—a dishonest and incoherent slur. . . . Those who cackle 'Chickenhawk!' are not making an argument. They are merely trying to stifle one, and deserve to be ignored."[6] Andrew Cline, in *The American Spectator*, claims, "The charge is a toothless epithet that nonetheless has gained currency among certain circles on the left because it has a seductive appeal to the illogical."[7] Professor Eliot Cohen wrote in September 2002, "Like most slurs, it works because it is both ugly and faintly amusing," while noting that "prominent Vietnam veterans have begun to hurl the epithet (or circumlocutions for it), and they are serious people."[8] *National Review* author Jonah Goldberg terms it a form of "bullying."[9]

Christopher Hitchens has gone so far as to charge that those who raise questions about the children of today's leaders are calling for a return to pagan rituals of child sacrifice. "Oh, Jesus," he states: "Another barrage of emotional tripe about sons. From every quarter, one hears that the willingness to donate a male child is the only test of integrity." All this talk about the children of leaders serving is only a "cheap emotional stunt."[10]

Many on the left have also voiced doubts about the charge. Matthew Yglesias writes in *The American Prospect*, "The simple cry of, 'If you like the war so much, why don't you fight it?' has become as disreputable among the pundit class as it is popular in the liberal blogosphere." He confesses, "As a matter of logic, the chicken-hawk argument is weak." It's a "tempting rhetorical ploy that in practice proves almost nothing."[11]

This book argues that the chickenhawk issue is a real one. It is not an incoherent slur, toothless epithet, or rhetorical ploy. Nor is it a purely partisan issue, involving a few politicians we don't like. The chickenhawk syndrome raises important ethical questions of war and personal responsibility. It raises basic political questions about the citizenry's connection—or lack thereof—to the wars that are fought in its name.

War and Personal Responsibility

This war must be personalized.

—Congressman Jack Murtha

How should we think of our responsibilities in wartime?

The most famous discussion of this, Henry David Thoreau's, approached the question from the standpoint of what it means to oppose a war. He asked about our responsibilities if our government is waging a war that we reject. He insisted that we must be ready to sacrifice for our own beliefs to bring the war to an end. Philosophers have had lots to say about Thoreau's question. But what if the war is one we *endorse*—or think we do? What are our responsibilities then? The question is a crucial one. War is society's most serious endeavor. Our support for a war can hinge on whether we accept the responsibilities it imposes. Yet political philosophers have had little to say about what those responsibilities are. They are no different than most people in ignoring the issue.

What does endorsing a war mean for my own personal sacrifice? The chickenhawk's answer is this: nothing at all. Figures like Bush, Quayle, Cheney, and others see *no* relation between their wholehearted support for a war and their own willingness to serve in it or have their children serve. Their position is that endorsing a war implies nothing about one's own sacrifices; indeed, one can do everything one can to avoid such sacrifices. But even speaking of their "position" may put things too positively. A striking fact about today's chickenhawks is how little they have thought about the issue of responsibility in the past or now. "I don't have to fight in the wars that I endorse. I don't even have to think about it."

Thus stated, many will be troubled by such thinking. In my view, the problem is that it makes war too *easy*. War is more attractive when it does not involve personal sacrifice. Endorsing war can be a casual, thoughtless affair when it is detached from any question of one's own responsibilities. This is why the founders of the republic sought to maintain a tight link between war and sacrifice. The monarchies of Europe had become casual about war because its costs were sheltered from people. Past philosophers like Kant held that the link between war and sacrifice made republics more peacelike than other societies. Concern about detaching war and sacrifice has been a recurring theme of antiwar thinkers. An astute critic of modern war, Randolph Bourne, wrote almost a century ago in his "A War Diary,"

> We are learning that war doesn't need enthusiasm, doesn't need conviction, doesn't need hope, to sustain it. And that is why this war, with apathy rampant, is probably going to act just as if every person in the country were filled with patriotic ardor. . . . Our war is teaching us that patriotism is

really a superfluous quality in war. The government of a modern organized
plutocracy does not have to ask whether the people want to fight or understand what they are fighting for, but only whether they will tolerate fighting.
America does not co-operate with the President's designs. She rather feebly
acquiesces.[12]

The disconnection of war and sacrifice has been a prominent issue in
the Iraq War, especially among the families of the fallen. Fiorela Valdez,
whose twenty-year-old sister Ramona was killed in Iraq, challenged
President Bush, "Why doesn't he send his daughters over there?" Rose
Gonzales, from Somerville, Massachusetts, whose mother was deployed
to Iraq, remarked, "I don't think you should be so 'rah-rah' for a war that
you aren't willing to send your own family members to."[13]

The challenge for political philosophy is to fill these worries out. What's
wrong with detaching the issue of war from one's own personal sacrifice?
Why shouldn't we *all* be chickenhawks—people who call for war and
then avoid its costs? The questions here are practical ones, but they raise
fundamental issues of political theory about the meaning of citizenship
and the nature of war as a collective endeavor. Addressing these questions is the first aim of this book.

My aims are not purely critical, though. By negative example, the chickenhawk challenges us to think about how we *should* think about war and
personal responsibility. If my country goes to war, for reasons I support,
should I offer my services or encourage my loved ones to do so? If I am
not willing to serve or have my loved ones do so, should this impact my
support for a war? My answer will echo the sentiments of Tim O'Brien,
cited previously. You should endorse a war only if you would be willing
to fight in, even die in, the war yourself (or have your loved ones do so).
I call this the "Murtha test" after Congressman Jack Murtha, who has
voiced similar sentiments. It is a demanding test—and purposefully so.
War has become too impersonal for most Americans. This test obliges us
to personalize it. Arguing for it is another aim of this book.

When I first started thinking about these matters, I didn't think they
needed much argument. Indeed, I thought they were trivial: "*Obviously*
endorsing a war means the willingness to fight in it yourself!" (Just as
endorsing a tax means the willingness to pay it oneself.) Talking to my
students, I discovered that it wasn't obvious at all to them. Many saw
no connection at all between supporting a war and their own sacrifice.
I learned that many in my own profession saw no connection either. A
distinguished philosopher charged that the logic behind the Murtha test
would mean "the end of society itself" since the whole *point* of society
was getting other people to do what you wouldn't do yourself. I realized
that there were larger issues involved about the nature of war and per-

sonal responsibility. I also learned, from exploring the matter historically, that my way of thinking was closer to how many of the founders of the United States thought about things. My argument thus appeals to both philosophical and historical considerations.

Alienated War

The normative issues I address raise larger political and historical questions about the country's relation to war making.

A chickenhawk, I've said, is someone who sees no relation between his wholehearted support for a war and his own willingness to sacrifice.[14] Thus construed, is today's average American so very different? Does the average citizen see any connection between endorsing a war and serving in it him- or herself? The evidence suggests not. War has become an abstraction for most people—something that other people fight, in lands they cannot identify, for reasons they barely understand. We have entered an age of *alienated war*. Exploring its nature and origins is another aim of this book.

Alienated war reflects America's schizophrenic attitude to war generally. The United States is currently the only advanced Western country where public figures routinely exalt the military. As Tony Judt has noted, "Politicians in the US surround themselves with the symbols and trappings of armed prowess; even in 2008 American commentators excoriate allies that hesitate to engage in armed conflict." Neoconservatives go so far as to claim that "war and conflict are things Americans understand— in contrast to naive Europeans with their pacifistic fantasies."[15] Yet the same neoconservatives—and Americans generally—evidence little interest in fighting war themselves. They increasingly turn to mercenaries to fight their wars for them. There is something pornographic in this fixation with practices from afar, performed by paid surrogates, with no interest in performing them oneself. The upshot is a form of national hypocrisy that verges on the obscene.

The specter of alienated war has been a recurring theme in antiwar circles. George Orwell's *1984* was one portrayal of it. He envisioned a world in which war was a constant presence and means of social control but no one knew whom the war was against or where it was being fought or even who was fighting it. One could not tell if there was really any war at all or if it was only a myth. Our most perceptive critic of alienated war was Randolph Bourne, who was both a moralist and a social theorist. Bourne was offended by alienated war but was convinced that moral appraisal needed augmenting by social analysis, lest all we have is moral indignation. I share this view. Explaining what's wrong with alienated war means exploring where it came from and how it became so accepted.

Bourne challenged the irresponsibility of alienated war. But his aim was not to make war "better" by improving its moral tone, nor is mine. Bad wars are not made better by being fought enthusiastically. Vietnam would still have been a tragedy if the chickenhawks of that era had stepped forward to fight it. Iraq would still be a disaster if the chicken-hawks of today behaved differently. We shall explore the significance of chickenhawk behavior, past and present. But the larger issue pertains to our relation to war generally. Americans like the idea of war but don't want to fight it themselves. Ours is a credit card mentality: we buy the war but avoid the cost. We are massively enabled in this regard by our government's efforts to obscure those costs. The solution lies in not buy-ing war in the first place. Americans are right to reject the sacrifices of needless war. We should simply be consistent and not impose those costs on others. The solution to alienated war is not *un*alienated war. The solu-tion lies in finding other ways to resolve our problems.

The (Alienated) War President

By the time these words are printed, the long dark night of George W. Bush's presidency will be over. It would be wrong to assume that these issues will disappear with him. Today's prowar youth who fail to serve should be held accountable for this in the future, especially if they are as-piring leaders. The same holds for parents that expect other people's chil-dren to fight and die in the wars that they endorse. Alienated war is not the product of George W. Bush's personality, nor will it disappear when more principled leaders are elected. It is the product of political decisions over decades that will not be unraveled soon. Finally, the chickenhawk problem is not a matter of Republicans versus Democrats. Liberal elites have no more interest than conservative ones in serving themselves or having their children serve. They differ on many issues. They agree that war is something to be fought by someone else.

It is important not to personalize issues too much. Yet presidents are symbols, especially in matters of war. George Washington affirmed the primacy of the civilian over the military in a republic by returning to pri-vate life after the Revolution. John F. Kennedy exemplified the "Greatest Generation's" ethic of shared sacrifice by serving in combat even though he was a child of privilege. Both symbolized aspects of our citizen-soldier tradition.

Bush's importance is like Richard Nixon's—in symbolizing where the nation has gone wrong. Most U.S. presidents never saw war. Nor was Bush the first president to have avoided war. Bill Clinton did. But Clinton avoided a war that he opposed. George W. Bush was the first president in our history to have strongly supported a war while doing everything he could to avoid fighting in it. Then he went on to fashion himself a "war president," with all the martial trappings. Sometimes the personality of a president is a prism through which the pathologies of the time can be perceived. The dark side of Andrew Jackson reflected the disturbing racial attitudes of the country that elected him. Bush's hypocrisy should be taken in the same way.

There are aspects of the Nixon presidency that students today find unbelievable. They cannot believe that Nixon was elected president in 1968 on the basis of a "secret plan" to end the war in Vietnam. How could the American people have been so gullible? I suspect that aspects of Bush and his administration will strike future students in the same way; perhaps this is why the American people were already trying to forget they elected him the last two years of his presidency. Shouldn't we forget him too? To me, this is all the more reason to reflect on what his presidency signified about the nation that elected him.

George W. Bush was the first true president of alienated war—an age in which bellicose leaders send others to die while their own children party, in which corporate warriors are paid to fight the wars that prowar youth avoid, and in which recruiting standards are relaxed via "moral waivers" to entice criminals, neo-Nazis, and skinheads into becoming "America's finest." He symbolized what society has become or will become if the corruption that he represented is not addressed.

WHATEVER HAPPENED TO THE CITIZEN-SOLDIER?

> Rich kids will not pay [for the war against Iraq]; their daddies' will get them deferments as big George did for George W.
>
> —Representative Peter Stark of California

War is society's most serious endeavor. No other government decision can affect the individual citizen more, and no other decision implicates every citizen more deeply. The question of war and personal responsibility stands at the center of sober citizenship. Yet that question is foreign to most Americans. My experience teaching in a large public university leads me to conclude that many young people find it strange, to the point of bizarre: what does my country's going to war have to do with *me*?

The Civic Republican Heritage

This was not always so. There is always a danger of romanticizing earlier times.[16] But at the nation's founding, the dominant "citizen-soldier" ethic held that war should be the responsibility of every citizen. War should be fought by ordinary citizens, and the country should go to war *only* if ordinary citizens were ready to fight it. Such thinking was a legacy of what political theorists call the "civic republican tradition" that influenced the founding generation. It was pervasive throughout the ranks of the Continental Army that fought the American Revolution.[17] In its original form, the ethic held that Americans would prove they *deserved* their own country by how they fought for it. Americans would not hire mercenaries, like the British. They would serve themselves and do so willingly. The "virtue of his service lay in his desire to serve," according to one commentator; "the worth of American ideals would be demonstrated by every citizen's willingness to fight for them in person."[18] For some, God himself had chosen America to exemplify this ethic of shared sacrifice. Hence, to forsake it would invite eternal damnation. "A man who forfeited his birthright of personal responsibility fell into a sleep which might doom him—in this world, or in the one to come."[19]

Today, most Americans know about the citizen-soldier tradition from the nostalgia for the so-called Greatest Generation that was strong in the 1990s. In Tom Brokaw's book and Steven Spielberg's *Saving Private Ryan*, the World War II generation was celebrated as the opposite of the chickenhawk generation. War meant everyone doing his or her part, without coercion or complaint, the privileged alongside the less advantaged. In a nationally broadcast speech of 1942, President Franklin Roosevelt spoke of how "every loyal American is aware of his individual responsibility":

> Whenever I hear anyone saying, "The American people are complacent— they need to be aroused," I feel like asking him to come to Washington to read the mail that floods into the White House and into all departments of this government. The one question that recurs through all these thousands of letters and messages is, "What more can I do to help my country in winning this war?"[20]

Roosevelt encouraged Americans to share in the financial burdens of war by changing their personal habits. They should avoid installment buying and pay off their debts, lest war spending have an inflationary impact.

The citizen-soldier ethic always had two sides to it. In early civic republican thinkers like James Harrington, its prowar dimension prevailed. Citizen-soldiers were praised for their manly "martial virtue" that sought fulfillment and excitement in battle. The citizen-soldier ethic rendered society as a whole more fit for war. People of my generation will associate this orientation with old John Wayne movies, where being a "real man" and a "real American" meant running off to war on a moment's notice. This actually had little to do with America's founding ideology. The citizen-soldier ethic ensconced in the American Constitution aimed to make war making more difficult, not less.[21] Empires like the British were seen as inherently warlike because hiring mercenaries shielded the country from war's true costs. By contrast, in a republic, war's costs in bodies and treasure would be born by ordinary citizens, thus ensuring that ordinary citizens would think twice about going to war needlessly.

Its antiwar dimension explains why the citizen-soldier model has always been favored by the antiwar left. The First International proclaimed that the decision to wage war should be made by those who would actually have to fight it. It railed against those who called for war but "exempted themselves from the impost of blood."[22] French socialist Jean Jaures, a leading European pacifist of the early twentieth century, held in *Democracy and Military Service* that a citizens militia would ensure that only defensive wars were fought. The major American antiwar voices of the time, William Jennings Bryan and Eugene Debs, held the same view.[23] Even Mohandas Gandhi maintained that if society insisted on a military, the citizen-soldier model was the least bellicose.[24]

The citizen-soldier ethic has meant that war *avoidance* has always been an issue. In a famous polemic that ignited our revolution, Thomas Paine wrote, "The summer soldier and the sunshine patriot will, in this crisis, shrink from the service of their country; but he that stands by it now, deserves the love and thanks of man and woman." The "sunshine patriot" was Paine's term for a chickenhawk—someone who talked the talk of patriotism but refused to walk the walk. Civil War General William Tecumseh Sherman said, "It is only those who have neither fired a shot nor heard the shrieks and groans of the wounded who cry aloud for blood, more vengeance, more desolation." At World War I's start, a leading congressman charged, "Let me once again remind the House that it takes neither moral nor physical courage to declare a war for others to fight." During the Korean War, Congressman Andrew Jacobs branded as "war wimps" zealous supporters of the Cold War who had avoided service there.

The question of the children of leaders serving has also been an issue. There was popular hostility in the American Revolution toward those who did not encourage their own children to serve.[25] During the Civil War, the reluctance of Abraham Lincoln's oldest son, Robert, to serve was the subject of much criticism, even from friendly press. When one senator pressed Mrs. Lincoln on the question, she replied, "Robert is making his preparations now to enter the Army; he is not a shirker—if fault there be it is mine."[26] The term "shirker," like "slacker," was coined for war avoiders. The affluent could buy their way out of the Civil War, a fact that later generations judged harshly. Theodore Roosevelt's father paid to avoid fighting. Roosevelt's shame at this drove his own desire to serve. When he was older than many of today's hawks, Roosevelt quit civilian life to organize a regiment for the Spanish-American War—the famous "Rough Riders." His sons agreed that service was not only for society's outcasts. One son, Quinton, was killed in action in World War I. Another, Theodore Roosevelt Jr., was wounded in World War I. He returned in World War II to land with the troops at Normandy and became the oldest soldier to earn the Congressional Medal of Honor at age fifty-four. His third son, Archie, was declared 100 percent disabled after World War I yet returned to serve in World War II, becoming the only soldier to be classified 100 percent disabled twice in his career. All of President Franklin Roosevelt's sons served in World War II. In her diary, Eleanor Roosevelt wrote,

> I think my husband would have been very much upset if the boys had not wanted to go into the war immediately, but he did not have to worry very much because they either were already in before the war began, or they went in immediately.[27]

Senator Leveret Saltonstall of Massachusetts; Governor Herbert Lehman of New York; Joseph Kennedy, former ambassador to Britain; and Harry Hopkins, one of Roosevelt's closest advisers, all had sons who died in the war.

Who Me?

Contrast these attitudes with those of today. In the 2008 primaries, presidential candidate Mitt Romney was challenged at an "Ask Mitt Anything" session on why none of his five military-aged sons were serving their country. Romney supported Iraq policies that required many more soldiers in a military already desperate for recruits. At the time of the question-and-answer session, 1,100 Massachusetts National Guard were serving in Iraq. As governor, Romney aggressively promoted National Guard recruitment. Yet when the issue of his own sons' serving was raised at the "Ask Mitt Anything" event, the question was met with loud hisses from the conservative crowd. When Romney replied, "No, I have not urged my own children to enlist. I don't know the status of my childrens' potentially enlisting in the Guard and Reserve," his voice was "tinged with anger."[28] Subsequent press accounts dwelled on the "unfairness" of the question. Conservative pundit Lisa De Pasquale wrote that the question proved that "liberals don't care whether a person is qualified because winning the war isn't their goal. It's not about victory for America, it's about making conservatives pay politically."[29] Romney subsequently defended his sons by insisting, "It's remarkable how we can show our support for our nation, and one of the ways my sons are showing support for our nation is helping to get me elected, because they think I'd be a great president."

He noted that one of his sons had recently bought a Winnebago and was visiting ninety-nine counties on his behalf.

Things have certainly changed. Mrs. Lincoln and Mrs. Roosevelt could be grilled on their sons' military service or lack thereof. But it's "unfair" to question Mitt Romney. Most striking of all is the fact that, judging from his response, Romney had never even thought about his sons' serving or thought to raise the issue with them. No one in the press thought to query him about this, either. What attitude does this express?

A strange one, I think. We still call military service "service." We invoke the language of the citizen-soldier tradition to praise it—the language of "sacrificing for one's country" and so on. In practice, the military is now regarded as an alternative lifestyle that people choose for idiosyncratic reasons and that does not admit of appraisal or even questioning. Asking about it is seen as inappropriate, in bad taste, and not done in polite circles, especially of public figures. In short, our society views military service much like liberals view sexual orientation. It is a purely private matter that no one should presume to question or influence.

This is an odd way to view what many regard as the highest form of public service. It is especially odd for conservatives. Columnist David Brooks praises fellow conservatives for having brought responsibility back into government. George Will bemoans the penchant of Americans to become "more individualistic, more self-absorbed, more whiny, in a sense, more of a crybaby nation."[30] Conservatives insist that parental guidance should be a major factor in shaping behavior. But when it comes to military service, their stance is "do your own thing." They insist that sexual behavior should be a matter of public scrutiny, but military service a private matter. They treat sex as a matter of principle but military service as a matter of lifestyle. They urge us to "support the troops." But lacking any sense of personal responsibility, this is like building an abstinence campaign around "support the abstinent."

Conservative hypocrisy on this is so familiar and all pervasive that we do not even notice it. The only parallel I can think of is legalized segregation prior to the civil rights movement, which had become such an entrenched part of American society that the hypocrisy it represented was taken for granted. Starting with Ronald Reagan, the modern conservative movement has been built around belief in a strong military and the virtues of personal initiative. It has never connected these two concerns, though, by encouraging people to join the military despite decades of trashing 1960s antiwar activists for their failure to serve. Conservatives sponsor scores of websites promoting abstinence that provide advice to young people on pursuing this difficult choice. They do not sponsor a single website encouraging military enlistment. George W. Bush completed his presidency without ever publicly asking young people to join the military. It's as if the modern liberal movement had been built around raising inheritance taxes, but when they were finally raised, liberals flatly refused to pay them.

The conservative discourse of responsibility has often had a racial dimension to it. Going back to Ronald Reagan's attack on "welfare queens," their values talk has inordinately stigmatized single mothers, minorities, and illegal aliens for not being responsible citizens. Yet these are the groups that are most willing to serve, while the children of conservative leaders stay home. The very first casualty in Iraq was Jose Guiterrez, a Guatemalan orphan and noncitizen raised in Los Angeles. As of November 2003, 36,000 members of the armed forces were noncitizens (5 percent of active-duty members), as were 12,000 members of the reserves. In the late spring of 2007, when the new immigration bill was stalled in Congress, senior U.S. defense officials urged Congress to fast-track a section of the bill that would allow them to recruit more illegal aliens into the military. The "Development, Relief and Education for Alien Minors," or "DREAM," provision in the bill was expected to boost military recruiting by allowing illegal aliens to enlist as a way to obtain citizenship. These are the very same groups the self-proclaimed "Minutemen" in the Southwest work to keep out. If they ever succeeded, some of these "Minutemen" might face the prospect of serving in Iraq themselves.[31]

Breaking the Silence

Conservatives may be hypocritical on these matters. But a central claim of this book is that the problem transcends political differences. I speak of a chickenhawk syndrome to mark the fact that it pervades the country as a whole, affecting both left and right.

Every major Democrat supported and still supports the war in Afghanistan. In 2007, all the major Democratic candidates supported the War on Terror. Hillary Clinton, John Edwards, and Barack Obama all promised that, if elected, they would expand the size of the military. Clinton declared it was "past time to increase the end-strength of the army and marines." Edwards called for a "substantial increase." Obama's program specified the addition of 92,000 soldiers. Both Clinton and Edwards had military-age children. Neither showed the slightest inclination to urge his or her own children to enlist.

In 2004, John Kerry ran against Bush promising to *raise* troop levels in Iraq by 40,000. That's a lot of troops when recruitment is down. Kerry made much of his own war record. He showed zero interest in encouraging his own military-age daughters to become one of those 40,000 new troops. Barack Obama's campaign called for a renewed focus on Afghanistan as the conflict escalated there. He has repeated this call since his election. Obama's appeal to youthful idealism has been likened to John F. Kennedy's. If Afghanistan is such a noble conflict, he should follow Kennedy's example and invoke that idealism in calling on young people to volunteer for Afghanistan, given the dearth of soldiers. One suspects that he didn't do this during the campaign because it would have been political suicide.

I have spoken of Romney's sons, but there is no discernible difference between them and secretary of state designate Hillary Clinton's daughter. Not long after 9/11, while attending Oxford University, Chelsea Clinton wrote in *Talk* magazine that "for most young Americans I know, 'serving' in the broadest sense now seems like the only thing to do." She voiced doubt about the importance of traditional careers given the challenges to America. "Is banking what's important right now?" she asked, skeptically.[32] Then, on leaving Oxford, she became—a banker. No one thought to query Senator Clinton about her daughter, even though, by the spring of 2007, 160,000 female soldiers had served in Iraq and Afghanistan (compared with 7,500 who served in Vietnam) and 10 percent of all soldiers in Iraq were female.

Any parent can understand the reluctance to have a child serve in wartime, especially a daughter. Statistics show an alarming rate of sexual abuse in combat zones. A Defense Department study of female veterans reported that 30 percent of a representative sample said they experienced rape or attempted rape during their service. Of them, 37 percent reported that they were raped multiple times, and 14 percent said they had been gang raped. Studies suggest that the rate of posttraumatic stress disorder (PTSD) among women soldiers is twice that of male soldiers. Twenty-five percent of female Vietnam vets suffered PTSD. Predictions are that the rate of Iraq female vets will be much higher given their closer relation to combat.[33] A study solicited by CBS News showed that veterans of the Middle East conflict were twice as likely to commit suicide as nonveterans. In 2007, a Veteran Affairs Department estimate said that 5,000 ex-servicemen and women would commit suicide that year because of postcombat problems.[34] We can understand why Clinton or Kerry did not want their daughters subjected to this. But endorsing war means asking *other* people's children to fight. The military might take these problems more seriously if it knew that the daughters of elites were affected. Male soldiers might think twice about sexual abuse if they knew the victim might be the daughter of a presidential contender.

Most discouraging to me personally has been the response of fellow progressives to the claim that if you endorse a war, you should be willing to fight it yourself. My experience is that many of them regard my raising the question of war and personal responsibility as a form of patriotic drumbeating, or a call for people to be *more* warlike. This concern might make sense if all progressives were pacifists, but they are not. Some of the strongest antiwar voices supported the war on Afghanistan. Almost all progressives support military action in some instances—to stop genocide or to address certain political injustices, as in the invasion of Haiti, and so on. This is fine, but then they too must consider their own responsibility to fight in these conflicts or encourage their loved ones to do so.[35] They condemn some wars and approve others. But, like everyone else, they do not want to discuss their own responsibility here.

More generally, the left has lost interest in how wars are fought. In the Vietnam era, the left was deeply critical of the draft. But it also worried about the alternative. Some of the strongest voices against ending the draft charged that it would create a military composed mainly of the poor and minorities, as it did to a great extent. After Vietnam, though, the question of who should fight our wars vanished from progressive thinking. Most leftists oppose a draft, and most find the volunteer approach inequitable, but none of them show the slightest interest in finding an alternative. If leftists think that war is a viable option, they should think about their own responsibility to serve. If war is not something they would serve in, they should cease regarding it as a viable option. In the meantime, calling for personal responsibility in these matters is no more an endorsement of militarism than calling for personal responsibility in drinking is an endorsement of alcoholism.

People can disagree about what supporting a war means in terms of personal responsibility. The most striking feature of alienated war is the silence surrounding the whole issue. Today, the question "Who's fighting our wars?" is like "Who's having sex?" was in Victorian times. It elicits awkwardness, annoyance, and anger.

Academia is as guilty as anyone. Political philosophers had lots to say about the legitimacy of the draft in the 1960s and early 1970s, when their children were affected. Like other privileged groups, they generally lost interest in the question of war and personal responsibility when the draft ended.[36] The decision to serve in the military is one of the most momentous choices a young person can make. It raises basic issues of citizenship, questions that were placed squarely on the individual when conscription ended. Yet political philosophers have had little to say on the decision to serve, in contrast to the thousands of pages they have generated on who you should have sex with. The pages that follow argue for a specific view on war and responsibility. Many may find it too strong. But this book will succeed if it serves to provoke more reflection on these matters.

ALIENATED WAR AND THE CHICKENHAWK SYNDROME

For too long our culture has said, "If it feels good, do it." Now America is embracing a new ethic and a new creed: "Let's roll." In the sacrifice of soldiers, the fierce brotherhood of firefighters, and the bravery and generosity of ordinary citizens, we have glimpsed what a new culture of responsibility could look like. We want to be a nation that serves goals larger than self. We've been offered a unique opportunity, and we must not let this moment pass.

—President Bush, State of the Union Address, January 2002

Alienated war denotes a set of both institutions and attitudes, and we need to explore both.

War and Detachment

The institutions of alienated war are ones that contemporary social theorists have identified as the "New War."[37] Militarily, they involve great emphasis on high technology and technical superiority over the enemy generally. War is no longer the massive battles and lumbering armies of the twentieth century. War is a matter of "smart bombs," swift strikes, and small mobile forces. We have witnessed these elements of the "New War" in Iraq. Such wars also aim to be short wars: they seek to avoid the long, drawn-out conflicts of World Wars I and II and Vietnam. The U.S. government hoped that this would be true of Afghanistan and Iraq, but it has not.

Politically, alienated war aims to isolate the ordinary citizen from the realities of war. Smaller armies and shorter wars are meant to serve this end, but there are other key factors. A major one is how war is financed. Governments have traditionally borrowed to fight wars. Indeed, the mechanisms of deficit financing first arose in England in the eighteenth-century in conjunction with the expansion of its military ventures. In America, though, such borrowing has generally been a temporary expedient. Starting with the Revolution, it was assumed that the cost of a war should not be handed down to the next generation. George Washington explicitly condemned deficit financing in his farewell address. The upshot was that fighting wars meant raising taxes, as in the two world wars. Franklin Roosevelt raised taxes even before it was necessary because he believed that Americans had to appreciate that war meant sacrifice. Kennedy acted likewise during the Berlin crisis. Lyndon Johnson raised taxes to finance the Vietnam War.

Alienated war changed all this. Bush's War on Terror is the first war to be accompanied by a reduction of taxes, along with numerous budgetary devices to hide the true cost of war. When people complained about this, they were accused of un-Americanism. In October 2007, Democratic House Appropriations Committee chairman David Obey proposed that the annual cost of the Iraq War, then estimated at $145 billion, be paid for by a war surtax that would range from 2 percent for low- and middle-income earners to 12 to 15 percent for upper-income earners. Said Obey,

> This war is draining the treasury dry. . . . There is a huge opportunity cost that is being paid by the same younger generation that is going to be asked to pay the bill because the president is paying for this war on the cuff. If you don't like the cost, then shut down the war.

"If you don't like the cost, then shut down the war": the thinking is as old as the republic itself. Today it is ridiculed. Fox News quoted a White House aide as saying, "What next? A tax on air?" White House Press Secretary Dana Perino stated, "We've always known that Democrats seem to revert to type, and they are willing to raise taxes on just about anything." Raise taxes to pay for war? "I just think it's completely fiscally irresponsible," she asserted.

For our purposes, the main feature of alienated war is how it procures its soldiers. Ultimately, it aims to replace the citizen-soldiers with professional soldiers so as to isolate the bodily cost of war from average citizens much as deficit financing hides the financial cost. This initially took the form of a professionalized military, our "volunteer" military. Over time, it has been augmented by the hiring of "corporate" soldiers working for private "security" firms. In Iraq, corporate soldiers quickly became the second-largest force after the U.S. military itself. By the fall of 2007, 20,000 to 30,000 private military contractors were working in Iraq, and the total number of private workers outnumbered military personnel. More private soldiers have died in Iraq than regular ones. This remained largely invisible to the American public until the highly publicized shooting of Iraqi citizens by employees of the Blackwater security firm in September 2007. Commenting on the event, the *New York Times* noted that corporate warriors in Iraq constituted "the most extensive use of private contractors on the battlefield since Renaissance princes hired private armies to fight their battles."[38]

The invisibility of this practice was no mere happenstance. Alienated war had its architects; a strong early champion of corporate war was Vice President Dick Cheney when he served in the Ford administration. Alienated war's proponents hoped that its mechanisms would dampen if not dispense with popular concern with American policies of the sort that ended the Vietnam War. When Nixon called for an end to the draft and the creation of a professional military, his aim was to stop the dissent that the draft generated. He remarked that ending the draft would ensure that academics and other professionals would lose interest in the question of who fights our wars and the injustices it involves.[39] History has proved him right about this.

Supporting the Troops versus Becoming One Yourself

Something I will stress throughout this book is the *surreal* nature of alienated war. Its discourse remains that of the citizen-soldier tradition, the discourse of personal responsibility and shared sacrifice. On Pearl Harbor Day 2002, President Bush urged Americans to "make the war their own." "Times of war are times of great sacrifice," he reminded us on July 4, 2004. In January 2007, he praised "the extraordinary and selfless men and women willing to step forward and defend us." He concluded, "Times of testing reveal the character of a nation." But such talk is totally disconnected from the realities of alienated war. We celebrate shared sacrifice while avoiding any thought of it ourselves. It's like celebrating Prohibition over drinks. Scholars of the Soviet Union used to joke that its ethic was, "We pretend to work, you pretend to pay us." Its cynical culture ultimately contributed to its implosion from within. America's ethic is, "You proclaim we are at war, we pretend to sacrifice." The upshot is a public culture pervaded by fraudulence.

This was clearly demonstrated in the 2004 presidential campaign. Near its end, John Kerry remarked that if you take advantage of your education and work hard, you can do well, but if you don't, "you get stuck in Iraq." Everyone knew he was right. The military itself acknowledges it when it recruits people by appealing to the opportunities they do not have at home. Yet Kerry was reviled for "not supporting the troops" and was compelled to apologize. During the Vietnam War, it was official policy to channel the uneducated into combat positions. Everyone of my generation knew that failing grades meant being drafted and going to Vietnam. But when General Lewis Hershey, director of the Selective Service, issued that policy, no one accused him of "not supporting the troops."

The citizen-soldier ethic was one of shared sacrifice. The ethic of alienated war is to "support the troops." Abstractly, it's a great idea. In reality, it's a substitute for a real ethic of personal responsibility. Does anyone know what it really means? It apparently doesn't mean that troops should be provided adequate equipment when they go to war or adequate medical treatment when they return. It doesn't even mean that they can come home when they were promised. Above all else, "supporting the troops" does not mean that I should become one myself, even if my services are needed. We "honor" their sacrifices so that we don't have to sacrifice ourselves.[40] The upshot is a silencing mechanism, another way that alienated war removes the topic from the public sphere. Consider how curious its logic is. Does questioning the War on Drugs mean "not supporting" the policemen who fight it? Would "honoring their sacrifices" be grounds for continuing a War on Drugs long after it had lost all sense? Did anyone argue that Prohibition should be continued to "honor" those who had died fighting liquor? This whole way of thinking personalizes politics in the worst way. The wisdom of the war becomes a matter of whether we "like" those involved in it. If a war is ill conceived, the only way to support the troops is to get them out of it.

As a teacher of the young, I am especially sensitive to the surreal nature of all this and the cynicism it induces. I have spent my life teaching in a public university. The hardest thing about it is getting students to take public issues seriously. Students may agree or disagree with any particular view, which is fine. But the greatest challenge is their attitude that none of it matters at all, that notions like patriotism and citizenship are so degraded by the pervasive hypocrisy in our culture that they lack all meaning. This is part of the passivity that Randolph Bourne identified, one that serves to sustain the government's criminal actions carried out in our name. Addressing alienated war means showing its ideology for what it is.

The Draft Diversion

> If there were ever serious talk about enacting a draft or raising taxes to fight it, you'd see quickly enough that the vast majority of Americans would not find it worth fighting.
>
> —Bob Herbert, "Another Thousand Lives,"
> *New York Times*, January 4, 2007

Other voices have challenged alienated war. The most persistent has been *New York Times* columnist Bob Herbert. He has not only questioned the integrity of individual chickenhawks but also related it to national concerns:

> There is something terribly wrong with this juxtaposition of gleeful Americans with fistfuls of dollars storming the department store barricades and the slaughter by the thousands of innocent Iraqi civilians, including old people, children and babies. The U.S. started the war, but most Americans feel absolutely no sense of personal responsibility for it. ("While Iraq Burns," *New York Times*, November 27, 2006)

Herbert cites one college student who said, "I get the feeling that most people at school don't even think about the war." Another said, "None of my friends even really care about what's going on in Iraq":

> This indifference is widespread. It enables most Americans to go about their daily lives completely unconcerned about the atrocities resulting from a war being waged in their name. While shoppers here are scrambling to put the perfect touch to their holidays with the purchase of a giant flat-screen TV or a PlayStation 3, the news out of Baghdad is of a society in the midst of a meltdown.

Another to bemoan this disconnection has been Congressman Charles Rangel, whose response has been to call for reviving the draft. "I don't see how anyone can support the war and not support the draft." To do so is "hypocritical," he has said.[41] Rangel's proposal has gone nowhere and has done nothing to shatter the silence around the larger issue. Here is Bob Herbert again, from the previously cited editorial:

> What struck me was not the uniform opposition to [Rangel's] proposal—it has long been clear that there is zero sentiment in favor of a draft in the U.S.—but the fact that it never provoked even the briefest discussion of the responsibilities and obligations of ordinary Americans in a time of war.

I share the frustrations of Herbert and Rangel and can understand the call for reviving the draft. What motivates it is the desire to revive the ethic of shared responsibility that characterized struggles like World War II. The hope is that the draft would bring about greater prudence in war-making policies of the kind that was so obviously absent with Iraq. If the *only* way to make the United States more prudent were to revive the draft, I would support it. Indeed, it would be narcissistic of Americans to privilege their own individual freedom over their responsibilities as global citizens, given the nation's enormous military power. But I do not believe that a draft is the only way to revive this ethic of shared responsibility. Even if there were a draft, people could still avoid reflecting on their responsibilities. Of the 26.8 million men eligible for the draft between 1964 and 1973, only 2.2 million were drafted.[42] If we revived a draft today, the overwhelming majority would still be personally unaffected. Moreover, I agree with the nation's founders that the ethic of shared responsibility draws its value from the fact that citizens are not forced into it. It should be part of our shared political morality.

In truth, I think that focusing on the draft *prevents* the discussion of personal responsibility that Herbert and Rangel desire. Fixating on the draft is one of alienated war's mechanisms for avoiding the discussion of personal responsibility. Hence, I call it the "draft diversion."

The draft diversion equates the question "Should we be more serious about sharing the sacrifices of war?" with the question "Should we reinstitute the draft?" Since everyone's answer to that is "No," equating the two issues means that the former one is forgotten. But this is like equating the question "Should we be more serious about how much we drink?" with the question "Should we reinstitute Prohibition?"

The draft diversion was a favorite ploy of Bush's. PBS's Jim Lehrer once asked Bush directly,

> Let me ask you a bottom-line question, Mr. President. If it is as important as you've just said—and you've said it many times—as all of this is, particularly the struggle in Iraq, if it's that important to all of us and to the future of our country, if not the world, why have you not, as president of the United States, asked more Americans to sacrifice something? The people who are now sacrificing are, you know, the volunteer military—the army and the marines and their families. They're the only people who are actually sacrificing anything at this point. (January 16, 2007)

Bush's response was that he did not believe in reviving the draft. He stressed that he did not believe in raising taxes either.

Again, we're so accustomed to such illogic that we overlook how strange it is. If someone were asked, "Should people be encouraged to donate more to Hurricane Katrina relief?" and his reply was, "I don't believe in forcing them"—we'd conclude that he didn't hear the question. If he repeated it over and over again, we'd assume he didn't know the meaning of "encourage" or "donate." It's not only illogical but also backward. Normally, when a society opts for a volunteer solution to a problem over a coercive one, it means that people should think *more* of their personal responsibility, not less. The end of Prohibition meant that people had to think more about their personal responsibility for drinking. The opposite has happened with military service. Americans take the end of the draft as grounds for forgetting the issue entirely.

It is because I oppose a draft that I think the question of personal responsibility needs to be taken *more* seriously. The issue is not whether to revive the draft. The issue is what it means to have a volunteer military. The United States has had a voluntary military for more than thirty years and will continue to do so. Yet America has never had a sustained discussion of what a volunteer military really means for the responsibilities of the average citizen. It is time that these issues are addressed.

Another avoidance mechanism is what I call the "national service diversion." You are more likely to find this on the liberal side of the spectrum. This responds to the problem of shared sacrifice in war by endorsing some kind of universal national service for youth. There may be sound reasons why every young person should spend several years serving his or her community. But this does not speak to the issue of shared sacrifice in war. Endorsing a war means the willingness to fight in it yourself if you can or to have your children fight in it. It does not mean the willingness to work in a recycling center while others fight it or a willingness to have your children work as forest rangers while other people's children die. The national service diversion takes the question "Why aren't you fighting in this war, if you endorse it?" and recasts it as "Why aren't you performing some form of public service?" These don't make up the same question. If fighting our wars is inordinately the job of minorities and the less advantaged, it does not change matters that the children of the privileged serve as playground supervisors. It is the link between *war* and sacrifice that has been severed. Addressing alienated war means addressing this.

AFTER 9/11

If one adds together the illegal immigrants, the jobless and the convicts, there is surely ample raw material for a larger American army.

—Niall Ferguson[43]

College professors like me are supposed to be totally clueless about the real world. Undoubtedly we are in many ways. But when you work at a large state university, issues of military service impact you more than many people, certainly more than people in most professions. My state, Oregon, is a small rural state. From the moment the United States pondered action in Afghanistan, I've had students in the reserves or ROTC facing imminent deployment. Oregon has lost more than one hundred of its citizens to Afghanistan and Iraq. One of the first marines to perish in Afghanistan was twenty-three-year-old Bryan Bertrand from Coos Bay, Oregon.

Several incidents in particular started me thinking about the ethical issues of war and personal responsibility.

War without Sacrifice

Not long after 9/11, one of the television networks held a "town hall" meeting with representatives of the administration and an audience of young adults. At several points, Bush administration proclamations about the importance of collective vigilance were met with vigorous and sustained applause.

One military man asked if the nation was truly ready for a "thirty-year effort against terrorism"—and there were resounding calls of "Yes!"

There was the same loud response when another Bush spokesman evoked John F. Kennedy's words about "no sacrifice being too great in the cause of freedom."

They all cheered when a well-dressed young man from the State Department said, "Let's show the terrorists what Americans are made of!"

But at the end, one remark more than any other got the most applause. It was when, in response to one anxious young man's question, a Bush spokesman proclaimed, "No, we have absolutely no intention of reviving the draft!"

Nobody found this strange but me. Yes, there are good reasons to oppose a draft. But if you thought fighting this war was such a great idea, why *wouldn't* you want to be drafted to fight it? This is how people felt in the past. In past wars the draft was a cause for celebration by many. Young men were proud of being the first chosen. They'd be photographed by newspapers smiling while their families beamed proudly. Movies made *fun* of people who couldn't be drafted because they were 4-F (medically unsuited to serve). In *It's a Wonderful Life*, George Bailey (Jimmy Stewart) can't be drafted because of his bad ear. He sees this as simply one more step in his life of hapless misfortune.

Believe it or not, up to the mid-1960s, polls showed that the draft was consistently one of the most popular institutions in America. Polls showed that 90 percent of Americans approved of conscription.[44] This was because it embodied an ideal of shared sacrifice that most Americans admired. As the enabling legislation of the draft stated, "Equality of obligation . . . is the essence of democracy" (Universal Military Training Act[45]). Most Americans sympathized with this egalitarian ethic, just as they sympathized with Chief Justice Edward White when he wrote, in the Supreme Court case affirming the draft, that participating in the national defense was the "supreme and noble duty" of all citizens. The draft was popular because it embodied this citizen-soldier ethic.

Maybe I was missing the point. Maybe all the gung-ho people in the audience did hope to fight in Bush's War on Terror. Their applause was not relief at avoiding service themselves and joy that others would be fighting for them. Rather, it was an expression of abstract political principle: "I myself am happy to go. But it's crucial that we continue to respect personal liberty by not reviving the draft!"

I doubt it.

Prior to the Iraq invasion, polls reported that while 80 percent of young people favored removing Saddam Hussein by military action, 60 percent said they'd evade a draft if asked to serve. Not long after the 2004 election, a majority of Americans polled by CNN agreed that bringing "democracy" to Iraq by military means was a good idea. It then reported that 90 percent of Americans would refuse to die for that goal themselves. If Americans' opposition to the draft were based solely on commitment to personal liberty, why hasn't there been more outcry about such blatant violations of liberty as the military's "stop-loss policy"?

Even if those applauding did intend to serve, I'd still find it strange. Imagine if a television network held a town hall meeting after Hurricane Katrina and one administration figure after another made pronouncements about how much the government would be doing to bring New Orleans back. All of it met with bursts of applause. Then, after a long list of expensive projects, the biggest ovation of all came when someone proclaimed, "And none of you will be taxed for it!"

I had first started thinking about alienated war a decade earlier during the first Gulf War. It was then that I realized how differently I thought about war than many of my students. I realized how many saw no connection at all between whether the country should go to war and whether they would be willing to fight in it. Newspapers started noticing the disconnection around the same time. David Marannis of the *Washington Post* interviewed seven Vanderbilt University undergraduates about the war. Five of the seven endorsed the Gulf War, and *seven* of the seven said that they were unwilling to fight in it. The reasons they gave were notable. One said, "I think it would be a shame to put America's best young minds on the front line." Another said, "I can't see myself shooting a gun."[46]

We were witnessing the birth of the chickenhawk syndrome.

Just Say Yes

Another incident was at the 2004 Republican National Convention. The convention, you may recall, began with several days of high-minded calls for sacrifice in wartime, some of them from people who had actually served—like Zell Miller, a former marine, and John McCain. This flag-waving was followed by an appearance of the Bush twins, their first appearance before a national audience.

What did they have to say? What words did they share with the American people in what every previous speaker had described as a "time of war"?

They joked about how "awesome" Arnold Schwarzenegger was as a model of someone to marry. They joked about *Sex and the City* and how their "Gammie" (grandmother) was not "hip" about sex. They joked about their drinking problems and how they kept trying to explain to their dad that "when you're young and irresponsible . . . well, you're young and irresponsible."

Then, bedecked in what the next day's newspapers described as their "trendy clothes," they topped it all off by giggling, "Since we've graduated from college, we're looking around for something to do for the next few years."[47]

How about serving in your father's war?

Imagine if, in the midst of World War II, Franklin Roosevelt's son had joked to the Democratic convention about his drinking problems and his mother Eleanor's sex attitudes and then concluded by musing about how he didn't know what he'd be doing for the next few years.

You're probably thinking that World War II and Iraq are hardly parallels. But George W. Bush thought they were. His administration constantly likened the Iraq conflict to fighting Hitler. His supporters characterized it as "World War IV."[48] Fox News Network's Sean Hannity wrote in his book *Deliver Us from Evil: Defeating Terrorism, Despotism and Liberalism*, "[The] threat they [the terrorists] represent is every bit as grave as the one we experienced during WW II."[49] Bush previewed the twins' speech prior to its delivery. Didn't he have the slightest concern about what they said?

Women of color are especially likely to serve today. They constitute more than 50 percent of the women serving. In the much-publicized Jessica Lynch incident at the start of the Iraq War, two other women were involved. One was killed—Private First Class Lori Ann Piestewa, who was not only one of the first Americans and first women to die in Iraq but also the first Native American woman to die in combat as a member of the U.S. military. The other was Shoshana Johnson, an African American who, unlike Lynch, fought to stave off her Iraqi captors, sustaining injuries in the process. Both Piestewa and Johnson were single mothers with young children back home.

Ask yourself, Who had better reason for *not* being in Iraq than Lori Ann Piestewa and Shoshana Johnson? If they could find reasons for serving their country, what possible reason could the Bush twins have for *not* serving?

Three Americans died in Iraq the day the twins spoke, two in combat. While the twins joked about their grandmother's sex attitudes Sergeant Monta S. Ruth, a twenty-six-year-old African American from Winston-Salem, North Carolina, was killed by an improvised explosive device. Soon after the twins were tittering about awesome Arnold, the news of Ruth's death was received by his wife Aylin and his daughter Zoe, age three.

After all their tee-heeing and sex jokes before a world audience, the president materialized on the large video screen behind them and told his daughters, "You make me so very proud."

Other countries' leaders have acted differently. On July 31, 2005, the *New York Times* reported how the U.S. military was "trolling" its territories in the Pacific for new recruits. Noting the strong sense of devotion to the United States among Pacific Island leaders, the article reported that the governor of American Samoa had a daughter serving in Iraq.[50] A *daughter.* Most of the leaders of the islands had close relatives serving in the military. The son of the immediate past president of the Federated States of Micronesia was a colonel in the Marine Corps. The article did note that a major incentive for Pacific Islanders to enlist was that the region's largest employer, the garment industry, had been laying off thousands of workers since the liberalization of import rules had opened the U.S. market to clothing made in China.

Conservatives preach the power of personal example on issues like drugs and sex. But the discussion stops at serving in the wars you support. The noted military sociologist Charles Moskos recounts how during the Clinton administration,

> I was once addressing a recruiting conference and I asked the recruiters—this was late in the Clinton administration—"Would you rather have Chelsea Clinton join the Army or have your advertising budget tripled?" What do you think they picked? Unanimously, Chelsea Clinton. If you have the privileged youth doing it then you know others will find that this must be a noble or worthwhile cause.[51]

Today's conservatives believe so much in the power of moral persuasion that they believe they can convince young people to swear off *sex* with a "just say no" campaign. Surely they must believe that they can persuade them to go to Iraq with a "just say yes" campaign. In the age of alienated war, the thought never occurs.

There is a terrible irony here. The nation's founders believed that a republic, unlike an empire, would be a society in which the privileged and the less privileged fought side by side. But today the children of our leaders don't give a thought to military service, while the children of British royalty affirm their civic duty. In the spring of 2005, the son of Prince Charles, Prince Harry, told the British press that he felt he should be serving alongside his fellow British soldiers in Iraq—to demonstrate that the sacrifice was being shared by all. On his graduation from the British military academy Sandhurst, he threatened to resign from the army if he was kept out of combat roles.[52] "There's no way I'm going to put myself through Sandhurst, and then sit on my arse back home while my boys are out fighting for their country," he stated in a television interview to mark his twenty-first birthday.[53] Pundits were quoted as saying, "If he doesn't go, [the public] will say, bad decision, because they're treating him with kid gloves." Prince Harry subsequently served in Afghanistan.

POSING THE MORAL QUESTIONS

As the war has dragged on, it is hard to give Americans en masse a pass.
We are too slow to notice, let alone protest, the calamities that have followed the original sin.

—Frank Rich, "The 'Good Germans' among Us,"
New York Times, October 14, 2007

Many people question whether supporting a war implies anything about
one's own responsibility. When I first published some of these thoughts
in a popular journal, the editors contacted several news organizations
about the piece—serious organizations like the *Christian Science Monitor* and the Associated Press. The reporters at such places are top-level,
highly informed professionals. They all found my position strange. What
they found most curious was my suggestion that if a leader like President
Bush asked other people's children to serve in the military, he should ask
his own children to serve as well.

One of them replied, "But couldn't they get *hurt*?"

I have also learned that time has dimmed people's understanding of
how things used to be. Many young people do not understand how the
draft worked or the thinking behind it. Many do not know about the
citizen-soldier ethic or the civic republican tradition from which it arose.
I didn't know much about them myself until I started researching these issues. The chapters that follow provide basic information about things like
the draft that some people, particularly of my generation, may already
know. They also provide historical details on the citizen-soldier tradition
and America's relation to war generally as background to the chickenhawk syndrome and the problem of alienated war.

Chapter 1 discusses how the events of 9/11 and their aftermath
brought home the reality of alienated war. Chapter 2 explores the
origins of alienated war by describing the rise and fall of the citizen-
soldier tradition. Special attention is paid to the problematic place of
the draft in American history. Together, these chapters provide the
political and historical background to the philosophical discussion that
follows. Chapters 3, 4, and 5 explore the logic of the chickenhawk syndrome. They distinguish different aspects of the problem and explore
the strengths and weaknesses of different views on it. The principle
that emerges from this critical discussion is what I have called the
Murtha test: endorse a war only if you would be willing to fight and
die in it yourself. The conclusion raises some larger issues about the
meaning of citizenship and community if they are uncoupled from the
duty to serve one's country.

The Moral Costs of Empire

> When those who benefit most from living in a country contribute the
> least to its defense and those who benefit least are asked to pay the ulti-
> mate price, something happens to the soul of that country.
>
> —Kathy Roth-Douquet and Frank Schaeffer, *AWOL*[54]

Much will be said in these pages about the chickenhawk's "moral failings," "character" flaws, and so on. I agree with Bob Herbert that our
current military adventures constitute a moral disaster, one that speaks
to our integrity as a people. After all, if Americans are indifferent to
domestic problems, like education, they are only hurting themselves. If
they want to dumb down their society, so be it. But the harmful impact
of American military actions falls chiefly on others. One would think that
this imposes a special burden of responsibility on Americans to follow
their government's actions with a critical eye. Yet in July 2006, half of all
Americans still believed that Iraq had possessed weapons of mass destruction (a 14 percent increase from the previous February), even though
the falsity of this view had been well-established two years before.

When figures like these are reported, people rush to blame "the media"
for such astounding ignorance. This is a cop-out. I don't see how newspapers and television news can be blamed for all the nation's faults when
many people pay so little attention to either. In this case *all* the media,
even Fox News, had reported the 2004 conclusion by the congressionally
appointed Iraq Survey Group that Saddam Hussein had no weapons of
mass destruction or plans to build them. Still, though 3,000 of their fellow
countrymen had died in Iraq, one out of every two Americans had little
interest in the truth. We're so accustomed to figures like these that they
no longer surprise us. But consider a parallel. What if, two years after
Pearl Harbor, half of all Americans still didn't know who attacked us?
What if they thought that Argentina had been the aggressor and that we
should now wage a long, expensive war to bring Juan Peron to justice?
I concur with Frank Rich, who wrote in November 2007 that as the war
has dragged on, it has gotten more difficult to give Americans en masse
a pass.

I think that progressive politics must reclaim moral discourse, especially the discourse of personal responsibility. Robert Bellah, Robert
Putnam, and others have called for a revitalized public realm in which
discourses like civic republicanism are reclaimed. More recently, George
Lakoff, Jim Wallis, and others have called for taking moral language back
from conservatives. Lacking such a language, critics of Bush harped on
his alleged "lack of intelligence." Bush's problem wasn't his stupidity. It

was his immorality—his lack of personal integrity as evidenced by his chickenhawk behavior. Does this put the point too harshly? Progressives have often been chastised by Bush supporters for their moral distaste for the man. I've always found this curious. Bush's conservative Christian followers claim that people like me are destined for eternal damnation for our flaws; then they call us "elitist" for harping on Bush's. The real problem with dwelling on Bush's flaws is if it detracts attention from our own. The question raised by Bush's failings is how they reflect our larger failings as a people.

Jim Wallis has written insightfully about how the left's concern with structural injustices should not obscure issues of personal responsibility.[55] The towering figures of twentieth-century progressive politics did not separate the two. Martin Luther King Jr. appreciated the structural nature of the problems he opposed, but he never lost sight of the personal responsibility question. Faced with the acquiescence of most Americans to segregation, he did not rush to blame the "media" for America's problems. He treated Americans like adults by holding them responsible for themselves and their society. He called them to abide by higher standards.

The problem of empire has received much attention since the start of the Iraq War. This work joins that discussion. A full account of alienated war would place its rise in the context of global transformations in the American imperial project in the latter half of the twentieth century. I am indebted to Andrew Bacevich's writings on the militarist bent of contemporary American society.[56] I will draw on the work of Chalmers Johnson in noting the parallels between America's situation today and Rome's in its age of imperial decline.[57] But my focal concern is to reclaim a theme dear to the civic republican ideology of the country's founders: the *moral* costs of empire. Imperialism is the source of many evils whose victims are overwhelmingly in other lands. It is also a source of moral rot at home, corroding the souls of its own citizens. It undermines their sense of personal responsibility and numbs them to the consequences of acts in which they are implicated. The revolutionaries of 1776 saw this happening in the ruling classes of imperial Britain. In his essay of civil disobedience, protesting America's imperial war on Mexico, Thoreau saw the same moral rot arising in his own country. The chickenhawk syndrome is part of the larger culture of empire.

Other empires have witnessed moral criticism from within. English men and women in the late nineteenth century were repelled by the immorality of their empire's actions. Some even joked about its chickenhawk dimensions, as in this popular music hall ditty ("Hindoo" referred to the Indian soldiers that did the empire's fighting for it):

> We don't want to fight
> But, by jingo if we do,
> We won't go to the front ourselves
> We'll send the mild Hindoo!

Civic republicanism had a good word for such moral rot: "corruption." Today, "corruption" evokes thoughts of sinfulness, specifically sex, but originally it had more political connotations. The corrupt society and the individuals that composed it were deeply irresponsible ones. Not only were they immoral, but they did not *care* about morality. This explains the astonishing superficiality of the corrupt group or individuals (the Bush twins). I have used the word "cluelessness," but ultimately someone who does not care about morality is someone incapable of shame, shameless. Our inquiry will show that this is not an incidental feature of the chicken-hawk syndrome but is central to its (im)moral character.

The Baby-Boomer Legacy

The moral burden of Iraq falls principally on my generation, the baby boomers. Our political consciousness was formed in the conflicts over the Vietnam War. Many of my generation prided themselves—and still do—on recognizing the wastefulness of that conflict early on. They think of themselves as a generation that, in the civil rights and antiwar movements, exhibited moral fiber in service of America's best values.

Has there ever been a generation that so catastrophically failed to live up to its moral promise? Thus far, our contribution to American political leadership has been Bill Clinton and George W. Bush. Clinton's presidency will be remembered as on par with Grover Cleveland's. Bush's may go down as the worst in our history. Our most recent contribution to the moral tone of our country has been to revive torture as an accepted practice of war. "Our most visible members are unrepentantly shameless self-promoters, intent on being someone rather than doing something. Given the choice between mingling with celebrities and bettering the human condition, we'll take the former every time." These are the words of Gregory Foster in "Baby Boomers: The Ungreatest Generation."[58] "We still don't have a clue how to get beyond the Cold War (much less how to extricate ourselves from the Iraq debacle with the country's dignity intact), or how to achieve comprehensive health care, reform education, or rid politics of the corrupting influence of money." Indeed, "in virtually every walk of American life—certainly in government, business, and academe—the Baby Boomers are fully in charge, and it isn't a pretty sight. In fact, it's downright ugly."

Has there ever been a generation that so casually and completely forgot the lessons of its youth? Prohibition was a huge mistake. My students find it hard to believe that the United States tried something as foolish as outlawing beer. But Prohibition made a good deal of sense at the time. It was the product of a century-long temperance movement that raised serious issues about public health and gender violence and engaged millions. In addition, the architects of Prohibition did not have the precedent of a disastrously failed attempt to control alcohol to learn from. The baby-boomer architects of the War on Terror *did* have the disastrous precedent of Vietnam to learn from, and they chose to ignore it. It is as if, barely three decades after Prohibition, the nation's political leadership decided to reinstitute it with no attention to how it failed before.

The subliminal awareness of this may contribute to the silence and discomfort around the whole issue of military service. During the 2004 presidential campaign, John Kerry remarked that he was not eager to "revive" the "divisive" Vietnam-era debate about who fights our wars. Why not? Especially when the debate over who should fight our wars was never really resolved. I would question whether that debate was really conducted in the first place; like the question of racial equality following the Civil War, it was shoved aside and forgotten. If anything can be salvaged from the mess of Iraq, perhaps it can be sober public reflection on the question of who fights our wars and how we should think about the decision to go to war generally.

THE FUTURE OF ALIENATED WAR

We're nowhere close to sharing the sacrifice. And it should be shared, because it's only in that sharing the society will care about what's going on over here.

—Sergeant Mike Krause, Army 101st Airborne Division, Iraq veteran[59]

As I write this, the nation is awaiting the inauguration of its new president. President-elect Obama has spoken eloquently of the need for a renewed spirit of shared sacrifice. Will this lead to a rethinking of alienated war and the spirit of irresponsibility embodied in the chickenhawk syndrome?

We have a long way to go. The total cost of the Iraq conflict is approaching that of the Vietnam War, which lasted more than a decade. Iraq has cost $648 billion, and Vietnam cost $686 billion. By contrast (these are rough estimates), the American Revolution cost $1.8 billion in adjusted figures, the Civil War $60.4 billion, and World War I $253 billion. Sometime in 2009, Iraq will become America's second most expensive war, after World War II ($4.1 trillion).[60] One would assume that a financial commitment of this magnitude involved great deliberation. Yet future historians will marvel at the thoughtlessness of our nation's leaders in the decision to go to war. This was in marked contrast to previous controversial conflicts, like World War I—a much harder war for politicians to oppose, yet they did so significantly. The grand old man of the Democratic Party's progressive wing, William Jennings Bryan, resigned as secretary of state over the issue and took to the road to campaign against the war. The party's own Speaker of the House opposed his president on it.

No such principles were evident in the run-up to the Iraq War. When the issue was brought to the Senate, that chamber was "hauntingly silent," in the words of one of the few voices to speak out, Senator Robert Byrd. A majority of Democrats were so anxious to support the war that they did not want to discuss it. The first day of "debate" saw the introduction of the Iraq resolution—and then no debate at all. Instead, one senator hailed the hundredth anniversary of the 4-H Club. Another commended the Future Farmers of America chapter in Caldwell County, Kentucky. Senator Barbara Boxer noted the hundredth anniversary of the city of Mountain View, California. Subsequent revelations confirmed how casually leaders approached the issue. Prior to the vote, every senator was given access to the National Intelligence Estimate (NIE), the most comprehensive judgment of the intelligence community on the issue of Iraqi weapons of mass destruction. The document was available two weeks before the debate, and it contained numerous caveats and dissents from the Bush picture. Only six senators read it. One of them, Bob Graham, forcefully urged his fellow Democrats to read it before voting since it undermined the Bush case for war. Yet neither Hillary Clinton nor John Edwards bothered to do so. Clinton stated she did not have time, though it was only ninety pages. On the floor of the Senate, she justified her support for Bush's Iraq policy by citing the alleged link between Saddam Hussein and al-Qaeda. Had she read the NIE report, she would have learned that no such links existed.

In time, the human costs of the endeavor meant that the public's turn against the Iraq War was swift and dramatic. As John Mueller observed in *Foreign Affairs*, broad public support in the postinvasion period eroded as American casualties rose. Indeed, "the only thing remarkable about the current war in Iraq is how precipitously American public support has dropped off. Casualty for casualty, support has declined far more quickly than it did during either the Korean War or the Vietnam War."[61] He added, "And if history is any indication, there is little the Bush administration can do to reverse this decline." An important factor was how the military itself had sought to counter alienated war through its "total force policy," which sought to link ordinary citizens and war policy, leading to the large numbers of National Guard and reserves who were mobilized for the Iraq venture in numbers unprecedented since World War II. This impacted certain segments of the country more than others. By February 2007, nearly half of American military fatalities were from towns of fewer than 25,000 people, and one-fifth were from towns of less than 5,000. And they were from poorer communities. Nearly three-quarters of those killed in Iraq came from towns where per capita income was below the national average.[62] This helped explain the shifting sentiment in those communities.

Politicians cautiously began to question the institutions of alienated war. In 2007, Senator Barbara Boxer challenged Secretary of State Condoleezza Rice on the question of who fights and dies in our wars. "Who pays the price? I'm not going to pay a personal price. My kids are too old and my grandchild is too young. You're not going to pay a particular price, as I understand it, with an immediate family. So who pays the price? The American military and their families." In the primaries, Senator Hillary Rodham Clinton raised the question of the volunteer army and its composition, stating that it "raises serious questions in a democracy, both [about] how we define ourselves [and] what the real risks politically and militarily of taking action might be."[63] But the question of who serves was absent from the contest between John McCain and Barack Obama. McCain was praised for his Vietnam service, and the sons of both Governor Sarah Palin and Senator Joe Biden were headed for military service. But none of this raised the larger questions of war and personal responsibility. Asked about the issue of shared sacrifice in the second presidential debate, McCain responded by stressing the importance of cutting taxes. In their televised debate, Governor Palin challenged Senator Biden's claim that paying taxes was patriotic. No one questioned the disparities of who served in the military. Indeed, Iraq seemed to fade from public consciousness as American military casualties declined. The news shows put it on the back burner. In June 2008, Andrew Tyndall, a television consultant who monitored the three network evening newscasts, reported that coverage of Iraq had been "massively scaled back this year." Almost halfway into 2008, the three newscasts had shown 181 weekday minutes of Iraq coverage, compared with 1,157 minutes for all of 2007. CBS News no longer stationed a single full-time correspondent in Iraq, where some 150,000 United States troops were deployed. Journalists at all three American television networks with evening newscasts expressed worries that their news organizations would withdraw from the Iraqi capital after the November presidential election.[64] My hometown newspaper in Oregon ran a guest editorial by a local high school student, Michelle Spresser, titled "War Seems So Distant to Me and My Peers." "Every time the term 'Iraq War' comes up during conversations among my friends, it's followed by heads shaking, eyeballs rolling, and laughter." "We observe war coverage with same distant gaze that we observe car commercials."

Alienated war has not triumphed completely. But it still could—it depends on us. "We are truly 'sleepwalking through history,'" said Senator Byrd on the floor of the Senate. "In my heart of hearts I pray that this great nation and its good and trusting citizens are not in for a rudest of awakenings."[65] Many of the politicians who led us into Iraq did so from political expediency. They did not want to appear unpatriotic, they did not want to hand the issue to Bush in the 2002 election, and so on. Would the fate of their own children or loved ones have tempered this expediency? Representative Charles Rangel has said that Congress would never have gone to war if there had been a draft. We can only wonder if Hillary Clinton or John Edwards would have taken the time to read the NIE if they knew their daughters would be deployed. We can only wonder if senators would have been less interested in the Future Farmers of America and more interested in Iraq if they knew their spouses, their loved ones, or they themselves might be fighting and dying there. To argue, as I do in this book, that war must be personalized is to ask our politicians to approach these matters as human beings and not just politicians.

NOTES

1. Cited in Allan Millet and Peter Maslowski, *For the Common Defense* (New York: Free Press, 1994), 79–80.

2. Ralph Nader has been credited with coining the term "chickenhawk."

3. Al Franken's 1996 book *Rush Limbaugh Is a Big Fat Idiot* included a chapter called "Operation Chickenhawk" depicting a fictional Vietnam War squad made up of Quayle, Newt Gingrich, Rush Limbaugh, Pat Buchanan, Phil Gramm, Clarence Thomas, and George Will, all of whom were of draft age during the Vietnam War but did not serve there. In the story, the cowardly incompetent unit is led by Oliver North, who actually served in Vietnam.

4. See, for example, Terry M. Neal, "Chickenhawk v. Chicken Little: Many Iraq Hawks Have Never Seen Military Service," *Washington Post*, September 6, 2002; John Sugg, "Roast the Chicken Hawks," *San Francisco Chronicle*, October 8, 2002; Ben Tripp, "A Bird Lover's Guide to Chickenhawks or Chickenhawk a la Mode," *CounterPunch*, October 15, 2002; "Chickenhawk Politics," *The Nation* (editorial), October 17, 2002; and Eric Alterman, "Why Chickenhawks Matter," *The Nation*, November 13, 2003.

5. Michael Kelly, "Chickenhawk Insult Sticks in My Craw," *Washington Post*, October 30, 2002.

6. Jeff Jacoby, "Are You a 'Chicken Hawk?,'" *Boston Globe*, July 23, 2006.

7. Andrew Cline, "Challenging the Chickenhawk Epithet," *American Spectator*, September 1, 2005.

8. Eliot A. Cohen, "Hunting 'Chicken Hawks,'" *Washington Post*, September 5, 2002.

9. Jonah Goldberg, "Playing 'Chickenhawk' Left-Wing Platitudes," *National Review Online*, August 17, 2005.

10. Christopher Hitchens, "Don't 'Son' Me—End This Silly Talk about Sacrificing Children," *Slate*, June 28, 2005. See also Christopher Hitchens, "'Armchair General': The Ugly Idea That Non-Soldiers Have Less Right to Argue for War," *Slate*, November 11, 2002.

11. Matthew Yglesias, "Manpower Meltdown," *The American Prospect*, August 8, 2005.

12. Randolph Bourne, *War and the Intellectuals*, ed. Carl Resek (New York: Harper and Row, 1964), 38.

13. Maggie Mulvihill, "Mitt Backs War, but His Boys Are Safe at Home," *Boston Herald*, August 27, 2005.

14. I will use the male pronoun throughout to refer to the chickenhawk since the overwhelming numbers are men.

15. Tony Judt, "What Have We Learned, If Anything?" *New York Review of Books* 55, no. 7 (May 1, 2008): 16–20.

16. The need for a regular army, over and above a people's militia, was an issue between the Federalists and Anti-Federalists. See Millet and Maslowski, *Common Defense*, chap. 4; see also Lawrence Cress, *Citizens in Arms: The Army and the Militia in American Society to the War of 1812* (Chapel Hill: University of North Carolina Press, 1982); Richard H. Kohn, *Eagle and Sword: The Federalists and the Creation of the Military Establishment in America, 1783–1802* (New York: Free Press, 1975); and Lois G. Schwoerer, *"No Standing Armies!" The Antiarmy Ideology in Seventeenth-Century England* (Baltimore: Johns Hopkins University Press, 1974).

17. I rely here on Charles Royster, *A Revolutionary People at War: The Continental Army and American Character, 1775–1783* (Chapel Hill: University of North Carolina Press, 1996).

18. Royster, *A Revolutionary People at War*, 17, 28.

19. Royster, *A Revolutionary People at War*, 7.

20. Franklin D. Roosevelt, "A Call for Sacrifice," April 28, 1942.

21. See Clare Snyder, "The Citizen-Soldier and the Tragedy of the Eighteenth Brumaire," *Strategies: Journal of Theory, Culture* 16, no. 1 (May 2003): 23–37.

22. This is quoted by Marx in Karl Marx and Friedrich Engels, *Selected Works* (New York: International Publishers, June 1986), 191–93.

23. See Debs's famous antiwar speech delivered Canton, Ohio, on June 16, 1918: "They are continually talking about your patriotic duty. It is not their but your patriotic duty that they are concerned about. There is a decided difference. Their patriotic duty never takes them to the firing line or chucks them into the trenches." For Bryan's views, see his speech "The Paralyzing Influence of Imperialism," Democratic National Convention, Kansas City, Missouri, July 6, 1900.

24. Gandhi, *Autobiography*, 666 (cited by Elaine Scarry, "War and the Social Contract: Nuclear Policy, Distribution, and the Right to Bear Arms," *University of Pennsylvania Law Review* 139 [May 1991]: 1270. Gandhi wrote, "Among the many misdeeds of the British rule in India, history will look upon the act of depriving a whole nation of arms, as the blackest" [446]).

25. Royster, *A Revolutionary People at War*, 135.

26. On the criticism of Robert Lincoln and Mary Todd Lincoln's response, see David Herbert Donald, *Lincoln* (New York: Simon and Schuster, 1995), 571. The quotation is from David Homer Bates, *Lincoln in the Telegraph Office: Recollections of the United States Military Telegraph Corps during the Civil War* (Whitefish, MT: Kessinger Publishing, 2008), 212–13. Lincoln resisted urging his son to enlist for fear of upsetting his wife's fragile mental state.

27. Cited in Kathy Roth-Douquet and Frank Schaeffer, *AWOL: The Unexcused Absence of America's Upper Classes from Military Service—and How It Hurts Our Country* (New York: Collins, 2007), 109.

28. Mulvihill, "Mitt Backs War."

29. Lisa De Pasquale, *Are We Hypocrites for Not Enlisting?* Townhall.com, August 15, 2007.

30. George Will, U.S. Naval Academy Forrestal Lecture, January 24, 2001. Will, who did not serve, bemoaned the fact that "we are developing, in a sense, a society that is strange to the military and the military is strange to it." He told the cadets, "Some Americans are morally superior to others and, frankly, that is why you are here, on the banks of the Chesapeake Bay."

31. In *What's the Matter with Kansas?* (New York: Holt Paperbacks, 2005), Thomas Franks has stressed the contradiction in modern conservatism between its populist ideology, claiming to champion traditional American values, and its pro–big business reality—serving the economic elite. The chickenhawk issue elicits such ire because it evokes this contradiction.

32. "Chelsea Clinton Speaks Out for the First Time in a Personal Account of the September 11 Tragedy and Its Aftermath," *Talk Magazine*, December 2001/January 2002, 12–13.

33. Sara Corbett, "The Women's War," *New York Times Magazine*, March 18, 2007, http://www.newyorktimes.com (accessed April 1, 2007).

34. Armen Keteyian, "Vets' Suicide Rate 'Stunning,'" *CBS News*, November 13, 2007.

35. If they do not want the American military to play this role, they should think about other ways to carry out these military actions, like the formation of international brigades during the Spanish Civil War. Progressives do none of these things.

36. For exceptions, see Robert K. Fullinwider, ed., *Conscripts and Volunteers: Military Requirements, Social Justice, and the All-Volunteer Force* (Totowa, NJ: Rowman & Allenheld, 1983). Communitarian thinkers like William Galston have continued to raise the issue, along with democratic theorists like Benjamin Barber. None of them gives it major importance.

37. See Martin Shaw, *The New Western Way of War: Risk-Transfer War and Its Crisis in Iraq* (Cambridge: Polity Press, 2005); Mary Kaldor, *New and Old Wars: Organized Violence in a Global Era* (Stanford, CA: Stanford University Press, 2007); and Herfried Münkler, *The New Wars* (Cambridge: Polity Press, 2004).

38. John Broder and James Risen, "Armed Guards in Iraq Occupy a Legal Limbo," *New York Times*, September 20, 2007.

39. See Aaron L. Friedberg, *In the Shadow of the Garrison State: America's Anti-Statism and Its Cold War Grand Strategy* (Princeton, NJ: Princeton University Press,

2000), 193–94, and Donald Smith, "The Volunteer Army," *Atlantic Monthly*, July 19, 1974, 89. See also George Q. Flynn, *The Draft, 1940–1973* (Lawrence: University Press of Kansas, 1993).

40. The mythology of veterans mistreatment by antiwar protestors in the Vietnam years is explored in Jerry Lembke, *The Spitting Image: Myth, Memory, and the Legacy of Vietnam* (New York: New York University Press, 2000). He has an excellent discussion of the citizen-soldier ideal in his final chapter, "We Are What We Remember."

41. Goeff Earle, "Rangel: Bring on the Draft," *New York Post*, November 19, 2006.

42. While 8.7 million joined voluntarily, according to Lawrence M. Baskir and William A. Strauss, *Chance and Circumstance: The Draft, the War, and the Vietnam Generation* (New York: Alfred A. Knopf, 1978).

43. Niall Ferguson, *Colossus* (New York: Penguin, 2004), 292.

44. Polls indicated that popular support for the draft was 90 percent in December 1965, dropping to 79 percent in August 1966 and to 5 percent by May 1968. See Michael Useem, *Conscription, Protest and Social Conflict* (New York: Wiley, 1973), 115.

45. Friedberg, *In the Shadow of the Garrison State*, 163.

46. Cited in David Halberstam, *War in a Time of Peace: Bush, Clinton, and the Generals* (New York: Scribner, 2002), 154.

47. Remarks by Barbara and Jenna Bush to the Republican National Convention, *Washington Post*, August 31, 2004.

48. World War III was the Cold War in their eyes.

49. Sean Hannity, *Deliver Us from Evil—Defeating Terrorism, Despotism, and Liberalism* (New York: HarperCollins, 2004), 6.

50. James Brooke, "On Farthest U.S. Shores, Iraq Is a Way to a Dream," *New York Times*, July 31, 2005.

51. Charles Moskos, Crain Lecture, De Paw University, September 30, 2004.

52. "Prince Harry to Be Sent to Iraq," *BBC News*, April 30, 2007.

53. Jennifer Quinn, "Prince Harry Says He Won't Sit Out Iraq," Associated Press, February 19, 2007.

54. Roth-Douquet and Schaeffer, *AWOL*, 128.

55. Jim Wallis, *The Soul of Politics: Beyond "Religious Right" and "Secular Left"* (San Diego, CA: Harvest Books, 1995).

56. Andrew J. Bacevich, *The New American Militarism: How Americans Are Seduced by War* (Oxford: Oxford University Press, 2006); *American Empire: The Realities and Consequences of U.S. Diplomacy* (Cambridge, MA: Harvard University Press, 2004); *The Limits of Power: The End of American Exceptionalism* (New York: Metropolitan Books, 2008).

57. Chalmers Johnson, *Nemesis: The Last Days of the American Republic* (New York: Metropolitan Books, 2006).

58. *Common Dreams*, July 16, 2006.

59. Quoted in Bob Herbert, "The Sacrifice of a Few," *New York Times*, October 12, 2006.

60. All estimates, adjusted for inflation, are based on the costs of military operations and don't include expenses for veterans benefits, interest on war-related

debts, or assistance to war allies, according to the nonpartisan Congressional Research Service. Christine Simmons, "Iraq War's Total Cost Nearing Vietnam's Price Tag," Associated Press, July 15, 2008.

61. John Mueller, "The Iraq Syndrome," *Foreign Affairs*, November/December 2005, 45.

62. "War Losses Mount for Nation's Small Towns," *USA Today*, February 20, 2007.

63. Tom Curry, "Clinton Questions Future of Volunteer Army," MSNBC, February 25, 2006.

64. Brian Stelter, "Reporters Say Networks Put Wars on Back Burner," *New York Times*, June 23, 2008.

65. U.S. Senator Robert Byrd, Senate floor speech, February 12, 2003.

1

⚜

"Mr. President, When Do We Enlist?": The Reality of Alienated War

"**W**atch my generation now, just watch us. This is our turn to be the greatest generation."

These are the words of a young man to Tom Brokaw, cited by *New York Times* columnist Thomas Friedman in one of his editorials championing 9/11 as a time for revitalization. Friedman concluded his piece, "This greatest generation has to win its stripes by making sure that the America that was passed onto us, and that now claims for itself the leadership of a legal war against evil terrorists, is worthy of that task."

"Mr. President, when do we enlist?"[1]

President Bush spoke similar words to Bob Woodward not long after 9/11. "Just like my father's generation was called in World War Two, now our generation is being called." Bush was confident that he had been placed in the presidency "for a reason." "This is going to be how we're going to be judged."[2]

Driving these appeals to the "Greatest Generation" was the widespread concern about political alienation in academia and popular culture of the 1990s. It received its pithiest expression in Harvard political scientist Robert Putnam's best-seller *Bowling Alone*.[3] Americans had traditionally thought of themselves as civically engaged. Alexis de Tocqueville made much of such engagement in *Democracy in America*. As recently as 1960, studies by political scientists Gabriel Almond and Sidney Verba seemed to confirm it. Drawing on research through the 1990s, though, Putnam's book documented a startling decline in all forms of political and community activity. Voting participation had plummeted. "Membership" in political organizations had increasingly become just a matter of sending contributions to pay for professionals to do what previously ordinary citizens had done together as members. There was a striking decline in the basic knowledge or even interest of average persons in the society around them. Putnam's title, *Bowling Alone*, referred to the fact that while previously most people had bowled together (e.g., as members of leagues), now they did so as solitary individuals. Now they bowled alone.

There was no agreement about what explained the rise of such alienation. In *Bowling Alone*, Putnam ascribed great importance to television and its socially isolating passivity-inducing effects. Others, like sociologist Theda Skocpol, looked to the link between citizenship and war. Charting the rise and fall of citizen involvement in *Diminished Democracy*, she noted that "ironically" major American wars had "proved surprisingly beneficial for popularly rooted associations."[4] The greatest increase in public involvement in our history, especially in nationwide associations, political and otherwise, came from the Civil War. Military mobilization prompted civic engagement in numerous ways. The largest women's organization of the nineteenth century, the Women's Christian Temperance Union, grew out of women's alarm at the amount of drinking among soldiers. Both World War I and World War II further boosted citizen activity and organizations.

The regenerative power of war is one of the oldest themes in our political culture. Starting with the War of 1812, political leaders have looked to war as a political "viagara," the magic pill for flagging patriotism and a flaccid populace.[5] Would Bush's War on Terror revitalize the land? Would we return to bowling together?

Many hoped it would. Robert Putnam remarked to the *Washington Post*, "I think there is the potential that Sept. 11 will turn out to be a turning point for civic America. It's a horrible tragedy, but there could be some good coming from it if it causes us to become . . . more aware of the obligations we have to other people and more open-minded about the role of government."[6] Putnam and coauthor Thomas Sander repeated these thoughts in a commentary of February 19, 2002, in the *Christian Science Monitor*, "Walking the Civic Talk after Sept 11th": "The tragedy of 9/11 dramatically led us to rediscover friends, neighbors, public institutions, and a shared fate." That tragedy "opened up a historic window of opportunity for civic renewal," they wrote, echoing Putnam's earlier remark to *Newsweek* (February 6, 2002) that "this is a once in a half century opportunity for President Bush."

No such civic renewal occurred. Americans remained disconnected. What the years since 9/11 have demonstrated is the depth of alienated war. They have revealed the centrality of the chickenhawk syndrome to what the country is all about.

"WE'RE LOOKING FOR A FEW GOOD GRANDPARENTS . . ."

Let's all take a deep breath and repeat after me: Give war a chance. This is Afghanistan we're talking about. Check the map. It's far away.

—Thomas Friedman[7]

The signs that 9/11 would not have a regenerative impact came quickly. Despite the public surveys reporting dramatic changes in attitudes, from declining cynicism to increased trust in the government, Putnam and others found no evidence of change in behavior. "Our ideas are outrunning our actions," they wrote. Polls reported a dramatic increase among children of baby boomers in their confidence in the U.S. military. But such confidence did not translate into any interest in serving themselves. One article laconically stated, "The growing popularity does not necessarily translate into a surge in enlistments."[8] Skocpol concluded her 2003 *Diminished Democracy,*

> Recurrently throughout U.S. history, wartime crises have triggered eras of civic renewal. But the martial conflicts themselves did not lead to civic revitalization—not in and of themselves, apart from leaders willing to seize the opportunity to engage, or create, popularly rooted organizations to undertake important public tasks. As of the early 21st century, the United States has too few associations and leaders able and willing to mobilize citizens for shared national undertakings. September 11th, 2001, sparked widespread yearnings for expanded public undertakings, but the chance for civic revitalization could all too easily dissipate before America's institutions and leaders catch up with America's people.[9]

Immediately liberal pundits announced that fault lay with President Bush. Writing in *The American Prospect*, Michael Lipsky remarked "the truly astonishing thing about the anticipated new 'war on terrorism' is the apparent indifference of our leaders to the need to cultivate a deep sense of national unity, on which long-term support for the war effort still relies."[10] In an article, "We, Not Me," Stanley Greenberg said of a plan to federalize airport security workers that "this is a Democratic dream" [!], but he went on to bemoan the fact that "the short-term, consumerist perspective" of Republicans prevented them from marshaling collective energies further.[11] Nine months after the event, David Gergen was opining in the *New York Times*,

> Give credit to Mr. Bush for adaptive leadership. But there is a big challenge that has so far received short shrift and needs a fresh look: the creation of a new sense of purpose in our national life. How can we transform the good

will and willingness to sacrifice since September 11th into meaningful and lasting changes in our communities and culture? Nine months after the attacks, our opportunity on that civic front is rapidly slipping away. (June 17, 2002)

One of the relentless proponents of popular involvement and a leading critic of Bush for not promoting it was Thomas Friedman. The man who on December 11, 2001, wrote that there was a "deep hunger in America in many people who feel that this is their war in their backyard and they would like to be summoned by the President to do something more than go shopping" was still voicing the theme in a February 2004 piece, "The Home Team." The occasion for the editorial was Janet Jackson's exposing herself to the world during halftime at the Super Bowl. This, conjoined with the wretched news from Iraq, prompted a series of reflections on the contradiction between fun at home and suffering abroad. Friedman recounted that after the Super Bowl he asked his wife, "How can we present something to America and the world that is this frivolous and gross when we have 115,000 U.S. soldiers in Iraq, dying at one per day?" "The whole burden is being borne by a small cadre of Americans—the soldiers, their families and reservists—and the rest of us are just sailing along, as if it has nothing to do with us." "We do not deserve these people," he said of the soldiers. He laid the blame on President Bush, quoting a friend, George Packer,

> We could not win the Cold War without our democratic allies abroad, and without real sacrifice at home, and we cannot win this one without both either. This is a huge, long-term war of ideas but it needs our public's participation and that of our allies. But this administration has never summoned that.

The "antiwar left" is wrong, Friedman concluded:

> However mangled was the Bush road to war, it is a war for the values of our civilization. But the Bush conservatives are also wrong. It can't be won with an idealism that is selfish, greedy, and arrogant.[12]

At some point in the future, social historians will ponder the immediate aftermath of 9/11—and how strange the reaction was. I'm not thinking of the horror felt at the events and the compassion for its victims, both of which were true and genuine. I have in mind the news-and-commentator class whose bafflement led to numerous statements of the kind they must surely regret now. It's as if they had never encountered a real crisis before. Even experienced CBS news anchorman Dan Rather made remarks like "George Bush is the president. And, you know, it's just one American, wherever he wants me to line up, just tell me where, and he'll make the call."[13] Is this the proper ethic for one of the nation's leading newsmen?[14]

Friedman was the most striking case, given his stature as the nation's leading foreign policy pundit. Reading him now, one senses someone driven by the wildest knee-jerk reactions to current events. He surely won't want to be remembered for statements like this:

> I was a critic of [Defense Secretary Donald] Rumsfeld before, but there's one thing . . . that I do like about Rumsfeld. He's just a little bit crazy, OK? He's just a little bit crazy, and in this kind of war, they always count on being able to out-crazy us, and *I'm glad we got some guy on our bench that's our quarterback—who's just little bit crazy, not totally, but you never know what that guy's got to do, and I say that's my guy.*[15]

Friedman repeated the thought in "Crazier than Thou."[16] "The terrorists and the states that harbor them thought we were soft, and they were right. They thought that they could always 'out-crazy' us, and they were right." Friedman acknowledged that Bush's Axis of Evil idea wasn't "thought through," "but that's what I like about it." That's what he liked about Rumsfeld too. "Meet Don Rumsfeld—he's even crazier than you are." There was much Friedman didn't like about Bush's foreign policy team, but their willingness to be "as crazy as some of our enemies, is one thing they have right." This is a novel theory of war leaders: they should be insane—or at least a "little bit" insane. Were Washington, Lincoln, Roosevelt, and Eisenhower flawed because they *weren't* mentally unstable?[17]

We now see the tragic consequences of having delusional people in charge. But Friedman was right about the skewed nature of the sacrifices. He was right that there was something morally bankrupt about "1 percent of America carrying the whole burden of this war," and he was right about the fraudulence of the president's calls to service. In an important work on political alienation published after 9/11, *Downsizing Democracy*, Matthew Crenson and Benjamin Ginsberg made the same point:

> President George W. Bush addressed the nation to calm fears, to inform Americans of his plans, and to call upon the citizenry to do its part in the face of the crisis. What exactly was the part the President assigned to ordinary Americans? We were advised to sing patriotic songs, and think patriotic thoughts, and, above all, to go shopping. In other words, the government held little need for citizens and could think of little for them to do besides buoy up the economy and stay out of the way.[18]

The sacrifice issue was later raised by the inaugural ceremonies for the president's second term.[19] The president's speechwriter, David Frum, stated that "the country wants some indication of how much sacrifice in international affairs he's [Bush] going to be asking." The inauguration's theme was "Celebrating Freedom and Honoring Service." It began with a tribute to the military and was followed, immediately after the taking of the oath of office, by a "Commander-in-Chief Ball"—for 2,000 troops who had served in Iraq or Afghanistan or were heading there. They were entertained by singer Lee Greenwood, famed for the patriotic anthem "God Bless the U.S.A." But then these faux calls for "sacrifice" were buried under the monstrous excesses of the event, at the price of $40 million (the most expensive inauguration in history), mainly from private corporate donations. The premier event of the festivities was the "Black Tie and Boots Ball," at which Republican luminaries consumed 21,000 enchiladas, 20,000 quesadillas, 25,000 pastries, and 3,000 pounds of barbecued beef. An appearance by Kid Rock was allegedly nixed by conservative Christians. President Bush defended it all by saying, "You can be equally concerned about our troops in Iraq and those who suffered in the tsunami while celebrating democracy." Laura Bush spent $3000.00 to get her hair done for the events.

Enlistment Problems

> This recruiting problem is not just an Army problem, this is America's problem. And what we have to really do is talk about service to this nation—and a sense of duty to this nation.
>
> —Army's Vice Chief of Staff General Richard Cody[20]

The most striking evidence of the absence of any civic rejuvenation was the deep and ongoing recruitment and retention problems of the military.

Not since the nineteenth century has the United States fought a war of any length using volunteer troops alone. Would people continue to volunteer if it actually meant going to war? Following the immediate post-Vietnam years, when military service was a hard sell, the military repackaged itself as a good career opportunity at a time when many blue-collar jobs were vanishing. For more than two decades, the army employed the slogan "Be All You Can Be" and later "An Army of One." Neither slogan had much to do with patriotism. Even before the Iraq War, a falloff in enlistment rates was evident. It became pronounced thereafter. Significantly, those branches not involved in combat (the navy and the air force) continued to meet recruiting goals, but report after report described the problem in other branches.

When the Pentagon called up substantial numbers of National Guard units for service in Iraq and Afghanistan in late 2003 and 2004, it elicited a strong backlash from communities throughout the country. In May 2005, the army reported that despite reducing its recruiting target from 8,000 to 6,700, it had still fallen 25 percent short.[21] Figures on the Army Reserve and National Guard were just as bad. In the fall of 2006, the army reported that it had met its yearly recruiting goal for the first time in several years by adding recruiters, sweetening enlistment bonuses, accepting older recruits, and even tolerating more tattoos. But experts pointed out that this meant drastically lowering the quality of new volunteers. "The real question is: how low are we willing to let the quality of the army decline while we continue in this war?" asked Lawrence Korb, assistant secretary of defense in charge of manpower issues under former President Ronald Reagan. In the fall of 2006, President Bush faced a growing revolt among his commanders around the overstretch issue. The army's top officer, General Peter Shoomaker, called for a nearly 50 percent increase in spending (to nearly $140 billion) to cope with Iraq. In what was deemed an "unprecedented protest" against previous budget rejections by the White House, the general refused to provide his budget request as scheduled.[22]

The situation remained bleak into 2008. The U.S. Army met its recruiting goals for fiscal 2007 but only by paying higher recruiting bonuses and lowering its standards. For the third year in a row, it failed to meet its benchmark for the educational level of new recruits. More were admitted with no high school diploma, lower aptitude scores, or criminal records. As a result, a higher percentage of recruits was expected to drop out before the end of their first term of enlistment, leading to more expenses for recruitment. The percentage of recruits from upper-middle- and higher-income neighborhoods continued to decline. In February 2008, the army's top general warned that the stress of repeated employments was causing a decline in the general quality of new recruits and retention of midlevel officers. It was also generating higher rates of desertions and suicide, among other problems. "That is a disturbing trend," he said.[23]

Much of the problem arose from the attitudes of minorities to Bush's policies. A major factor in the all-volunteer military's success in the 1980s and 1990s had been African Americans seeing it as a good career opportunity. Although racial tensions in Vietnam had left a bad legacy, the military had come to be seen—correctly—as offering equal opportunity. At the end of the twentieth century, minorities represented 42 percent of enlisted soldiers in the army. African Americans constituted 29 percent of army enlistees despite constituting 13 percent of the population as a whole. But after 9/11, they proved reluctant to enlist in the administration's War on Terror. Major General Michael Rochelle, commander of army recruiting, stated in August 2005, "We saw a most precipitous drop [of African Americans enlisting] immediately after September 11th."

Noting that the army had long enjoyed a "special relation" with blacks, he bemoaned the fact that the relation might be over.[24] In fiscal 2001, African Americans constituted 23 percent of all new army recruits, as they had in each of the previous five years. In fiscal 2005 they constituted only 14 percent. That's a decline of nearly 40 percent. From 2000 to 2004, the number of black enlisted troops declined significantly in all three military branches. New recruits fell from 38,034 in 2000 to 26,170 in 2004, a decline of nearly a third. The sharpest decline in black recruitment was experienced by the army, which had the most troops deployed in Iraq. In the marines, the second-largest force in Iraq, the share of black recruits decreased to 8 percent from 12 percent in the same period. All commentators ascribed this to the greater unpopularity of the Afghanistan and Iraq wars among African Americans.[25] A CBS News telephone poll in late 2007 reported that 83 percent of the blacks surveyed said the United States should have stayed out of Iraq; only 14 percent said it had done the right thing in taking military action. DeTorrian Rhone, age eighteen, a recent high school graduate, stated,

> A lot of black kids, they don't want to be in it. Most of the kids say they don't want to fight for a country that's pickin' on other countries. I don't want to fight because this [Iraq] war was stupid, it wasted money. Army people are getting killed for nothing, and we should have stayed in our own business.[26]

Whites, by contrast, were closely divided: 48 percent said military action had been right, and 46 percent said the United States should have stayed out.[27]

Another key factor was the attitudes of parents. A Department of Defense survey in November 2005 reported that only 25 percent of parents would recommend military service to their children, down from 42 percent in August 2003. The problem was not just lack of encouragement but also outright hostility. Said one recruiter in Ohio, "Parents are the biggest hurdle we face." General Rochelle, the previously mentioned commander of army recruiting, stated that parental resistance could put the all-volunteer force in jeopardy. When parents and other influential adults dissuade young people from enlisting, he said, "it begs the question of what our national staying power might be for what certainly appears to be a long fight." Part of the problem resulted from the law that was supposed to make recruiting easier. The No Child Left Behind Act, passed in 2001, required schools to turn over students' phone numbers and addresses unless parents opted out. This was a spark that ignited parental resistance. Some recruiters have even been threatened with violence. "I had one father say if he saw me on his doorstep I better have some protection on me," said a recruiter in Ohio. "We see a lot of hostility."[28]

The problems continued. At the end of 2006, just a month before Bush's call for an increase of troops in Iraq, the army asked for new authority to send National Guard and Reserve soldiers back to that conflict for repeat deployments, including those who had already served the maximum time allowed by the Pentagon. The plan was pushed by the Army Chief of Staff, who continued to raise the alarm about the military "breaking" under the strain of the Iraq War. More and more people noted the disparity between the grandiosity of American war policy and its limited troops to carry it out. "This is not an Army that was built to sustain a 'long war,'" America's top general in charge of Iraq, John Abizaid, told students at Harvard.[29] The Bush administration's defense policy committed the U.S. military to defending its homeland, sustain two major wars, and the presence in key regions abroad to fight the global War on Terror. Since the Carter administration, the United States had been committed to whatever was necessary to maintain its interest in the Middle East. The massive military budget reflected these priorities. Yet military leaders worried that we had been brought to the breaking point by insurgencies in two small countries, where we had committed only half the troops we sent to Korea and a third of those we sent to Vietnam.

The problem of troop retention came into bizarre focus in the spring 2008 debate over a new GI bill. A proposed bill with wide bipartisan support aimed to expand benefits significantly for men and women who had served in the military at least three years since the attacks of 9/11. In what would be the biggest expansion of GI benefits in a quarter of a century, the bill included substantial educational benefits for returning soldiers, paying tuition and other expenses at a four-year public university. But the proposal ran into trouble in the Senate when the administration warned that it would cause serious retention issues since soldiers would have more incentive to leave the military and return to college. President Bush threatened to veto the new military benefits, with the support of Senator John McCain, apparently on the grounds that rewarding soldiers for their service was incompatible with keeping them on the job.[30]

Reponses to the Problem

The administration's responses to the decline were multifold:

1. *Spend more money*: The military began offering bonuses up to $20,000 as it sent more and more recruiters into the field. There was talk of raising this to $40,000. The army raised college scholarship offers from $50,000 to $70,000 and offered up to $50,000 in "mortgage assistance." As a result, the cost of recruiting soldiers increased from $7,600 per soldier in 1996 to more than $14,000 in 2004. In 2003 the Pentagon spent almost $4 billion

targeting high-achieving low-income youth, especially on enlistment bonuses, commercials, video games, personal visits, and slick brochures.

In its attempt to become more media savvy, the Pentagon contracted companies like Teenage Research Unlimited for advice on getting inside kids' heads. The Department of Defense acknowledged that, with the aid of marketing firm BeNow, it had created a database of 12 million youth, some only sixteen years old, as potential recruits. In the summer of 2005, the air force launched its own personal profile on MySpace.com, the popular website that reached 49 percent of all Internet users between the ages of eighteen and twenty-four. "In order to reach young men and women today, we need to be in tune and engaged in their circles," said Colonel Brian Madtes, Air Force Recruiting Service's strategic communications director. "MySpace.com is a great way to get the word out to the public about the amazing things people are doing in the Air Force."[31] In addition to the thirty-second commercials, users would be able to view expanded videos of Airmen as they fly and fight, call in air strikes, navigate satellites, and jump out of airplanes.

2. *Target minorities*: Minorities have been crucial to filling the military ranks since the desegregation of the armed forces in 1948. The government has made special efforts to draw them in, especially when the more privileged had little interest in fighting. During the Vietnam War, a program called Project 100,000 was created specifically to recruit southern black youths to the war's front lines. Secretary of Defense Robert McNamara had standards lowered to recruit and "rehabilitate" 100,000 youths annually that had previously been rejected for failing mental or physical requirements. This resulted in several hundred thousand men being sent to Vietnam and several thousands to their deaths who otherwise would have been spared. (By 1970, a Defense Department study found 41 percent of the soldiers were black as compared to 12 percent of the army as a whole, and 40 percent were trained for combat as compared to 25 percent in the services generally.[32])

Accordingly, today's troop shortfall led to increased efforts to target minorities, especially Latinos, whose overall enlistment lagged behind its population percentage and which, as a community, was less hostile to the administration's war policies than African Americans. Latinos constituted 13.5 percent of the population as a whole but only 9 percent of army enlistees (though they were overrepresented in combat-related positions at 17.5 percent). Puerto Rico was the army's number one recruiting territory. Capitalizing on that island's 40 percent unemployment rate, recruiting offices averaged four times the rate in the United States. The military sought to recruit noncitizens in Mexico—but not without protest. In May 2003, the Mexican government formally complained about recruiters crossing the border into Mexico to "prey" on youth.[33]

In an April 2005 article, "Military Recruiters Targeting Minority Teens," *Los Angeles Times* reporter Erika Hayasaki described the approach of one recruiter—Carloss—who had spent seven weeks in recruiting classes to hone his marketing and communication skills. His techniques were those endorsed in the army's *School Recruiting Program Handbook* of 2004. Carloss made a point of delivering doughnuts and coffee to school staff once a month, attending faculty and parent meetings, chaperoning dances, participating in Hispanic Heritage Month events, meeting with student governments, and even leading the football team in calisthenics—the overall aim to make himself "indispensable" on campus. The previously mentioned handbook encourages recruiters like Carloss to ingratiate himself to student leaders like the student body president or captain of the football team not because they are likely to choose the military but because they will "provide you with referrals who will enlist."[34]

3. *Target parents*: Attempts to change parental attitudes were crucial. A study by the firm Millward Brown commissioned by the government reported that "opposition to . . . military service is increasing significantly among both moms and dads." Another study by GfK Custom Research placed the problem mainly on the mothers. Eighty-one percent of young respondents identified their mothers as the key influence compared with 70 percent for the fathers. The conclusion: "Reach the parents with the army's new message, particularly moms."

Key to the "new message" was convincing parents that serving in the military was not a "death sentence." Indeed, the Iraq War was not even mentioned as part of the message. New ads were directed at parents as well as coaches and ministers. A nine-minute video, *Parents Speak,* showed parents of marines describing how good the Marine Corps had been for their children. Commercials shifted from high-tech, hectic imagery to heart-to-heart talks describing the army's virtues for building character. "You're a changed man," a father said to a son in the commercial. "You shook my hand, and you looked me square in the eye." "I get training in just about any field that I want. And besides, it's time for me to be the man," the actor portraying the son said.[35]

"What we are communicating—that the army will enable your son or daughter to be successful in anything that they choose to do in life," said Colonel Tom Nickerson, in charge of the army's recruiting outreach program. As Colonel Nickerson was touting the military as a path to future success, the *New York Times* reported that experts were predicting a "potential deluge" of former soldiers into the nation's medical system to cope with mental health problems caused by the stress of war. "About one in six soldiers in Iraq report symptoms of major depression, serious anxiety, or posttraumatic stress disorder; but some experts say it could eventually climb to one in three, the rate ultimately found in Vietnam veterans."[36]

The attempts to reach parental "influencers" were singularly unsuccessful. A story by Dan Harris on ABC's *World News Tonight* reported that military leaders had concluded privately that the recruiting challenge was too big for them to fix on their own. They had asked President Bush to step in. The president refused. To the discontent of many in the military, Harris noted, the president had left it to the military "to do the convincing."[37]

4. *Change the slogan*: In 2005, the army retained the services of the New York–based ad agency McCann Worldgroup to "rework its image" and improve its outreach. The agency was behind such triumphs as McDonald's "You deserve a break today." The army signed a $1 billion four-year contract in the hope that McCann could market soldiering the same way it had marketed Egg McMuffins and Happy Meals.

The upshot was a new slogan, "Army Strong," linked with an advertising blitz commencing Veterans Day 2006 involving television, radio, and the Internet. Officials hoped to appeal to young people with a minimalist phrase that "got right to the point." Forsaking what former Army Secretary Louis Caldera called the "me-now" approach, the slogan was seen as speaking to "an essential truth of being a soldier," in the words of current Army Secretary Francis Harvey. According to Army Public Affairs, the new slogan was meant to emphasize "skills, leadership, teamwork and selfless service" and the "transformative power of the U.S. Army." The service branches not involved in combat were happy with the status quo. Their slogans, by the way, are "Do something amazing" (air force), "Accelerate your life" (navy), and "Ready today, preparing for tomorrow" (coast guard).[38]

5. *Change the military*: The military transformed itself significantly with the creation of the all-volunteer force, almost entirely for the better. Recruitment problems spurred further changes. For example, in July 2005, the *New York Times* reported a diligent effort to rein in abuses at boot camps. The story told of a staff sergeant chastised for what he described as just doing his normal job: punching new recruits in the stomach, hitting them repeatedly on the chest, throwing them on the floor, and calling them "fat nasty." The sixteen-year veteran was court-martialed and found guilty of cruelty. The army said that if it did not stop this sort of thing, "we won't get the support of the mothers and fathers."[39]

6. *Expand the pool*: In the summer of 2005, the Pentagon announced it was raising the age limit for recruits to forty-two.[40] A military spokesperson explained by insisting that "age should not be a basis for discrimination." This led to a spate of human interest stories describing the military's new middle-aged members, numbering in the thousands by some reports. Forty-one-year-old Lauri Ann Fouca, a mother of four from Arizona, followed her son into the military. "My son was like, 'You're

crazy, moms don't join the military,'" she said. Despite being a grandmother, Margie Black of West Columbia, Texas, also served alongside
her twenty-one-year-old daughter. A spokesman for the local recruiting
office remarked, "Lots of people [over thirty-five] are fit and are living
longer, and they figure they can do this." Private First Class Kimberly
Brown "couldn't resist" cupping her eighteen-year-old son Derek's face
in "jubilation" after they both successfully graduated from basic training.
With five children to support at home, Ms. Brown said that the work in
the army was welcome.[41]

The army also continued to lower its standards for who was morally
fit to serve. One wry commentator observed that the new slogan "Army
Strong" was accompanied by a weakening in its standards for enlistment.[42] It instituted a system of "moral waivers" to bypass existing regulations. Recruits with serious criminal records, drug problems, histories
of gang membership, and other questionable factors that would have
excluded them before were now accepted. From 2001 to 2006, the army's
acceptance of moral waivers increased about 40 percent; from 2004 to
2005, the number of recruits brought in with serious criminal misconduct
waivers jumped 54 percent, and drug and alcohol waivers increased 13
percent.

In the fall of 2007, the military was looking to relax further its standards, the Associated Press reported:

> Faced with higher recruiting goals, the Pentagon is quietly looking for ways
> to make it easier for people with minor criminal records to join the mili-
> tary. The review, in its early stages, comes as the number of Army recruits
> needing waivers for bad behavior—such as trying drugs, stealing, carrying
> weapons on school grounds and fighting—rose from 15 percent in 2006 to
> 18 percent this year. And it reflects the services' growing use of criminal,
> health and other waivers to build their ranks. Overall, about three in every 10
> recruits must get a waiver, according to Pentagon statistics obtained by AP
> [Associated Press], and about two-thirds of those approved in recent years
> have been for criminal behavior.[43]

The article noted that "according to the Pentagon data, the bulk of all
conduct waivers are for recruits involved in either drug offenses or serious misdemeanors. Over the past five years, the overall percentage of recruits involved in serious misdemeanors has grown." Relaxing standards
was necessary to meet Pentagon targets of increasing the army by about
65,000 soldiers to a total of 547,000 and the marines by 27,000 to 202,000.
But many were not enthusiastic about the prospect. Army officers complained that they already spent too much time dealing with discipline
problems. "In a meeting with Adm. Mike Mullen, chairman of the Joint
Chiefs of Staff, a number of officers vigorously nodded their heads when

he asked if that was a concern. One officer told Mullen that when he was in Iraq he would spend long hours into the night dealing with 'problem children.'"[44]

Congressional voices responded sharply. After Congress voted to increase the size of the U.S. Army and the Marine Corps, Representative Ellen Tauscher, chairman of the House Armed Services Subcommittee on Strategic Forces, charged that the wars in Iraq and Afghanistan had made the military so unattractive that "moms and dads and spouses have voted with their feet," urging soldiers to get out of uniform and discouraging young people from joining in the first place. She specifically cited problems raised by lowering moral standards. "I'm all for rehab and giving people a second chance, but that's not why we're doing this. This is about the fact that we need people with pulses that are willing to come into the military," she said. "If you have—as the nuns used to say—comportment issues, if you can't sit quietly and listen, if you can't be trained and if you have a predilection to pilfering—or bigger things—you're going to be a detriment to your unit."[45]

7. *Sign up immigrants, illegals, foreigners, and so on*: Measures were instituted to expand the number of legal immigrants allowed to enlist. Noncitizens were increasingly enticed to join by the promise of a fast track to citizenship under a law approved by Bush in 2003 and enacted in 2004. Prior to 9/11, American naturalization ceremonies had taken place on foreign soil only twice: in the Korean conflict and in the 1990s with Filipino veterans of World War II. Now teams of immigration officers flew around the world to carry out such naturalization ceremonies. From 2002 to 2005, 20,000 military service members became citizens this way.[46]

In late 2006, reports surfaced about the military's plans to recruit foreigners directly.[47] From 9/11 to 2005, the number of immigrants in uniform who had become U.S. citizens increased from 750 to 4,600, a spike of more than 500 percent, and by December 2006, there were 30,000 noncitizens serving in the U.S. military, about 2 percent of the active-duty force (about a hundred noncitizens had been killed in combat). Enlistment shortfalls led to the consideration of more aggressive measures, though, as one report noted, the military was quiet about foreign citizens' serving since it could expose the Pentagon to criticism that "it is essentially using mercenaries to defend the country" and would reflect "badly on Americans' willingness to serve in uniform." Still, measures were considered, such as opening recruiting stations overseas to create the American equivalent of a French Foreign Legion.

A vocal champion of such measures was Max Boot of the Council of Foreign Relations. Boot drew attention for calling on the United States to establish a colonial office to administer its "new possessions" in the Middle East and Asia.[48] In a 2005 *Los Angeles Times* commentary,[49] Boot argued that America's enlistment woes and the flat disinterest of Americans themselves to serve called for some "outside-the-box thinking": "In this regard, I note that there is a pretty big pool of manpower that's not being tapped: everyone on the planet who is not a U.S. citizen or permanent resident." He bemoaned the fact that there were so few noncitizens serving in Iraq and Afghanistan. "In the 19th century, when the foreign-born population of the United States was much higher, so was the percentage of foreigners serving in the military":

> No doubt many would be willing to serve for some set period in return for one of the world's most precious commodities—U.S. citizenship. Open up recruiting stations from Budapest to Bangkok, Cape Town to Cairo, Montreal to Mexico City. *Some might deride those who sign up as mercenaries,* but these troops would have significantly different motives than the usual soldier of fortune.
>
> The simplest thing to do would be to sign up foreigners for the regular U.S. military, but it would also make sense to create a unit whose enlisted ranks would be composed entirely of non-Americans, led by U.S. officers and NCOs. (emphasis added)

In "Call It the Freedom Legion," Boot wrote,

> It would have as its mission defending and advancing freedom across the world. U.S. politicians, so wary (and rightly so) of casualties among U.S. citizens, might take a more lenient attitude toward the employment of a force not made up of their constituents. An added benefit is that by recruiting foreigners, the U.S. military could address its most pressing strategic deficit in the war on terrorism—lack of knowledge about other cultures. The most efficient way to expand the government's corps of Pashto or Arabic speakers isn't to send native-born Americans to language schools; it's to recruit native speakers of those languages.

Perhaps there are still a few Hessians or Nepalese Gurkhas still around, unemployed since the British Empire no longer hires them to fight its wars.

8. *The stop-loss policy*: Especially dramatic—and controversial—was the government's employment of the so-called stop-loss policy. In essence, this policy forced regular soldiers and reservists to stay in the military after their terms of service were supposed to end. (Stop-movement orders can also bar soldiers from moving to new assignments.) Congress first gave the military stop-loss authority after the Vietnam War when the Pentagon faced difficulties replacing combat soldiers, but the Pentagon did not use the authority until 1990 during the first Gulf War buildup. The Pentagon issued stop-loss orders in November 2002 for Reserve and National Guard units activated for the War on Terror. An order for active

troops was issued in February 2003. Despite bonuses up to $10,000 for re-enlistment, the army needed the stop-loss approach. Although estimates were inexact, tens of thousands of soldiers were prevented from retiring or leaving the military so that they could be deployed to Afghanistan or Iraq.[50] The total number affected was surely more than 50,000.

These were not faceless numbers. Consider a case for my own community in Oregon. Emeliano Santiago was the child of farmworkers and a Mexican immigrant who had been in the country five years when a National Guard recruiter came to his high school in Stanfield, Oregon. "I was really excited to see the uniform," he said. "I wanted to wear the same uniform, to be a part of that." The recruiter informed him that National Guard service was "a little off-side thing that you could do," almost guaranteed not to result in deployment. "The only reason the National Guard would get deployed is if there was, like, a World War III," Santiago remembered being told. Eighteen years old, he signed up for eight years and became a helicopter refueler for a unit based in Pendleton, Oregon. He got married, moved to Pasco, Washington, and became an electronics technician at a laboratory run by Battelle Memorial Institute for the U.S. Department of Energy.

In April 2004, less than three months before he was to be discharged, the army informed him that his unit might be mobilized and that the termination date of his service was being extended by more than *twenty-seven* years—to December 2031. Now married with a family, the twenty-seven-year-old filed suit in federal court claiming that he was improperly being called back to active duty. But court decisions went against him, with one judge ruling that the harm the military would endure if blocked from keeping soldiers like Santiago in its ranks merited the burden on him and his family. Supporters pointed out that the stop-loss approach was nothing less than a "backdoor draft."[51]

In the fall of 2007, the Associated Press reported that "the U.S. Army will continue to rely on an unpopular program that forces some soldiers to stay on beyond their retirement or re-enlistment dates, despite repeated pressure from Defense Secretary Robert Gates to reduce and eventually eliminate the practice." The number of soldiers forced to remain in the military increased by almost 30 percent after Bush's "surge." There is little chance of the situation changing. "Until there is some reduction in the demand, we're going to have to rely, unfortunately . . . on stop loss," military officials told reporters. "Until the demand comes down a bit, we can't do it without it."[52]

9. *The consequences*: A result of such attempts to boost recruiting numbers was a host of problems that are unlikely to go away. In August 2006, Reuters reported that allegations of wrongdoing by military recruiters jumped 50 percent from 2004 to 2005 and that criminal violations such as

sexual harassment and falsifying documents had more than doubled.[53] The source of these reports, the Government Accountability Office, Congress's investigative agency, acknowledged that the full extent of violations by recruiters was unknown since the Defense Department refused to institute an oversight system. If anything, its estimate of almost 4,500 incidents of wrongdoing in 2005 understated the problem. An Associated Press report of the same month noted that more than eighty military recruiters had been disciplined the previous year for sexual misconduct. Since 1996, more than 700 army recruiters had been disciplined for actions as serious as rape.[54]

As the military continued to lower its enlistments standards to meet its quotas, it acknowledged that a higher percentage of new recruits barely passed its standard aptitude tests. In the fall of 2005, the army reported that the number scoring at the very bottom of its aptitude test tripled. Twelve percent scored between sixteen and thirty points out of a possible ninety-nine. In the first years of the all-volunteer force, as much as 50 percent of new recruits had been low scoring. Then Congress and successive administrations imposed quality controls so that by 1990 the percentage scoring at the bottom was only 2 percent. Today that figure has climbed back to 12 percent with every indication that it will continue to rise. Former Army Secretary Thomas E. White said that the service was making a mistake by lowering its standards. "I think it's disastrous. You are throwing the towel in on recruiting quality," said White, a retired general whom Defense Secretary Donald H. Rumsfeld fired in 2003 over policy differences.[55]

The strain on soldiers in uniform manifested itself in numerous ways. In 2005 the Pentagon estimated that since the start of the Iraq conflict, more than 5,500 U.S. military personnel had deserted.[56] The already hard-pressed system of health care for veterans faced a potential deluge of thousands of returning soldiers with mental health problems. Some estimated that the wars in Afghanistan and Iraq would generate more than 100,000 troops needing mental health treatment. Increasing attention was paid to the problems of posttraumatic stress disorder (PTSD). A study released on April 17, 2008, by the Rand Corporation reported that 18.5 percent of the 1.6 million U.S. troops who had served in Iraq or Afghanistan, or 300,000 people, said they had symptoms of depression or PTSD because of their overseas service. Nineteen percent (320,000) reported they had suffered head injuries, which, research showed, sharply increased these troops' likelihood of later developing PTSD. Only about half the troops had sought treatment for their mental health or head wounds, according to the report.[57]

The most dramatic consequence was the increase of elements like skinheads and neo-Nazis in the armed forces. In the 1990s, the Pentagon had toughened policies on admitting such elements after the Oklahoma City bombing by Timothy McVeigh, a decorated Gulf War veteran, and the murder of a black couple by a skinhead gang in the elite 82nd Airborne Division. Recruiters were given advice on how to identify such young men and exclude them. The Pentagon eventually launched a massive investigation and crackdown within its own ranks. One general ordered all 19,000 soldiers at Fort Lewis, Washington, strip-searched for extremist tattoos. But with the difficulties in recruiting after Iraq, they looked the other way. "Recruiters are knowingly allowing neo-Nazis and white supremacists to join the armed forces, and commanders don't remove them from the military even after we positively identify them as extremists or gang members," said Department of Defense investigator Scott Barfield.[58]

Cases in point included one former skinhead who, before attending counterinsurgency training, had attended Nazi festivals as leader of a hate rock band. Another was an army engineer who, before he joined the invasion of Iraq, fantasized about fighting a war on Jews as a member of the neo-Nazi National Alliance. "Ever since my youth—when I watched WWII footage and saw how well-disciplined and sharply dressed the German forces were—I have wanted to be a soldier," he said in a winter 2004 interview with the National Alliance magazine *Resistance*. "Joining the American military was as close as I could get."

Neo-Nazis "stretch across all branches of service, they are linking up across the branches once they're inside, and they are hard-core," Department of Defense gang detective Scott Barfield told the *Intelligence Report*. "We've got Aryan Nations graffiti in Baghdad," he added. "That's a problem."[59]

Where's the Sacrifice?

By the summer of 2005, when the failures of the Iraq effort were becoming evident to all, voices complained about the lack of sacrifice among citizens generally. In an article of July 24, "Soldiers Starting to Ask, Where's the Sacrifice?" the *New York Times* reported, "From bases in Iraq and across the United States to the Pentagon and the military's war colleges, officers and enlisted personnel quietly raise a question for political leaders: If America is truly on a war footing, why is so little sacrifice asked of the nation at large?" No one is proposing a tax increase to cover the $60 billion annual cost of the Iraq and Afghan wars, the author, Tom Shaner, continued. "There are no World War II-style war bond drives, no victory gardens, not even gas rationing. Back here in the fatherland, only 'support our troops' car ribbons indicate that we're at war—and they aren't even bumper stickers, they're magnetic. Apparently Americans aren't even willing to sacrifice the finish on their automobiles to promote the cause." One brigadier general added, "There has to be more. The absence of a call for broader national sacrifice in a time of war has become a near constant topic of discussion among officers and enlisted personnel."

By the end of 2005, commentators generally were bemoaning the fact that instead of a new age of idealism, Bush's wars were ushering in a new age of skepticism, in *New York Times* columnist David Brooks's phrase,

> The chief cultural effect of the Iraq war is that we are now entering a period of skepticism. Many Americans are going to be skeptical that their government can know enough to accomplish large tasks or be competent enough to execute ambitious policies. More people are going to be skeptical of plans to mold reality according to our designs or to solve the deep problems that are rooted in history and culture. ("The Age of Skepticism," December 1, 2005)

This was a striking turnaround in such a short time. It took a decade for the Vietnam experience to drive the American public into a state of cynicism. Brooks, the in-house Bush champion at the *New York Times*, detailed the depths of despair. Americans were in an awful mood, he wrote, despite rising consumer confidence and strong economic growth. They were increasingly cynical about politics and parties, explaining why Democrats did not necessarily benefit from the travails of Republicans. Only 24 percent of Americans said the Republicans represented them, and only 26 percent said the Democrats did, according to an NBC/Wall Street Journal poll. Roughly two-thirds of Americans said the country was headed in the wrong direction. Iraq was not the only issue driving this "sour pessimism," Brooks noted, but it was the main one.

RESPONSES TO ALIENATED WAR: LIBERAL, CONSERVATIVE, ETCETERA

> What's at stake in Iraq is not only the future of that country, but the future of American self-confidence.
>
> —David Brooks

The aftermath of 9/11 affirmed the reality of alienated war. How did people respond to this fact? The liberal response focused on President Bush, and rightly so. From the start of his War on Terror, there was something disconnected about the clash between his strong public calls to duty and his other behavior. Consider, for example, the March 2004 annual dinner of the Radio and Television Correspondents Association when he entertained the crowd by showing humorous photos of him on his hands and knees searching the Oval Office for weapons of mass destruction. Six hundred Americans had died in Iraq by then. The question remained, though, of whether the American people would have responded any more if Bush had exercised stronger leadership. Perhaps Bush had his finger on the true pulse of the American people when he made patriotic pronouncements without any specific proposals for sacrifice. If Bush's liberal critics had really wanted to counter his example and promote sacrifice, the best way would have been by setting an example themselves—enlisting themselves or publicly encouraging their children to do so. Bush's liberal critics could have started campaigns similar to the war bond drives of World War II encouraging people to donate money to the War on Terror or spend their time in other specific activities supporting the war. But none of his critics did. Instead, it remained an abstract policy dispute, with critics of the president chastising him for failing to support vague notions of national service and the like.

A prominent response from conservatives was to diagnose the problem as a lingering effect of the 1960s slacker ethic. One proponent of this was self-proclaimed virtue czar William Bennett, often cited as one of the more prominent chickenhawks of the right. Another was *National Review* author Stanley Kurtz, who, proclaiming a theme we'll meet shortly, wrote that America was entering an era of imperialism—but "reluctant imperialism," with President Bush the "ultimate reluctant imperialist."[60] Kurtz maintained that much as "we like to think that America has already been put to the test" and had evidenced a "restored spirit of patriotism and willingness to sacrifice," the sad fact was that the patriotism and sacrifice that were "lost in the 1960s" had not been regained. Faced with the threat of Islamic terrorism, we were still bedeviled by the legacy of Woodstock, *Hair*, and *Laugh-In*. The "heightened cultural individualism" of those years continued to be our sad fate.

Another group to bemoan America's resistance to self-sacrifice was those who believed it would be the best thing for everyone if America established itself as the new global empire. The most articulate of these was Niall Ferguson, an economic historian from Great Britain now at Harvard. Ferguson was one of several historians who saw disturbing parallels between the beginning of the twenty-first century and the beginning of the twentieth century, a century of unprecedented conflict and carnage due to war. But while others saw the parallels as confirming the importance of strengthening international organizations like the United Nations, Ferguson's conclusion was that the British had bungled it and that now the Americans had a chance to do it right—"it" being the creation of a "liberal empire" spreading capitalism and democracy throughout the globe. Unfortunately, despite its promise, there were substantial barriers to achieving this. Ferguson characterized them as "deficits." Taken together, these deficits placed America in the problematic if not pathetic position of looking immensely strong while not actually being strong.

One such deficit was economic—the fact that America was probably unable to financially sustain an empire. Ferguson disputed the views of Paul Kennedy that America's economic problems derived from an over-stretched military.[61] In Ferguson's view, war making did not actually cost that much. The problem was the irrational commitment by Americans to social services like Social Security and Medicare. Ferguson had no soft spot in his heart for the Greatest Generation and its children, the chief beneficiaries of these services. Like most conservatives, he did not enter-tain the thought that such deficits could be addressed on the revenue side, for example, by rescinding Bush's tax cuts, except to say that it was not politically viable.[62]

The second great deficit was "manpower." It included, for starters, the lack of talented Americans to carry on the administrative and orga-nizational tasks of empire. Unlike the British Empire, whose children of the elite looked forward to careers serving overseas, the children of the American elite had no intention of spending their time in places like the Middle East serving the American Empire. You simply could not have an empire without imperialists—out there, on the spot—to run it, he proclaimed. "Until there are more U.S. citizens not just willing but eager to shoulder the 'nation builder's burden,' ventures like the occupation of Iraq will lack a vital ingredient."[63]

The bigger "manpower" problem involved who was going to fight these wars and to police the countries that are occupied. Ferguson was somewhat mystified about this:

> There is undoubtedly something perplexing about the apparent lack of American combat effective troops at a time when the U.S. population is growing at 1.25 percent per annum, unemployment is proving stubbornly resistant to economic recovery (by one estimate there are 4 million victims of the current "job gap") and the American prison population exceeds 2 million—1 in every 142 American residents. If one adds together the illegal immigrants, the jobless and the convicts, there is surely ample raw material for a larger American army. One of the keys to the expansion of the Roman Empire was, after all, the opportunity offered to non-Romans to earn citizen-ship through military service. One of the mainsprings of British colonization was the policy of transportation that emptied the prison hulks of 18th-cen-tury England into ships bound for Australia. Reviving the draft would not necessarily be unpopular, so long as it was appropriately targeted.[64]

Note the lack of romanticism. Finding soldiers to fight for liberty and democracy is approached as an issue of "ample raw material," the pos-sible sources of such raw material being the unemployed, prisoners, and illegal immigrants. Ferguson was not bothered by the racialized character of today's military or the increasingly racialized profile it would acquire drawing from such groups. The idea of shipping prisoners directly to Iraq was a novel one, though Ferguson seemed unconcerned that it would violate the Thirteenth Amendment to the Constitution. Note also the potential impact on African American communities, already decimated by the disproportionate numbers of young African American males in prison, of shipping more of them overseas. Ferguson saw only the silver lining in all this. "If the occupation of Iraq is to be continued for any length of time," he writes, "it can hardly fail to create career opportunities for the growing number of African-American officers in the army."[65]

The obvious alternative was to rely on non-Americans to fight our wars, as the British Empire did in the past. Ferguson smiled on this possibility. "If Americans themselves are reluctant peacekeepers, they must be the peacekeepers paymasters, and strike such bargains as the mercenaries of the 'international community' may demand."[66]

But were Americans even willing to pay for it? Here the third and most insurmountable "deficit" kicked in.

That deficit, "the most serious of the three," was the "attention" deficit. The term suggested an inability to stay focused on much of anything very long, including the project of warfare. Was this really the problem? Depending on how you date it, the United States was involved in the Vietnam conflict for ten or fifteen years at least; in the end, the problem with that war was not impatience to get out of it but the pigheadedness at staying in it. Perhaps the problem was not one of attention span but one of political values, the fact that the history of the United States included a tradition of strong opposition to foreign military interventions. Of such normative issues, Ferguson wrote, "The idea of invading a country, deposing its dictators and imposing free elections at gunpoint is generally dismissed as incompatible with American 'values.'"[67] Ferguson was careful to put quotation marks around "values," as one does around "phlogiston" or "ectoplasm," to suggest their basic unreality.

In the end, the problem for Ferguson was that America had become a nation of *slackers*. In his book, *Colossus: The Price of America's Empire*, he wrote,

> The United States has acquired an empire, but Americans lack the imperial cast of mind. They would rather consume than conquer. They would rather build shopping malls than nations. They crave for themselves protracted old age and dread, even for other Americans who have volunteered for military service, untimely death in battle.[68]

It's bad enough that Americans at home wish a comfortable old age for themselves. They even wish it for those who have volunteered for military service. In an earlier book, *The Cash Nexus*, Ferguson spoke even more bluntly in condemning the "pusillanimous fear [of the United States] of military casualties":

> Perhaps that is the greatest disappointment facing the world in the 21st century: that the leaders of the one state with the economic resources to make the world a better place lack the guts to do it.[69]

Now that he resides in the United States, Ferguson has a chance to walk his talk and encourage his Harvard students to become not just administrators but real fighters in the model of Winston Churchill.

These responses have truth to them. The Bush administration could have asked more in real self-sacrifice. The legacy of the 1960s does live on in matters of self-indulgence. President Bush was the best example of this. And so on.

My own view is that alienated war requires responses of two sorts. One is historical. Alienated war is a dramatic departure from the citizen-soldier ethic of the past. The demise of the latter and the rise of the former is a long story, as yet uncompleted. But any response to the alienated arrangements of today must situate itself in historical understanding. In the next chapter, I offer a sketch of this story—but only a sketch. Other scholars are noted who have dealt with these matters. These are large issues that speak to the fundamental character of American society. Much work remains to be done.

Another response is moral. I think this should be our main response. The proper reaction to alienated war is one of moral outrage. Above all else, alienated war is a sign of deep moral casualness if not moral *rot*. This outrage must be informed by an understanding of how we got where we are, something I'll address in the next chapter. This historical understanding only heightens the moral concern since it shows how drastically we have departed from the orientation of the nation's founders.

As noted at the outset, the founding generation had a good name for the moral rot of today: corruption. "Corruption" is not a common word these days. When most people think of it, they think of it as characterizing individuals: the corrupt politician, say. For the founding generation, corruption was a societal matter pertaining to political culture as a whole. In the words of Henry Knox, one of the first secretaries of war, a corrupt culture was one of "vice, luxury, and laziness"—especially in reference to one's civic obligations.[70] A corrupt culture (like the British in the founders' eyes) was an irresponsible one. It did not only shirk its responsibilities. It did so thoughtlessly, even shamelessly. After all, people can disagree about the specific responsibilities they have. Some will disagree with the claims I'm making about our responsibilities with respect to war.

A corrupt culture is not one of thoughtful disagreement but one in which people don't think about these matters at all.

Corruption is a moral *cluelessness* that the nation's founders identified with overprivileged aristocratic society. A central concern of theirs was to prevent such corruption from corroding the new republic. They did not think a republic could survive widespread corruption since its health required that there be active informed citizens who took their civic responsibilities seriously. A culture of civic virtue could not be enforced from above. It was necessarily a matter of shared public morality, the "habits of the heart" of the average citizen in Tocqueville's words, though this made it all the more essential that citizens be provided good moral exemplars by those who aspire to be their leaders.

In the eyes of the founders, a republic like that of America was a fragile thing since what defined a republic was not its number of bombs or the size of its bank account but the civic virtue of its citizens. A threat to that virtue was the temptation of empire, and that temptation was an enduring one. Empire not only held out the promise of ever more wealth and power. Like all truly evil temptations, it had an element of idealism. Empires have always claimed to bring great benefits to others by their military adventures: bringing "peace" to others (by waging war on them), bringing "civilization" to others (by treating them like savages), and bringing "democracy" to others (by imposing governments on them and so on). Peace, civilization, and democracy are worthy goals, but as the aims of empire, they are illusory. They do not bring these benefits to others. But in the course of claiming to do so, what the imperial impulse does accomplish is undermining republican ideals and arrangements at home—so that ultimately republics are turned into empires and become the disease for which they were originally the cure.

John Quincy Adams remarked that republics "should not go chasing monsters." Republics can spread their ideals through the power of example, but otherwise their orientations should be grounded in humility. This is where the secular enlightenment tradition of republicanism aligns with the Christian heritage: nations, like individuals, should be most feared when they become arrogant. And with nations, such arrogance follows corruption: the greatest check on the grandiose delusional schemes of our government's leaders is a citizenry that takes the question of war seriously by taking the question of war as a personal one: we should fight only those wars for which we as citizens are willing to bear the bodily and financial cost.

NOTES

1. Thomas Friedman, "Ask Not What . . . ," *New York Times*, December 9, 2001.

2. Bob Woodward, *Bush at War* (New York: Simon & Schuster, 2003), 205.

3. Robert Putnam, *Bowling Alone: The Collapse and Revival of American Community* (New York: Simon & Schuster, 2000).

4. Theda Skocpol, *Diminished Democracy: From Membership to Management in American Civic Life* (Norman: University of Oklahoma Press, 2004), 33.

5. See Steven Watts, *The Republic Reborn: War and the Making of Liberal America, 1790–1820* (Baltimore: Johns Hopkins University Press, 1989).

6. Quoted in Dana Milbank and Richard Morin, "Public Is Unyielding in War against Terror," *Washington Post*, September 29, 2001. Putnam returned to the theme in "The Rebirth of American Civic Life," *Boston Globe*, March 2, 2008, to argue that there had been an enduring revitalization of civic engagement among young people. He acknowledged that no one could tell how much this was due to the Obama campaign rather than 9/11.

7. Thomas Friedman, "Foreign Affairs; One War, Two Fronts," *New York Times*, November 2, 2001.

8. Robin Toner, "Trust in the Military Heightens among Baby Boomers' Children," *New York Times*, May 27, 2003.

9. Skocpol, *Diminished Democracy*, 251.

10. "The War at Home," *The American Prospect*, January 28, 2002.

11. *The American Prospect*, December 17, 2002.

12. *New York Times*, February 8, 2004.

13. *Late Show with David Letterman*, September 17, 2001.

14. Rather later regretted his attitude; see Stephen Gowans, "Dan Rather's Change of Heart," Media Monitors Network, May 22, 2002.

15. CNBC, October 13, 2001 (emphasis added).

16. *New York Times*, February 13, 2002.

17. To his credit, Friedman quickly recognized his errors in judgment. He was one of the first to call for Rumsfeld's resignation.

18. Matthew A. Crenson and Benjamin Ginsberg, *Downsizing Democracy: How America Sidelined Its Citizens and Privatized Its Public* (Baltimore: Johns Hopkins University Press, 2004) xii.

19. John Tierney, "For Inauguration in Wartime, a Lingering Question of Tone," *New York Times*, January 16, 2005.

20. Quoted in Jim Miklaszewski, "Army, Marines Miss Recruiting Goals Again," MSNBC, May 10, 2006.

21. Andrew Bacevich, "Who's Bearing the Burden?" *Commonweal*, July 15, 2005.

22. Jim Lobe, "Overstretched Army Brings Bush New Grief," Inter Press Service News Agency, September 26, 2006.

23. Tom Vanden Brook, "Casey: Deployments Strain Army Recruiting, Retention," *USA Today*, February 19, 2008; Andrea Seabrook and Tom Bowman, "Army Faces Tougher Recruitment in 2008," *All Things Considered*, December 22, 2007.

24. Army Recruiting Commander Briefing by Major General Michael D. Rochelle, Office of the Assistant Secretary of Defense (Public Affairs), May 20, 2005, http://www.defenselink.mil/transcripts/transcript.aspx?transcriptid=3274.html (accessed June 6, 2007). An excellent collection of articles on problems in minority recruiting in the military can be found at http://www.countermilitary.org/Articles/MilitaryRecruiting/PeopleOfColor/article_list.html.

25. Dave Moniz, "Black Americans Make Up Smaller Share of Military," *USA Today*, November 4, 2005.

26. Richard Whittle, "Army Battling Decline in Black Recruits," *Dallas Morning News*, August 2, 2005.

27. Sarah Abruzzese, "Iraq War Brings Drop in Black Enlistees," *New York Times*, August 22, 2007.

28. Damien Cave, "Growing Problem for Military Recruiters: Parents," *New York Times*, June 3, 2005.

29. Kevin Ryan, "Stretched Too Thin; We Don't Have Enough Troops to Meet Defense Demands," *Washington Post*, December 18, 2006.

30. Steven Lee Myers, "Fear of Troop Exodus Fuels Debate on G.I. Bill," *New York Times*, May 22, 2008. Recruiting figures were up at the end of 2008, mainly because of the horrible economic conditions in the country. "Good news for the Army has coincided with terrible news elsewhere," the *Washington Post* reported (Christian Davenport, "Downturn Drives Military Rolls Up," *Washington Post*, November 29, 2008). The article cited the remark of David Chu, undersecretary of defense for personnel and readiness, that the military does "benefit when things look less positive in civil society. I don't have the Dow Jones banner running up behind me here this morning, but that is a situation where more people are willing to give us a chance. And I think that's the big difference: People are willing to listen to us." It was reported that the military was using Obama's election and the fact that he was pledging to get the United States out of Iraq as a recruiting tactic.

31. Nick Turse, "An Army of (No) One: An Inside Look at the Military's Internet Recruiting War," *TomDispatch.com*, July 13, 2005.

32. Myra MacPherson, *Long Time Passing: Vietnam and the Haunted Generation* (Garden City, NY: Anchor/Doubleday, 1984), 9.

33. Report from American Friends Service Committee, "Eight Things You Need to Know about the Draft," http://www.afsc.org/youthmil/thinking-of-enlisting/poverty-draft.html (accessed October 7, 2007).

34. Erika Hayasaki, "Military Recruiters Targeting Minority Teens," *Los Angeles Times*, April 5, 2005.

35. Rick Jervis, "Army, Marine Recruiters Shift Focus to Wary Parents," *USA Today*, April 4, 2006.

36. Scott Shane, "A Flood of Troubled Soldiers Is in the Offing, Experts Predict," *New York Times*, December 16, 2004.

37. Dan Harris, "Army Tries to Recruit Soldiers by Winning Over Parents," *World News Tonight*, August 26, 2005.

38. "'Army Strong' to Be New Recruiting Slogan," *Washington Times*, October 9, 2006.

39. Erik Eckholm, "As Recruiting Suffers, Military Reigns in Abuses at Boot Camp," *New York Times*, July 26, 2005.

40. Damien Cave, "Pentagon Proposes Rise in the Age Limits for Recruits," *New York Times*, July 22, 2005.

41. Susanne M. Schafer, "Army Accepting Older Recruits," Associated Press, July 19, 2006.

42. Rick Sallinger, "Army Recruits' 'Moral Waivers,'" CBS 4 Denver, August 6, 2007. See also Lizette Alvarez, "Army Giving More Waivers in Recruiting," *New York Times*, February 14, 2007, and Jim Michaels, "1 in 8 Army Recruits Needs Conduct Waiver," *USA Today*, April 9, 2008.

43. Lolita Baldor, "Military May Ease Standards for Recruits," *USA Today*, November 6, 2007.

44. Baldor, "Military May Ease Standards for Recruits."

45. William Matthews, "Lawmaker: Recruiting Criminals Unwise," *Army Times*, November 9, 2007.

46. Edward Wong, "Swift Road for U.S. Citizen-Soldiers Already Fighting in Iraq," *New York Times*, August 9, 2005.

47. Bryan Bender, "A U.S. Military 'at Its Breaking Point' Considers Foreign Recruits," *Boston Globe*, December 26, 2006.

48. Max Boot, "Washington Needs a Colonial Office," *Financial Times*, July 3, 2003.

49. Max Boot, "Uncle Sam Wants Tu," February 24, 2005.

50. Tom Squitieri, "Army Expanding 'Stop Loss' Order to Keep Soldiers from Leaving," *USA Today*, January 5, 2004.

51. Nina Shapiro, "Stopping 'Stop-Loss,'" *Seattle Times*, March 30, 2005.

52. "Army to Keep Forcibly Re-enlisting Soldiers 'Stop Loss' Program Still Needed, General Says in Response to Gates," Associated Press, October 18, 2007.

53. "Allegations of Wrongdoing by U.S. Military Recruiters Jumped by 50% from 2004 to 2005," Reuters, August 14, 2006.

54. Martha Mendozam, "Recruiters Force Sex on Women," Associated Press, August 21, 2006.

55. Tom Bowman, "Army Reaches Low, Fills Ranks 12% of Recruits in October Had Lowest Acceptable Scores," *Baltimore Sun*, November 8, 2005.

56. Kathy Dobie, "AWOL in America, When Desertion Is the Only Option," *Harper's Magazine*, March 2005.

57. Mike Fitzgerald, "The War Within: Post Traumatic Stress Disorder," *St. Louis News Democrat*, April 29, 2008.

58. John Kifner, "Hate Groups Are Infiltrating the Military, Group Asserts," *New York Times*, July 7, 2006.

59. David Holthouse, "A Few Bad Men, Ten Years after a Scandal over Neo-Nazis in the Armed Forces, Extremists Are Once Again Worming Their Way into a Recruit-Starved Military," Intelligence Project, Southern Poverty Law Center, July 7, 2006.

60. Stanley Kurtz, "Finishing the Job: The Clash at the End of History," *National Review*, February 12, 2002.

61. Paul Kennedy, *The Rise and Fall of the Great Powers* (New York: Vintage Books, 1989).

62. Niall Ferguson, *Colossus: The Rise and Fall of the American Empire* (New York: Penguin, 2005), 272.

63. Ferguson, *Colossus*, 213.

64. Ferguson, *Colossus*, 292.

65. Ferguson, *Colossus*, 210.

66. Ferguson, *Colossus*, 293.

67. Ferguson, *Colossus*, 300.

68. Ferguson, *Colossus*, 29.

69. Niall Ferguson, *The Cash Nexus: Money and Power in the Modern World, 1700–2000* (New York: Basic Books, 2002), 418.

70. These words are cited in Lois G. Schwoerer, *"No Standing Armies!" The Anti-army Ideology in Seventeenth-Century England* (Baltimore: Johns Hopkins University Press, 1974), 199.

2

◈

The Rise and Fall
of the Citizen-Soldier;
or, Bye-Bye, Elvis

When citizen and soldier shall be synonymous terms, then you will be safe.

—John Randolph[1]

From the moment he became famous, reporters asked Elvis about his plans for military service. Today, the media is reluctant to raise the issue of the Bush twins or the Romney sons. Back then, no one was too high and mighty to serve his or her country. Elvis would eventually receive offers from all three service branches for easy ways to meet his military obligation. The navy proposed a special "Elvis Presley Company" to exploit his performing skills. The air force proposed he entertain at recruiting stations around the country. But Elvis agreed with his manager, Colonel Tom Parker, that public opinion would be upset if he received special treatment.

He wasn't entirely happy about going into the military (who is?). But when his draft notice arrived, he commented, with sincerity (according to his biographer), "I am grateful for what this country has given me. And now I'm ready to return a little. *It's the only adult way to look at it.*"[2] On the day of his induction, he went on to say, "If I seem nervous it's because I am." But he looked forward to having a good experience in the army. "The army can do anything it wants with me," he remarked. "Millions of other guys had been drafted, and I don't want to be different from anyone else."[3] Columnist Hy Gardner commemorated the occasion with a column in the form of a letter to his fellow soldiers.

In what other nation in the world would such a rich and famous man serve alongside you other draftees without trying to use influence to buy his way out? In my book this is American democracy at its best—the blessed way of life for whose protection you and Elvis have been called upon to contribute 18 to 24 months of your young lives.[4]

Not long after, a musical debuted on Broadway celebrating Elvis's being drafted. It became a major hit and later a popular movie. Titled *Bye-Bye Birdie*, it recounted the tale of a fictionalized Elvis character, Conrad Birdie, whose induction into the military is exploited by his manager for one last hit song before he goes. The show made a star of Dick Van Dyke; its most popular song was "Kids!" It included a hymn to the virtues of conscription. Titled "Normal American Boy," the song spoke of how the character about to be inducted was "proud" to be a "plain GI," who would "gladly face those bullets" because he was "not afraid to die."

The top star of his day expressing his desire to serve. A hit Broadway show singing of how normal American boys are not afraid to die for their country. We seem to be describing a distant land as foreign to ours as it could be.

Yet we are describing the United States of America just a few generations ago.

It was a world in which young males assumed that what it *meant* to be American was that everyone served if needed. In the words of Elvis Presley, this was how you showed your gratitude for what society had given you. If society had given you a great deal, your thanks should be even more. Elvis's political orientation seemed so natural at the time because it was one that had prevailed for years. The draft was at its heart, embodying the citizen-soldier ethic tracing back to the origins of the republic.

The demise of the draft—not just its official end but also the intense hostility that now surrounds it—is one of the most striking events of twentieth-century America. It is hard to name another institution in American history that was once so popular but whose fall from grace was so quick and total. Prohibition comes to mind. But Prohibition was never very popular. Its creation after World War I was a fluke. When it ended in the 1930s, people looked back on it as an oddity. No one—except perhaps for the extreme advocates—imagined that Prohibition spoke to the heart of what America was all about.

People *did* regard the draft as embodying the citizen-soldier ideal. They no longer regard that ideal as embodying what America's all about.

I don't romanticize the draft. Its coerciveness was always an odd fit for this country. Its left-wing critics rightly regarded it as an instrument of state centralization, crucial to the mass wars and mass slaughters of the twentieth century. Still, the story of the draft's demise is the flip side of the rise of alienated war. We of the baby-boom generation have a unique perspective on it because we lived through this transformation. We are the last generation in American history to regard the draft's ethic of shared responsibility as reasonable. Today it is inconceivable that Britney Spears or Justin Timberlake would suspend their careers to fight alongside Lori Ann Piestewa or Shoshana Johnson.

Let's begin our brief account of the rise and fall of the citizen-soldier ethic.

THE CIVIC REPUBLICAN BACKGROUND

Ralph Waldo Emerson's "Concord Hymn" was one of the most famous poems of the nineteenth century. It spoke of an "embattled farmer"—an ordinary citizen stepping forth reluctantly but steadfastly to defend his ideals against the British mercenaries.[5] Emerson's poem tapped a powerful strain in our political heritage. Political theorists call it the civic republican tradition.[6] It is the tradition that gives us our citizen-soldier ethic. Perhaps I should call it the citizen-soldier *syndrome* to mark the fact that it too signified an entire political culture.

It held several key convictions:

1. How a country fights its wars—especially, *who* fights its wars—is a key to its character generally. Republics do not simply ensure civilian control of the military. They require that ordinary citizens do the fighting. Empires (like the British) hire mercenaries or recruit from an underclass that has no other options. A republic's wars are fought by ordinary citizens who approach war as a matter of personal responsibility. Clare Snyder writes, "In keeping with the basic republican premise that 'what affects all must be decided by all,' the citizen-soldier tradition maintains that the decision to wage war should be decided by those who will actually have to fight."[7] They fight their own fights, and they pick only fights that they themselves are willing to fight.

Citizens of the early republic gave the citizen-soldier tradition, with its ethic of fighting your own fights, almost sacred significance. In the words of Charles Royster, "The refusal to hide behind corruptible mercenary soldiers, made war the proof of Americans' moral . . . survival." This ethic of personal responsibility led some to endorse short terms of military service as insurance against a corrupt permanent military. In Congress, Roger Sherman argued, "Long enlistment is a state of slavery."[8] For many, all this had a religious sanction. God had chosen Americans to exemplify the ideals of personal responsibility. To forsake them invited "eternal scorn."

2. This is why republics are more peace oriented than empires. The citizens of a republic do not casually call for war since they *themselves* will be doing the fighting. It is a constraint on political leaders who would otherwise wage irresponsible wars. This is the crux of the "Democratic Peace Thesis" as propounded in Immanuel Kant's essay "On Perpetual Peace." It harkens back to the views of earlier republican thinkers like Machiavelli, who wrote that while professional soldiers "are obliged to hope that there will be no peace," citizen-soldiers only wish "to come home and live by their profession." A citizen-soldier "will gladly make war in order to have peace" but "will not seek to disturb the peace in order to have war."[9]

3. Implicit in this political ideal is the conviction that war is not just another unpleasant job—like garbage collecting—that can be hired out. It is a shared endeavor in which all are implicated; hence, all must play a part. The parallel is the justice system and the conception of jury duty as something that everything citizen can be called to perform. It is not something we hire people to do.

In ascribing this ideal to America's founders, I don't want to idealize or simplify things too much. George Washington was skeptical of a citizen's militia and favorably disposed to a professional military. But after the Revolution, he was diligent in endorsing the citizen-soldiers ideal (as the quote at the beginning of the introduction shows). When former officers of the Continental Army launched the Society of the Cincinnati in 1783, it was met with widespread criticism for portending a military elite à la Caesar or Cromwell. Washington was quick to disavow such notions.[10] Alexander Hamilton favored a professional military as part of favoring a strong centralized government generally. But even Hamilton, in the *Federalist Papers*, endorsed the citizen-soldier model. Moreover, in a class-divided society like ours, military service will always be skewed to the poor and outcast, though it is remarkable how little this was true of World War II.[11] The main point is that the citizen-soldier ideal was an *ideal* identified in theory—if not always in practice—with what America was all about.

Standing Armies and Militias

> What, sir, is the use of a militia? It is to prevent the establishment of a standing army, the bane of liberty.
>
> —Elbridge Gerry

The ideal was often stated most forcefully in complaints against other practices.

Every American has read the Declaration of Independence. At the time, what made that document so powerful was its articulating ideals dear to the Republican political tradition in language that ordinary people could grasp. At the heart of these ideals were worries about the *military*. The Declaration is constructed around a series of grievances against the British Empire that crucially involved military transgressions.

Here are two of them:

> "He [King George III] has kept among us, in times of peace, Standing Armies without the consent of our legislatures."
> "He [the King] has affected to render the Military independent of and superior to the Civil power."

The focal worry here is "standing armies." It is echoed later in complaints about how the King is transporting "large Armies of foreign Mercenaries" to our shores. The charge that the military has become independent of and superior to civilian power is another aspect of this worry. This concern persisted well after the Revolution. When the authors of the Constitution presented it to the general public, the chief objection from the Anti-Federalist was that it opened the door to a "standing army" and a full-time military establishment.[12] Hence, the essays written favoring the Constitution, the *Federalist Papers*, devoted more attention to these issues than any other.

Reading the political literature of the founding era one constantly encounters the specter of the standing army.[13] At the Constitutional Convention, James Madison spoke of "large standing armies" as "the *greatest* danger to liberty."[14] Yet the term has vanished from our political vocabulary.

A standing army is a full-time professional army. To say it is a "professional" army does not simply mean that its soldiers are paid to serve. Some form of payment is part of most armies. It means that they serve only because they are paid. The idea that wars are fought for love of country became prominent only after the American and French revolutions. And a standing army is more than just a mercenary force. It is a *full-time* military force—a perpetual army, if you will. Fighting for pay is all that its soldiers do. They don't have any other job, and that job is a long-term one. A "standing army" was the eighteenth century's term for an entrenched military establishment of the kind that President Eisenhower bemoaned in his famous farewell speech on the "military-industrial complex." While Eisenhower identified it with corporate power, the early civic republicans identified it with the kingly power of monarchs.

A standing army is dangerous because it makes wars too *easy*. Kings— or executives (presidents)—are always inclined to start wars. There are lots of reasons for this: wars are more interesting than the other boring stuff they have to do, wars bring them lots of praise and attention from their own people who otherwise gripe about how things are going, and unlike the negotiating and haggling of domestic pursuits, war gives leaders a free hand—to mobilize troops, browbeat their subjects, and so on. It's the ultimate power trip.

Just as there has been a long history of anxiety about standing armies for making war too easy, there has been a history of similar worry about paying for war through borrowing. The British in the eighteenth century developed the practice of financing war through debt.[15] From the start, civic republicans criticized it for making war too easy (this is another theme in Kant's "On Perpetual Peace"). Another criticism of it was its unfairness. Borrowing to pay for war meant shifting the financial cost of the conflict to later generations. If this generation wants war (the thinking went), then it should be willing to bear its financial burden.

The very existence of a standing army creates its own momentum for war. Civic republicans assumed that a professional military establishment would want to put its skills and technologies into practice and that pretty much any war would do. In addition, there was its impact on relations between countries. The very existence of standing armies leads to a perpetual arms race where countries create ever-larger armies to keep up with potential foes. Kant spoke of how, by giving the appearance they are preparing for war, standing armies goad countries into military projects that know "no bounds."[16] In another piece, "Speculative Beginning of Human History" (1786), he wrote,

> All must understand that the greatest evil that can oppress civilized peoples derives from wars, not, indeed, so much from actual present or past wars, as from the never ending and constantly increasing arming for the future. To this all of the nation's powers are devoted, as are all those fruits of its culture that could be used to build a still greater culture; freedom will in many areas be largely destroyed, and the nation's motherly care for individual members will be changed into perilously hard demands that will be justified by concern over external dangers.[17]

In "On the Proverb: That May Be True in Theory, but Is of No Practical Use," Kant speaks of how "the preparation for defense often makes peace more repressive and destructive of internal welfare than even war."[18]

The alternative to a standing army was one of ordinary citizens, a "people's militia." A militia was everything a standing army was not. It was composed of ordinary citizens with ordinary jobs and families who had no professional interest in starting wars or sustaining them. It was not directed by some centralized authority but rather was under local control of the town or colony. Finally, it came into existence only when needed and was not there to be used as the plaything of the sovereign. Service in the militia was a duty. Training was regular, and failure to show up often resulted in a fine. But there was nothing like the coercion associated with the modern conscripted army, where long jail terms faced those who refused. The premise of the militia was that no one would refuse to fight if the conflict were truly one of self-defense. If standing armies made war too easy, militias made them more difficult. Ordinary citizens would consent to be called out only if the reasons for fighting were very good ones. And its virtues extended to the political culture as a whole. Its proponents claimed that the more the ordinary citizens were responsible for their own defense, the more *responsible* they would be as citizens generally—the more attentive they would be to the issues of the day that could lead to war and the more jealous they would be of their rights and prerogatives as citizens in other matters.

Ancient Anxieties

The concern of the founders about military matters was rooted in their reading of history. The fate of Rome obsessed civic republicanism.[19] From the names of its institutions—like the "Senate"—to the architecture of its buildings, the influence of the Roman republic was omnipresent. The fact that America was founded as a "republic" speaks to it. But it also brought anxieties. The iconography of the republic suggests solidity and durability: massive impressive buildings and statues to endure throughout the ages. The U.S. Constitution is remarkable for how long it has endured. But for the founders, as for earlier civic republicans, republics were fragile things. Many in this tradition assumed that the life of a republic was necessarily finite.

What threatened republics? The Roman precedent suggested that what threatened republics most was the specter of empire and the corruption that came with it. A "republic" was defined by a set of institutions developed by Rome. Central were the separation of powers, checks and balances, and government by constitutional law. So powerful was this model for the founders that their debates were conducted in terms of who most represented this precedent. In the debates over the Constitution, the Federalists signed their essays "Publius," the first consul of the Roman republic, while the Anti-Federalists used "Brutus," who defended republican principles against the tyranny that would destroy the republic in 27 B.C. The source of that downfall concerns us here.

Drawing on Aristotle, thinkers like Cicero stressed how republican government rested on the political engagement of its citizens, the skills of self-rule, and the commitment to exercise those skills the republican tradition termed "civic virtue." Essential to such virtue was the role of ordinary citizens in the defense of the realm. In the Roman republic's most vital years, the Roman legions were a true citizen army of landowners. All citizens between the ages of seventeen and forty-six could be called for military service. As Chalmers Johnson notes in *Nemesis: The Last Days of the American Republic*, a notable feature of that system was that only citizens possessing property could serve.[20] Those who benefited most from the state were most responsible for its defense.

Johnson notes another feature. After military victory, the returning farmers who constituted the military marched into Rome behind their general in a "triumph." The general, who paid for the parade out of his own pocket, rode in a chariot. But he was accompanied by a slave boy who stood behind him whispering in his ear—"Remember that you are human." After the general came his prisoners in chains and then his legions of ordinary citizens—who by ancient custom sang obscene songs making fun of him. President Bush expressed boundless admiration for the founding principles of our republic. Perhaps he should have reinstituted this practice.

The collapse of the Roman republic and its replacement by an empire was a complex event. A central factor was the contradiction between republicanism and a large military empire. After consolidating its power over Italy, the republic inexorably extended its conquests so that by the first century its dominion extended over all that is now France, much of Spain, as well as northern Africa and parts of Asia Minor. One result of the vast wealth generated was that Roman citizens were relieved of the burden of paying taxes; this served individual self-interest, but its net effect was to lessen citizens' concern with the doings of the government—along with increasing the arrogance that unearned wealth involves. The most important change was the replacement of the citizen's army by a professional military force—a standing army—accompanied by the growth of militaristic values. Eventually the burdens of maintaining an expansive and expensive empire proved too great for the principles and arrangements on which the republic was founded. It was just a matter of time until the forces of tyranny overthrew the republic in the name of bringing about law and order. The great Roman legal thinker Cicero observed the dismantling of the Roman republic with horror and wrote some of the classic texts warning of the dangers to the republic from excessive militarism. His head and hands would be chopped off for opposing military dictatorship.

The story of how republican sentiments migrated to the United States is a fascinating one that historians have been exploring for decades.[21] Republican thinking was revived in England in the seventeenth century in the years of turmoil of its civil war. Opponents of the tyrannical Stuarts sought some framework for opposing their abuses. Thinkers like those of the "Commonwealth" school turned to the tradition of Cicero to understand how concentrated power could destroy liberty. In a historical twist, when colonists sought to understand why they were being oppressed by King George, they turned to these English thinkers and to older Roman principles.

From its first emergence in England, this revived civic republicanism fretted about standing armies. Opponents of the Stuarts in the English Civil War identified their tyranny with their creation of a full-time military. After the triumph of Parliament and Cromwell, the latter's rule again raised the specter of military tyranny. Hatred of a standing army was a driving factor in the Glorious Revolution of 1689. Article VI of the Bill of Rights asserted that no standing army could be established in peacetime without the consent of Parliament. The concern endured into the eighteenth century among those who feared that the Glorious Revolution was being betrayed by Hanoverian monarchs and London financial interests—committed to large armies and large debts. Bolingbroke wrote that standing armies posed a central threat to liberty not so much by threatening coups d'état as by the slow "corruption" of government.[22] David Hume and William Robertson suggested that despotism in Europe followed from the use of paid troops.

English antimilitary tracts circulated in America as early as the 1720s. Attacks on standing armies as inimical to liberty were found in the writings of John Adams, Samuel Adams, John Dickinson, and George Mason, as well as Thomas Jefferson. Annual orations commemorating the Boston Massacre were devoted to preserving "in the minds of the people a lively sense of the dangers of standing armies."[23] The issue of "corruption" remained primary. Standing armies were seen as expressions of "vice, luxury, and laziness" that were incompatible with a democratic culture.[24]

Such concerns eventually found their way into the U.S. Constitution.[25] As one historian, Walter Millis, remarks,

> Though the point has not often been noticed, the Constitution was as much a military as a political and economic charter. . . . The problem was to provide for an effective defense against both foreign war and domestic upheaval without trenching too far upon the jealous sovereignty of the states or rousing the universal fear and loathing of irresponsible standing armies.[26]

Some people worried that the new Constitution would pave the way for the creation of a standing army by its centralization of military authority. These were the previously mentioned "Anti-Federalists." Here are the words of one of them, writing under the name "Brutus":

> Standing armies are dangerous to the liberties of a people. . . . If necessary, the truth of the position might be confirmed by the history of almost every nation in the world. A cloud of the most illustrious patriots of every age and country, where freedom has been enjoyed, might be adduced as witnesses in

support of the sentiment. But I presume it would be useless, to enter into a labored argument, to prove to the people of America, a position which has so long and so generally been received by them as a kind of axiom. (*New York Journal*, January 17, 1788)

The most significant upshot of this debate was the Second Amendment to the Constitution: "A well regulated militia being necessary to the security of a free State, the right of the People to keep and bear arms shall not be infringed." Today, when people think of this amendment, they think of disputes over gun control laws. The National Rifle Association maintains that any law restricting firearms infringes on this amendment and must be opposed. The pros and cons of gun control are not our concern here.[27] Originally, the Second Amendment expressed the fear of a standing army and of centralized military power generally. There was a lot of controversy around the Constitution when it was first proposed for adoption by the states. The opponents were the previously mentioned Anti-Federalists, who held that the Constitution vested too much power in the federal government over the individual states. The Anti-Federalists were not able to block the adoption of the Constitution. But their agitation led to the quick adoption of the first ten amendments to the Constitution, which sought to affirm the limits of federal power. Central to these limits was the prohibition of a standing army via the endorsement of the militia system.

When the amendment speaks of what is necessary to the "security of a free state," such security should be understood in two senses: the security from attack by other governments and the security of citizens from the actions of their own government enabled by the existence of a standing army. The Constitution contained numerous other provisions driven by this fear of centralized military power. The most well known are the checks on executive war-making power, almost all of which are now ignored. The chief example is vesting the power to declare war in Congress rather than the president. There are additional constraints, though, like the fact that the military budget is the only one constitutionally required to undergo full review every two years. All these provisions arise from the civic republican insistence that the project of war making remain closely connected with the concerns of average citizens and their representatives.

The Division of Labor

More must be said, finally, about the civic republican attitude toward hiring people to fight our wars. The experience of the American Revolution made this an especially charged issue. The colonists regarded the British redcoats as an archetypal standing army that, like imperial armies generally, contained substantial numbers of mercenaries. A substantial portion of the British army was so-called Hessians: German soldiers hired by King George to quell the colonial revolt. Throughout history, mercenary soldiers have been more the rule than the exception. But to the civic republican consciousness of the colonists, mercenaries exemplified political corruption.

This marks a crucial tension between the civic republican view of politics and a capitalist faith in the marketplace. A capitalist society like ours generally meets its needs through market mechanisms, or what early economists called the division of labor. But not all social needs are met this way. We do not have a professional class of paid jurors, and we are suspicious enough of professional politicians that some of our states effectively ban them through term limits. Our civic republican tradition has always been suspicious of professionalization for political goals. It was seen as a source of corruption.

The notion of the division of labor was first formulated in the late eighteenth century in such works as Adam Smith's *The Wealth of Nations*. Observers were impressed with the productive powers of market relations that theorists like Smith attributed to the specialization of tasks. But there was immediately disagreement about the appropriateness of the division of labor for military purposes, with civic republican thinkers deeply skeptical of its role.[28] This partly reflected their larger conception of war.

The idea that war, like many other things, may be pursued by division-of-labor principles rests on the view that fighting a war is akin to fighting a fire: just as we hire firemen to do the latter, we may hire soldiers to do the former. But civic republicanism regarded war as an intrinsically *political* act, that is, one about which there would invariably be disagreement about whether to fight it and how to fight it. The U.S. Constitution reflected this fact in numerous ways, mainly in how difficult it made the act of declaring war. Because there is no disagreement about the necessity of fighting fires, firefighting is something we want to make as easy as possible. But the Constitution was novel in how difficult it made war making. In contrast to the practice of its times, the Constitution divided the war-making power between the executive and the legislature—and gave the latter the authority to make war not only because it was the more popular body but because its workings would make the decision to go to war slow and deliberate. If war is a political act, it follows that every citizen should be implicated in that act in ways that would make them weigh the decision seriously, and the way to do this is to ensure that the burden of war making is shared generally—in ways it is not when it is fought by professional soldiers.

FROM THE MILITIA TO THE DRAFT

In the twentieth century, the citizen-soldier ethic became identified with the draft. The end of the draft meant the end of the citizen-soldier ethic as a general orientation to thinking about war and sacrifice. The story of "Whatever Happened to the Embattled Farmer," then, involves the story of what happened to the draft. But keep in mind that the two are not identical. One can approach the issue of war and sacrifice responsibly without the government's forcing you to do so. Civic republican ideals are valuable independent of institutional realities.

The Peculiar Institution

The citizen-soldier ethic was first identified with the militia. A militia was not a conscripted army as we have come to understand it, mainly in that it was more voluntary. Citizens were expected to serve in the militia, and there were penalties for not showing up involving fines and even jail. But the sanctions never approached anything like those for evading the draft. Finally, militias were organized on the local level, while the twentieth-century draft was a federal draft, administered by local boards but directed by Washington.

The idea of a draft was always an uneasy fit with American values, which is why I call it "the peculiar institution." What's surprising is how it came to be so accepted despite traditional objections to it. This attests to the popularity of the citizen-soldier ideal of fairness that conscription instituted. The chief problem with the draft has always been its violation of personal liberty. That great observer of nineteenth-century America, Alexis de Tocqueville, stated forthrightly that the habits of Americans were flatly opposed to a draft.[29] He was not only speaking of Americans' love of personal independence. He was referring to the deep suspicion of centralized government basic to its fear of standing armies. A federal draft invests extraordinary power in the centralized state. This was a main basis of opposition to it when it was first introduced in the Civil War, and it remained a concern of opponents up to the early 1950s.

The American Revolution was typical of American wars up to the Civil War in relying on volunteer militias and some conscripted soldiers. But in keeping with republican worries, the power to draft remained vested in local state governments. Even in the darkest days of the Revolution, General Washington was consistently denied his request that the national government be empowered to conscript. Although the Constitution would give the federal government the right to "raise armies," the explicit power to conscript was withheld. Edmund Randolph spoke of how the power to conscript "stretched the strings of government too violently to be adopted."[30] Thomas Jefferson remarked of how "in Virginia a draft was ever the most unpopular and impracticable thing that could ever be attempted. Our people . . . had learned to consider it as the last of all oppressions."[31] The Constitution effectively established the nation's "two-army tradition," with a small regular army to be augmented by cadres of volunteers in the case of actual conflict.

Conscription became a focus of intense debate in the War of 1812 when President Madison tried and failed to enact a national draft. Opponents assailed the plan as unconstitutional and a harbinger of Napoleonic despotism. Senator David Daggett of Connecticut proclaimed it "utterly inconsistent with the principles [of civil liberty] to compel any man to become a soldier for life, during a war, or for any fixed time."[32] The most famous words were spoken by the renowned Daniel Webster before the House of Representatives. "The question is nothing less, than whether the most essential rights of personal liberty shall be surrendered, and despotism embraced in its worst form," he intoned, attacking conscription. "Is this, Sir, consistent with the character of a free Government?"

> Where is it written in the Constitution, in what article or section is it contained, that you may take children from their parents, and parents from their children, and compel them to fight the battles of any war, in which the folly or the wickedness of Government may engage it?

He went on to attack the vast power that conscription would invest in a centralized state, no longer constrained:

> Nor is it, sir, for the defense of his own house and home, that he who is the subject of military draft is to perform the task allotted to him. You will put him upon a service equally foreign to his interests and abhorrent to his feelings. *With his aid you are to push your purposes of conquest. The battles which used to fight are the battles of invasion.*[33]

It was America's first truly "modern" war, the Civil War, that witnessed the first federal draft. Volunteerism sufficed at first. But as the massive battles consumed larger numbers, both North and South concluded that a draft was necessary. Indeed, with a smaller total population to draw on, the Confederacy's draft was much more extensive. In all, 21 percent of the 1 million Confederate soldiers were conscripts. In both regions widespread protest ensued. In the South, resistance to the draft led to the virtual secession of some counties from the Confederacy. In the North, thirty-eight officers in charge of conscription were assassinated, and sixty others were wounded.[34] The most dramatic resistance was the New York City draft riots that followed Lincoln's call for 300,000 new conscripts—in a conjunction with graphic accounts in the newspapers of the carnage at Gettysburg. These remain the largest civil disturbance in our history. Following the newspaper publication of draftees' names, mob violence erupted throughout the poorer neighborhoods of the city and then spread to wealthier ones. African Americans were a special target of violence; more than $1.5 million in damage occurred, leading Lincoln to deploy combat troops from the Federal Army of the Potomac to restore order.

The inequities of the draft provoked special ire. Most notorious was the provision allowing those with money to hire a substitute if their name was chosen. The so-called commutation fee was equal to about half the annual salary of the average working-class American. In addition, the affluent could find doctors to provide medical excuses for them, as in the Vietnam War. The draft's coercive and inequitable nature meant that the Union emerged from the Civil War with a profound distaste for conscription. The late 1860s and 1870s were the years when the success of Prussia's conscripted army led some on the Continent to introduce similar measures. These were years of waning support for the draft in the United States.

World War I was the great dividing point. Conscription in the United States was largely a product of Northeast elites allied with the business classes. The father of American conscription, Leonard Wood, had seen it at work in Prussia. What really made the difference was the link between conscription and efficiency as touted, most loudly, by theorists of Progressivism. The draft would do for the military what the corporation had done for the market economy—streamline it and rationalize it in ways that would render it more amenable to intelligent central decision. Conscription was praised as an instrument of modernization in serving as a school for the nation, inculcating patriotic virtues and inoculating the young against anarchism and other noxious sentiments.

The role of Progressive intellectuals in countering traditional suspicions of the draft bears stressing. Both John Dewey and Walter Lippmann voiced strong support for it in the pages of *The New Republic* as part of their call for "tough-minded" thinking in the "national emergency" posed by World War I.[35] The ensuing conflict over the draft was very much a regional one, with rural areas of the Midwest most opposed. Prodraft thinking involved a redefinition of citizenship away from one's primary ties to family, local, and ethnic groups to the nation-state as a whole. As the distinguished promilitary Harvard philosopher Ralph Barton Perry wrote in 1916,

> Nothing short of national safety or some higher design of international justice and order, can make it reasonable to cultivate the art of destruction. But since military service is so justified, as a painful necessity like surgery, capital punishment or self sacrifice, it is reasonable that it should be done well, and

soberly undertaken as a function of the state. In a democracy this means that should be acknowledged and assumed as an obligation by all citizens. For democracy implies that there shall be neither privilege nor immunity.

Perry concluded that conscription was fully compatible with liberty. "There must be a place secured for freedom, and to secure that freedom, free men may be soldiers."[36]

The institution of the draft was met with dramatic protest, mainly through evasion. Between 2 million and 3 million men never registered, and 338,000 (about 12 percent of those drafted) never reported or deserted soon after arrival. Almost 65,000 of those who registered sought conscientious objector status. Conscription was challenged in court, leading to the Supreme Court decision of 1918 that is still the controlling decision on these matters. The decision merits study by anyone interested in the politics, philosophy, and law of military service. The crucial point for our purposes is that the right of the national government to conscript was unanimously affirmed by the court, with Chief Justice White arguing that the right to force its citizens to fight for it was implicit in the very concept of sovereignty. He tellingly wrote that if the power to raise armies relied solely on the consent of its citizens, it would be no power at all.

The draft's reputation declined dramatically after World War I, only to rise even more dramatically with the onset of World War II. There was some dissent when draft mechanisms were put in place after the fall of France, but it disappeared with Pearl Harbor. Men from eighteen to thirty-eight were eligible to be drafted to serve for the duration of the war. Inequities that characterized the Civil War draft and later the Vietnam draft were largely absent. Ultimately, about 10 million men were called by the Selective Service System, and about 6 million enlisted, mainly in the navy and air corps. The Justice Department investigated 373,000 cases of alleged draft evaders but obtained convictions of only 16,000.

The last serious debate over the draft occurred in the late 1940s with the proposal to create the first peacetime draft. The proposal was supported mainly by Democrats. The principal skeptics came from the Midwest. The chief skeptic was a leading Senate Republican, Robert Taft, son of the former President and Supreme Court Chief Justice William Howard Taft. Taft's opposition harkened back to Daniel Webster. A peacetime draft, Taft proclaimed, was "contrary to the whole concept of American liberty." "It is hard to think of a more drastic limitation on personal freedom," he asserted, worrying that it would transform the U.S. into a "militaristic and totalitarian country."[37] Nevertheless, the peacetime draft was instituted and became increasingly popular up to about the midpoint of the Vietnam War.

The Vietnam War was a turning point for the draft, as it was for American politics generally. After Lyndon Johnson committed ground troops to the conflict in 1965, draft calls rose from 100,000 in 1964 to 400,000 in 1966. Although draftees were a minority of the armed forces as a whole (only 16 percent), they were the bulk of infantry riflemen in Vietnam (88 percent in 1969) and accounted for more than half of army battle deaths. Although African Americans were only 11 percent of the population, they were 16 percent of the army's casualties. In addition to various forms of draft avoidance, of the sort cultivated by chickenhawks, the number of draft resisters reached unprecedented proportions. Approximately 570,000 of those eligible between 1964 and 1973 evaded the draft illegally. Of those, 360,000 were never caught, 200,000 had their cases dismissed, 9,000 were convicted, and 4,000 went to prison. An estimated 30,000 to 50,000 fled into exile, mainly to Canada, Britain, and Sweden.[38]

The draft came under increasing pressure to reform, but General Lewis Hershey, the head of the Selective Service System, blocked all change until 1969. With Richard Nixon's election, occupational and dependency deferments were soon ended, and an annual lottery among eighteen-year-olds was instituted in December 1969. Nixon appointed former Secretary of Defense Thomas Gates to head a commission that in 1970 urged the creation of an all-volunteer armed force. Congress reluctantly agreed to extend the draft for two more years in 1971 but ended student deferments and dramatically increased pay for soldiers to encourage volunteers. During his 1972 reelection campaign, Nixon reduced draft calls to 50,000 and stopped forcing draftees to serve in Vietnam. On January 27, 1973, the day the cease-fire was announced, the administration officially stopped drafting young Americans.[39]

It's not surprising, given this contentious history, that the draft was ended. As I've said, it may be more surprising that it was ever embraced. It continues to be embraced, interestingly enough, in all the nostalgia around the Greatest Generation. In the books and films lionizing that generation's ethic of shared sacrifice, there is no griping about the fact that young men had no choice about fighting fascism. It was a civic duty that, like other civic duties (e.g., paying taxes), was enforced by law.

Since the ethic of shared sacrifice pre-dated the draft, though, it is logical to ask why that ethic disappeared with the draft. An answer lies in looking at the debates that ended it.

Ending the Draft

The first thing to note is how little substantive debate there was about ending the draft. A cynic might say that privileged people on both the left and the right had come to agree that their children should no longer be asked to fight our wars. Hence, the issue was shrouded by silence, like the issue of who serves today. It's hard to find a parallel to how little substantive discussion there was at the time, given its political importance. Other institutions have been identified with the meaning of American citizenship, like the federal income tax. There was a long debate over instituting the federal income tax, raising some of the same issues as a draft. (Significantly, the federal power to tax required a constitutional amendment, while the power to conscript was judged by the Supreme Court to be implicit in the notion of sovereignty; you would think that one would be as necessary as the other.) Eventually, the citizenry came to agree that being an American meant paying your fair share in taxes. So one would expect that ending the federal income tax, were that ever to occur, would involve a substantial debate about the meaning of citizenship, a debate that might linger on once the decision was made.

No such debate happened with conscription. There was little debate at all, and the discussion that did occur was notable for the poverty of its content.

The antiwar movement is often credited with ending the draft. But the antiwar movement's stance was complex, a fact that time has obscured. Libertarian concerns were a factor, but equally important was the draft's unfairness. The popular slogan of the time, "Rich Man's Battle, Poor Man's Fight," harkened to the hypocrisy of claiming that this was a war in which all Americans sacrificed. We were still near enough to World War II to remember when the draft really was equitable in its implementation. The libertarian concern might be met by creating a paid military. But no one in the antiwar movement imagined that a paid military would make matters *fairer* in who served.

Official discussion began in the summer of 1966 when President Johnson appointed a commission to study the problem of Selective Service since the law was to expire later that year. The committee was headed by former Assistant Attorney General Burke Marshall. It focused on what was regarded as the principal complaint about the draft—its *unfairness*.[40] In March 1967, Johnson sent a message to Congress explaining his conclusions from that study and his decision to renew the draft, with changes. From the start, his principal concern was fairness. He began by quoting President Franklin Roosevelt's statement of 1940:

> America has adopted selective service in time of peace, and, in doing so, has broadened and enriched our basic concept of citizenship. Beside the clear democratic ideals of equal rights, equal privileges and equal opportunities, we have set forth the underlying other duties, obligations, and responsibilities of equal service.[41]

He noted that fairness had always been the goal of the Selective Service System. "When the present act was passed in 1948, one of its underlying assumptions, was that the obligation and benefits of military service would be equitably born."[42] The message concluded by wishing that society did not have to impose this burden on the young but that, as long as the burden existed, it had to be shared equitably.[43] Unlike the debate of the late 1940s, traditional Republican concerns about the draft and centralized power were not voiced. Even liberal-minded figures like Burke Marshall saw nothing intrinsically worrisome about a large military establishment.

From the mid-1960s on, a major opponent of the draft was conservative economist Milton Friedman. A leading authority states that Friedman's free-market arguments were definitive in bringing about the draft's demise.[44] Friedman himself regarded ending the draft as one of his greatest policy achievements. In retrospect, what is striking about his arguments is how completely they rejected the fairness issue that had been definitive up to that time. After him, the issue of shared sacrifice was simply forgotten in how we fight wars. Freidman himself did not believe that "fairness" should be a political consideration at all. Typical are these remarks from an editorial lambasting the Federal Communications Commission's fairness doctrine:

> The modern tendency to substitute "fair" for "free" reveals how far we have moved from the initial conception of the Founding Fathers. . . . Yet, scrutinize word for word the Declaration of Independence, the Constitution, and the Bill of Rights, and you will not find the word "fair."[45]

He may have been right on the linguistic point. None of these documents speaks of honesty either, but it does not follow that honesty was not a concern. But to conclude that the nation's founders were not concerned with fairness in how we fight our wars revealed a striking ignorance of their civic republican heritage. Friedman was highly selective in what he found in these documents. In one early statement, he acknowledged, "It's always a puzzle to me why people should think that the term 'mercenary' somehow has a negative connotation."[46] Having scoured the Declaration of Independence for the word "fairness," he never wondered why that document was so exercised about "standing armies" or why it ensured a "well-regulated militia." To Friedman, "all these words mean exactly the same thing": "volunteer" army, "professional" army, and "mercenary" army. "I think mercenary motives are among the least unattractive that we have." His arguments proceeded to focus entirely on matters of cost, arguing that a professional military would provide a more efficient use of society's resources.

President Johnson's 1966 call for a review of the draft led to Senate hearings in 1967 that saw a telling exchange between Friedman and Senator Robert Kennedy. Kennedy continually pressed Friedman on the idea that the obligation to defend one's country was a national responsibility that should not become the province of one particular class. Kennedy was appealing to the citizen-soldier ethic of shared sacrifice. Friedman had no idea of what Kennedy was talking about. Friedman returned again and again to the claim that there would be something unfair about "telling" an African American or anyone else that one could *not* enlist in the military—because the obligation was one for all citizens. This response was silly. The existence of a draft never prevented anyone from enlisting. Draft board quotas were a matter of how many young men were still needed after volunteers had been accounted for.

The Sounds of Silence

Periodically in American history, the nation's relation to war making has undergone redefinition. Our Revolution redefined war in relation to the practices of the British Empire, adopting the republican model. The Civil War inaugurated the era of the mass-conscript military that came to fruition in World Wars I and II. The first change was widely discussed, if not debated. The second change was hotly debated. In the years that America had a draft, the question of how society should generate its soldiers remained a legitimate one.

But the end of the draft and the rise of alienated war cast this issue in silence. After Vietnam, one might have expected a serious discussion of democracy's relation to the military, one that might have begun by returning to the ideals embodied in the Constitution. This did not occur. In the twilight of the Vietnam conflict, Robert J. Lifton bemoaned the possibility that instead of deep reflection on the matter, our culture would go into deep *denial* about the complex political—and moral—problems surrounding America's military stature.[47]

His worst fears have come true.

AFTER THE DRAFT

America must never outsource America's national security.

—George W. Bush

Frankly, I'd like to see the government get out of war altogether and leave the whole feud to private industry.

—Major Milo Minder Binder, in Joseph Heller's *Catch-22*

The end of the Vietnam War saw a strong consensus on ending the draft.[48] At that point, several possibilities presented themselves.

Privatizing Private Ryan

One was to press the Milton Friedman–libertarian logic to its full conclusion: give up the draft as part of giving up the whole idea of society as a shared project involving shared sacrifice. This would mean giving up the whole idea of "citizenship" as a viable category. Politics is just another market endeavor in which individuals pursue their private ends. "National defense" (if the notion of "nation" makes sense at all) is just another economic good to be pursued through market channels. As Friedman said, calling it a "professional" army or a "mercenary" army amounts to the same thing.

The reality of our military practices has matched this mercenary model to some extent. The question is whether this model will ever triumph completely. The specter of such a triumph is raised by the new phenomenon of *corporate warfare*.[49]

An early champion of corporate warfare was Dick Cheney when he was secretary of defense for the senior President Bush. He urged privatizing the logistical side of military operations. On leaving Washington, he became chief of Halliburton, a key player in the growth of privatized war. At the time, there were about ten private military corporations in the United States. Today there are more than thirty, and worldwide there are several hundred firms doing about $100 billion a year in business. The initial focus of private firms was logistical, providing food, clothing, and other essentials (and not-so-essentials) to those in uniform. Over time their activities expanded to include combat and combat-related activities.

Corporate war as a global phenomenon was a product of the end of the Cold War when the downsizing of national militaries left huge numbers of military personnel looking for work. A leading scholar of the topic, Peter Singer, writes, "In the wake of globalization and the end of the Cold War the private military market has expanded in a way not seen since the 1700s."[50] He is referring to the age of mercenary warfare. But today's corporate warfare differs from the older mercenary warfare where individuals contracted themselves out to the highest bidder in being corporate, hence driven by corporate profit rather than private gain. And it is multinational, meaning that its services go to the highest bidder whatever their nationality. Hence, it is possible that the allegiance of a corporation might change in the midst of a conflict, or it could end up fighting for both sides should profit mandate it. In Joseph Heller's *Catch-22*, Milo Minderbinder wages privatized war in the waning days of World War II and ends up bombing his own base because there is money in it.

At the time Iraq achieved so-called sovereignty, there were about 30,000 privately contracted soldiers in the country, making them the second-largest military force behind the United States and ahead of Great Britain. The ratio of private contractors to regular soldiers was about ten times what it was in the first Gulf War. Corporate soldiers were hired to provide protection around the "Green Zone" in a contract worth about $1 billion. Corporate operatives trained the new Iraqi military. In August 2003, independent experts estimated that as much as one-third of the $4 billion monthly cost of keeping U.S. troops in Iraq was going to private contractors.

Corporate soldiers first gained attention when four employees of the Blackwater firm were killed, burned, and dismembered in Faluja. Even more dramatic has been the role of mercenaries in military scandals. In the notorious Abu Ghraib scandal, sixteen of the identified incidents of abuse were linked to private contractors. Such contractors continued to play shady roles because they provided deniability to government officials. In May 2004, the compound of former U.S. client Ahmed Chalabi was raided in Baghdad in an action that revealed the splits among the newly installed Iraqi leadership and brought renewed focus on Chalabi himself, now an embarrassment to the U.S. endeavor. Officials hurried to distance themselves from the operation, insisting that it was entirely an Iraqi affair and claiming that no U.S. government employees were involved. This was only technically true since eight armed private contractors paid by the U.S. State Department went on the raid to direct and encourage the Iraqi police officers.

This was foreshadowed in earlier uses of private forces. In Bosnia, employees of DynCorps, a major player now training the Iraqi police force, were accused of "perverse, illegal, and inhumane behavior" for engaging in trucking in prostitution, purchasing illegal weapons, forging false passports, and other illegal acts. The employees, who included the firm's Bosnia supervisor, were caught videotaping themselves while raping young Bosnian women. None of the employees were prosecuted because there were no relevant laws that applied to them. As private contractors, they were not subject to military justice—they could only be fired. The two employees who reported the crime were terminated by the company. But their employer was not affected. Its contract to train Iraqi police is worth more than $50 million.[51] In Afghanistan, a mercenary employed by the United States was instructed to get information from a detainee named Abdul Wali. He ended up beating the man to death with a heavy metal flashlight, an act that got him a prison term but only because, as in other similar cases, the event was brought to public light.

The most notorious corporate warrior is Halliburton and its division Brown and Root Services. The turning point for Halliburton was the first Gulf War, in which it was contracted to bring 320 burning oil wells under control and repair damaged public buildings in Kuwait. Soon it made a major expansion into the military services market that became a significant portion of all its activities. In 2007 its employees in that area numbered around 20,000 with its gross revenues about $6 billion a year. Military planners were said to no longer even envision a military action without a major role for Halliburton. In Kosovo, Halliburton provided such services as construction, engineering, base camp operations and maintenance, transportation, road repair and vehicle maintenance, water production and distribution, food services, laundry, power generation, refueling, firefighting, and mail delivery, among others. Dick Cheney joked that Halliburton employees were the first people our soldiers saw when they arrived in Kosovo and the last they waved good-bye to when they left. Soldiers themselves joked that their uniform patches should say, "Sponsored by Brown and Root."

Bush's War on Terror was an economic bonanza for Halliburton and the industry as a whole. After 9/11, when the stock market was generally in a state of collapse, corporate warfare stocks jumped 50 percent in value. In 2003, Halliburton Pentagon contracts increased from $900 million to $3.9 billion, almost 700 percent. The company now has more than $8 billion in contracts for Iraqi rebuilding, a figure that could grow as high as $18 billion. As one Defense Department official remarked, the war effort is a "full employment act" for these companies, a "gravy train."[52]

Halliburton was hit by public scandal, though its economic clout was so substantial that one doubts that the Washington establishment will ever do much absent substantial public outcry. Halliburton was found to have overcharged for gasoline brought into Iraq from Kuwait by more than a dollar a gallon. It charged for three times as many meals as it served to troops in Kuwait, and at some of the mess halls the food was so bad that soldiers refused to eat it. While soldiers suffered from shortages of sufficiently armored Humvees and body armor, Halliburton was wasting money in Kuwait on luxury items like monogrammed towels for the company's health club and sport-utility vehicles for its executives. It was cited for not issuing proper bills for the $8 billion in work it had performed for the Pentagon thus far, and the General Accounting Office suggested that its contracts, including those to manage Iraqi oil fields, had been improperly awarded. This led to some of the first public questioning of the whole practice. Senator Richard Durbin of Illinois publicly called Halliburton to task for wasteful spending at a time when ordinary soldiers went wanting.

The problems posed by corporate warfare run from the very bottom to the very top. Regular soldiers are often required to risk their lives in defense of privatized soldiers performing their duties. Consider how it feels to be a regular grunt, paid $20,000 a year, and be asked to risk your life for a privatized soldier doing exactly the same thing (or something less risky) for $85,000 a year. If private soldiers are captured or killed, the U.S. military is under no obligation to find them or retrieve their bodies, and the corporation alone is responsible for notifying the families and shipping the bodies home. Corporate soldiers do not take an oath of allegiance to the U.S. Constitution, nor are they subject to the Uniform Code of Military Justice, as the Bosnian incident showed. At the same time, there are often no *local* legal standards to which they are answerable either. In Iraq, when there was effectively no legal system at all, the Coalition Provisional Authority still insisted that contractors and other foreign personnel would not be subject to any Iraqi criminal processes. If an employee commited a crime, there was little a firm could do but fire him or her and little the military could do to the firm but not renew its contract.

Figures in the military recognized that the whole idea of corporate soldiers grated against the traditional military ethos of shared sacrifice. Keep in mind that there was nothing in corporate war to ensure that soldiers hired to fight were even American citizens. U.S. Army Colonel Bruce Grant stated, "When former officers sell their skills on the international market for profit the entire profession loses its moral high ground with the American people."[53] The "moral high ground" in this case was the citizen-soldier ethic. (Private contractors now run more than 200 ROTC programs. They wear military uniforms and train the soldiers of the future but are not in the military themselves, nor are they subject to military discipline.)

How do we explain the rise of such warfare?

As the military increasingly relied on high technology, it became increasingly efficient to hire private parties to operate it rather than provide expensive training to new recruits. There are undoubtedly such efficiencies elsewhere. But scholars agree that there is no evidence that outsourcing *generally* saves money in military matters. Here's an example of the problems that arise. As the conditions of privatized soldiers become more dismal, the insurance premiums that corporations must carry skyrocket. When I did this research, forty cents of every dollar spent by private contractors in Iraq when to insurance premiums. There are very few mechanisms to police the vast sums spent on corporate war despite the fact that such corporate war accounts for more than 30 percent of total American expenditures in Iraq. Corporate firms are not subject to Freedom of Information Act issues like other government agencies. Congress is not even notified of individual military contracts if they are under $15 million, as many contracts are. The Defense Department is legally required to answer congressional inquiries about the deployment of U.S. forces, but private firms are not. The upshot of this is the creation of a private military arm of the government with almost no accountability under the Constitution.

Corporate warfare is not more efficient. It has arisen from the political exigencies of alienated war—to distance the average American from the realities of military conflict. Singer cites the desire to insulate average citizens from the import of war as determinative. The military acknowledges it, too, off the record. Sometimes this involves straightforward subterfuge. When Congress imposed a cap of 20,000 soldiers in Bosnia, the military turned around and hired private contractors to do the same thing. Speaking of the role of such contractors in Colombia, a military officer told the *Dallas Morning News* off the record that the purpose was to minimize so-called official casualties. If something goes wrong, he said, it's important that Washington be able to say that "there wasn't a soldier killed."

Many people have heard of "privateers" who figured prominently in the transition from mercenary war to the citizens' war of modern times. They were private sailors on private ships who were given license by a country, like Britain, to wage war against the ships of another country. Often their payment—or "prize"—was the right to keep some if not all of what they captured when they destroyed a foreign vessel. This approach had its efficiencies. Instead of maintaining a full-time navy, you could commission privateers to do the dirty work. Commissioning them involved giving them "letters of marques" that allowed them to privateer against another country for a certain period of time. The status of such letters was an issue in the creation of the Constitution. It is another instance of limiting executive power since Congress, not the executive, is vested by the Constitution with the power to issue "letters of marques." But such letters were already falling out of favor in the new republic since privateers were little else than government sponsored pirates. The very idea of them clashed with the citizen-soldier ideal and republican notions of accountability to the citizenry.

Corporate warfare received unprecedented scrutiny in the fall of 2007 when employees of Blackwater killed seventeen Iraqi civilians in Baghdad's Nisour Square. By then the security firm had been implicated in nearly 200 other shootings since 2005. Immediately thereafter, private security forces gunned down two Iraqi women, both Armenian Christians. From the extensive coverage of these events, many Americans learned for the first time that during the initial occupation of the country, the U.S. government had unilaterally exempted security firms like Blackwater from Iraqi law, an exemption that continued after the United States reinstated Iraqi sovereignty. Hence, the Iraq government could not prosecute the perpetrators of the Nisour Square action, so it announced that Blackwater would be expelled from the country. The United States resisted this doggedly, fearing that the practice of corporate warfare generally would be targeted.[54] By the fall of 2007, payments to private security firms had jumped to $4 billion a year from $1 billion just four years earlier. The Iraqi government was eventually forced to compromise with the United States on Blackwater activities in the country.

In 2008, reliance on corporate warriors was stronger than ever, as indicated by the first official estimates of its cost. The Congressional Budget Office (CBO) reported that, since 2003, the United States had spent $100 billion or more on contractors in Iraq since the invasion in 2003. One out of every five dollars spent on the war in Iraq had gone to contractors in a war zone where employees of private contractors, at least 180,000, outnumbered U.S. soldiers. The CBO report repeated concerns that such outsourcing had led to overbilling, fraud, and shoddy and unsafe work that had endangered and even killed U.S. soldiers. Senator Byron L. Dorgan (D-ND) pushed for the Senate to create a special war-contracting committee, like the panel that Harry Truman led in the Senate during World War II before he was tapped to be President Roosevelt's running mate in 1944. "The Truman Committee held 60 hearings on waste, fraud and abuse," Dorgan said. "It's unfathomable to me that we don't have a bipartisan investigative committee on contracting in Iraq."[55]

Corporate warfare will be indispensable as long as young people who support America's wars refuse to fight in them. Presidential candidate and libertarian Representative Ron Paul of Texas has introduced a bill that explicitly calls for the reauthorization of eighteenth-century privateering.[56]

Sustaining the Citizen-Soldier

A second alternative after the end of the draft would have been to *reaffirm* the citizen-soldier ideal but without a draft. This could have taken a number of forms. One might have been taking the notion of a "volunteer" military seriously by stressing the volunteer component of service. A campaign to this effect might have been built around the philosophy of Elvis Presley: people should give back to society when society has given them so much. Our society has many successful models of encouraging volunteerism. Every year the United Way conducts public campaigns to encourage volunteer giving. The Red Cross elicits public support constantly. Other groups engage in such practices especially around Christmastime. If the government truly regarded military service as a form of public service, it could have learned from these groups—identifying famous people or their children who were willing to enlist themselves and urge others to do so.

But the government did nothing of the sort. It promoted military service not as a form of public service but as a career opportunity. It is as if the Red Cross conducted a blood campaign on the basis that selling your blood was a good way to pick up some extra money.

The most notable effort at sustaining the citizen-soldier connection came from within the military itself. I noted in the introduction to this book that it has proved an important factor in the Iraq conflict. At the start of the Vietnam War, President Johnson ignored the urgings of the Joint Chiefs of Staff to mobilize the Reserves. The mobilization of reserves had been crucial in previous wars in demonstrating the full commitment of the nation, but Johnson sought to dampen the war's impact on the average person. The draft's impact fell on younger men. Older men in the Reserves were never required to go overseas, nor were privileged younger men, like George W. Bush, who found spaces in the National Guard.

The American military was honestly distressed at its alienation from the ordinary public during the Vietnam conflict. It felt that the civilian leaders had irresponsibly ignored the advice of military leaders in ways that augmented its isolation. The upshot was the "total force policy," developed by General Creighton Abrams in the waning years of the Vietnam conflict and identified with him ever since.[57] The idea was to link full-time military and Reserve and National Guard forces so that a mobilization like that of Vietnam would not be possible. War would require the involvement of ordinary citizens so that it would require the support of the citizenry. The means included policies like "mirror imaging" that called for keeping the same kind of combat units in both the active forces and the National Guard so that the latter would be a more equal and relevant partner when war occurred. There were other reasons for the policy, of course. Secretary of Defense Melvin Laird supported it because, in his view, the so-called volunteer approach would never generate enough soldiers for the regular military, and it was a less expensive way of maintaining a substantial fighting force.

Some of the problems encountered in Iraq are offshoots of this total force policy. Reserve forces have often not been sufficiently trained for the tasks required of them. The total force policy is also responsible for the outdated, inadequate equipment that National Guard and Reserves have been saddled with. Still, the policy has maintained a citizen-soldier link in ways that have led its critics to claim that it ties the hands of the executive.

Neoconservatives like Vice President Cheney opposed the total force policy, favoring instead full privatization of the military. Secretary of Defense Donald Rumsfeld was notoriously quoted demeaning the fighting abilities of ordinary draftees of World War II, Korea, and Vietnam; he was later compelled to recant. The total force policy was of a piece with the so-called Powell Doctrine in aiming to keep the military out of endless stalemated quagmires where the whole distinction between war and peace became blurred.[58] After a substantial call-up of the Reserves in

2003, by the way, the Bush administration refrained from doing so again because of the widespread popular outcry it engendered.

California Dreamin'

Cheney's dreams of privatization may ultimately come to pass. But the system we have in place today is a hodgepodge of rhetoric and reality contributing to what I've termed the surreal character of today's politics. The author of this hodgepodge was Ronald Reagan.

Reagan ascended to the presidency on a tide of renewed patriotism that included clarion calls to sacrifice. His first inaugural address concluded with an extended reference to one of the soldiers buried in Arlington National Cemetery, World War I veteran Martin Treptow. Consummate speaker that he was, Reagan evoked all the imagery of the civic republican citizen-soldier heritage. Treptow, he told the nation, "left his job in a small town barber shop" in 1917 to join his fellow citizens in France. Killed on the Western Front, he was found to be carrying a diary whose words Reagan quoted:

> America must win this war. Therefore, I will work, I will save, I will sacrifice, I will endure, I will fight cheerfully and do my utmost, as if the issue of the whole struggle depended on me alone.

The new president concluded that our struggle too requires "our best effort, and our willingness to believe in ourselves and to believe in our capacity to perform great deeds."

Reagan's calls to national purpose were reminiscent of John F. Kennedy's. The success of his presidency lay in reviving this sense of shared purpose. But Reagan's genius was to sever the ideal of shared struggle from any reality of shared sacrifice.[59] Kennedy had ended his inaugural speech, "Ask not what your country can do for you, ask what you can do for your country." Reagan's concluding reference to Martin Treptow's commitment to "sacrifice," "save," and "fight" for his country carried no suggestion that his listeners would be asked to sacrifice or fight—or even save, for that matter.

Reagan wrapped himself in the mantle of military purpose in ways both large and small. Some of them have persisted ever since. Here's one small example. Reagan instituted the practice of saluting uniformed personnel when greeted, often with a jaunty snap of the hand. The practice is completely inappropriate. Real soldiers salute only while in uniform, and keep in mind that while the president is commander in chief of the armed forces, he is not a member of them. His saluting betrays the principles of civilian control when it pretends that he is. Real former soldiers like Eisenhower never saluted others while president, nor did he feel the need to don himself in military jackets or other regalia.[60]

Reagan invested extraordinary amounts of money in the military in ways that improved the lives of the professional soldiers enormously. Behind it was the assumption that military service was no longer something that average people would be involved in. Reagan began the drive for a military that would use fewer and fewer soldiers by relying on high-tech weapons and fantasies, like the Strategic Defense Initiative ("Star Wars"). The struggle that he championed was one in which no one had to serve in the military or even pay for it. Reagan did not raise taxes to pay for his extraordinary military buildup; rather, he cut them. The economic sacrifices were to be born by later generations.

The upshot was an extraordinary shift in attitudes that persists to this day. Andrew Bacevich puts it this way: Reagan made *support* for the troops rather than *becoming* one of them the standard of civic virtue.[61] A true American celebrates Rambo when he comes home; the true American also assumes that when war comes, Rambo will do the fighting, not him.

THE GREATEST GENERATION AND AFTER

The 1990s saw a good deal of military activity but no discussion of the larger questions about the place of the military in American life. Perhaps the American public was so exhausted by the conflicts of Vietnam and the Cold War that it didn't want to think about these matters. In retrospect, what is striking about this decade's attitudes to war is the nostalgia that swept the country in the decade's second half for the so-called Greatest Generation and the experience of World War II. It provided a continuing rhetorical trope for thinking about the issue of sacrifice. Fittingly, it also had a dimension of unreality that spoke to our disconnected relation to these matters.

The celebration of the Greatest Generation was an exercise in nostalgia. What is nostalgia? Nostalgia and memory are not the same thing. Nostalgia has an idealized dimension, often an excessive one that bespeaks of a longing for values that were once held precious but that have now disappeared or are disappearing. There was a legitimate homage to the deeds of the past in the chief artifacts of the Greatest Generation celebration like Tom Brokaw's book *The Greatest Generation* and Steven Spielberg's film *Saving Private Ryan*. But there was an over-the-top dimension to them that speaks to how much the ideal of shared sacrifice they celebrated has vanished from our midst.

Brokaw's *The Greatest Generation*

Brokaw's *The Greatest Generation* was a powerful celebration of the unsung heroism of ordinary men and women in World War II. It did not dwell on the overall achievements of the World War II generation. No one needed reminding of how the Depression was endured or the Axis defeated. Brokaw focused instead on the acts of personal sacrifice, small and large, in achieving victory. The message was a good one: the Greatest Generation represented a personal moral ideal, the civic republican notion of "civic virtue." When a war is being fought that you believe in, you don't sit on the sidelines or twist the regulations to excuse yourself: you join in.

But there was an excessiveness to the claims, bespeaking of the idealizations of nostalgia: the idea of a "greatest" generation to begin with. The author didn't just claim that the World War II cohort was the greatest generation America had produced (what about the founding generation—without whom we wouldn't even have an America?). He claimed that it was "the greatest generation any society had produced, ever."[62] Really—*any* society, *ever*? How about the Jews that Moses led out of Egypt? They were pretty good. Or the Christians that survived Roman repression to propound the Good News. They weren't bad.

Or consider Brokaw's account of that generation's character. He writes at the start of the book,

> It is not surprising that the horrors of war give birth to a new generation of good Samaritans. Young men and women who have been so intensely exposed to such inhumanity often make a silent pledge that if they ever escape this dark world of death and injuries, this universe of cruelty, they will devote their lives to good works. Sometimes this pledge is a conscious thought. Sometimes it is a subconscious reaction to their experience.[63]

Brokaw endorses the view that military service builds character of the right kind. But as a characterization of an entire generation, the claim is problematic. More than 90 percent of those who served got nowhere near the fighting, hence, nowhere near any firsthand experience with "the dark world of death and injuries." In addition, if the World War II cohort gave us civic-minded altruists, it also gave us criminals and scoundrels. Yes, the young men of this generation won World War II, our "good" war. Then they turned around and started Vietnam, our worst war (prior to Iraq). Yes, many devoted themselves to good works. Others became Richard Nixon and conspired to create the greatest political scandal in American history, the Watergate affair.

Still, it is certainly true of this generation that compared to *later* ones, the "idea of personal responsibility [was] a defining characteristic." For this generation it *was* important to stay true to values of "personal responsibility, duty, and honor."[64]

As a side note, the first President George Bush is featured in Brokaw's book. The path from the senior Bush to the younger Bush seems to confirm Mark Twain's remark that evolution works backward. The senior Bush volunteered for service and achieved distinction as a pilot. But I didn't know before reading Brokaw's book that what he mainly did in the military was censor the mail of other enlisted men on his aircraft carrier. The senior Bush, a product of cloistered privilege, credits this with teaching him much that he knows about life. "When I would see a man whose letter I had censored," he tells Brokaw, "I would look to him with more understanding and I felt richer" [richer!].[65] His stint as head of the Central Intelligence Agency must have helped him have even more "understanding" and feel even "richer."

Spielberg's *Saving Private Ryan*

Spielberg's *Saving Private Ryan* was an homage to both the citizen-soldier ethic and the World War II movies celebrating that ethic. Hollywood had given up on war films when Spielberg's movie came along. The last successful World War II film had been *Patton* in 1970. That film was atypical of World War II films in focusing on a single great general rather than a bunch of ordinary citizen-soldiers. Spielberg returned us to the generic form of ordinary guys just doing their job for democracy. The 1980s had seen the emergence of Vietnam War films, some of which fit the traditional World War II format of ordinary guys thrown together and trying to survive (*Platoon* and *The Deer Hunter*). But the most commercially successful 1980s war films were the Rambo films, which had little in common with the traditional genre. John Rambo was *not* a citizen-soldier but a professional killer for whom ideology (like "democracy") was irrelevant—beyond the fact that "we" should "win." Rambo was a James Bond figure, more buff and less debonair.

"Rambo" reinforced the emerging 1980s view that war was no longer something to be fought by ordinary normal people. Let Rambo do it. Spielberg returned us to the citizen-soldier ethic whose ideology was embodied in his characters. Consider Tom Hanks's lieutenant: the ongoing speculation of his fellow soldiers about what he really did back home evoked two things: this was a war that people fought no matter what their civilian job—no one was special, but soldiering was not their real job— and they were not members of a professional army. As in most World War II films, the platoon's makeup reinforced this message. Its mixed membership was a metaphor for the racial, class, and regional melting pot democracy ideally involves. Guys from Brooklyn fought alongside country boys from the South, and Jews and Italians fought alongside midwesterners. The film accurately portrayed the army's exclusion of African Americans.

The "embattled farmer" was embattled because he really did not want to fight. His spirit was peacelike, which is why for the founding fathers a military composed of such persons would be a reluctant one. Accordingly, Spielberg celebrated democracy at war but does not engage in rah-rah.[66] The most striking aspect of Spielberg's film was its graphic portrayal of battle. Its realism was an implicit comment on the extraordinary lengths to which governments have gone to hide the realities of war. In World War I, photographs of dead soldiers were banned. In World War II, films of soldiers being shot were not allowed. Eventually magazines like *Life* were allowed to show photos of fallen GIs but only if they were shown as peaceful—with bodies intact. It has been more than ten years since the Defense Department has allowed Americans to see photos of coffins and body bags returning from overseas. When the picture of flag-draped coffins of Americans in Iraq appeared in the *Seattle Times*, the worker who had sent it to her mother (to show their families "respect and honor") was immediately fired by the military contractor she worked for.[67] In the Iraq War, the denial has even extended to whether Americans are actually dying. When soldiers from the 507th Maintenance Company were attacked at the very start of the war, the Pentagon refused to respond to reports that Americans had been killed or captured. All the major networks went along with the charade so that the families of prisoners of war had to see their loved ones on foreign language television. Not surprisingly, Spielberg's film would become politically suspect in the eyes of the powers that be. In 2004, sixty-six ABC affiliates decided not to run Spielberg's film on Veterans Day for fear of government reprisals to its graphic depictions of battle. This was despite the fact that the film had been shown twice before, with the first broadcast in 2001 seen by almost 18 million people.

The Films of Alienated War

As the culture of the citizen-soldier tradition recedes, the culture of alienated war has begun to define itself. Rambo led the way, but Rambo was still an identifiable American. A better glimpse of the future is found in two films directed by the talented Paul Verhoeven: *RoboCop* and *Starship Troopers*.

Both films are science fiction, but science fiction has always had a special place in the literature of war, especially in capturing contemporary anxieties and anticipating the future. As Niall Ferguson has observed, H. G. Wells's "The War of the Worlds" foreshadowed the logic of twentieth-century world war, which Ferguson terms the "War of the World." An additional factor today is the degree to which the military aspires to be and certainly presents itself as science fiction come to life. Alienated war's emphasis on high technology seeks to convince us that war can be something fought entirely by robots, at least on our side, with the speed and precision of video games. The upshot is a mechanized warrior that the average citizen cannot possibly identify with—or needs to identify with—since the wars of their nation have as much personal impact as *Star Wars*.

Verhoeven's films are interesting for how they capture the transitional nature of alienated war and the anxiety it generates. The earlier of the two, *RoboCop*, transplants the war zone into a future Detroit, Michigan, which is experiencing all the effects of what Martin Shaw has termed "degenerative war." Chaos rules and the city is in financial ruin. In response, the politicians adopt the domestic equivalent of today's corporate warfare, essentially privatizing law enforcement by contracting out to the mega-corporation Omni Consumer Products. The story gets going when the corporation wheels out the robot it hopes to substitute for real people in fighting crime. But law enforcement droid ED-209 quickly demonstrates that its massively lethal firepower is not informed by comparable powers of discrimination in who to kill and who not to kill. ED-209 is a fitting image of today's high-tech destructive power unburdened by political wisdom. After it kills a hapless employee in a demonstration, the company turns to the RoboCop program instead, in which a recently killed police officer is resurrected as half man, half machine. In the early days of the Iraq conflict, reporters observed the similarity between America's high-tech warriors roaming the streets and the fictional RoboCop. In the film, though, the cyborg was the only character who achieved any humanity.

Starship Troopers is even more interesting for our purposes insofar as it is a sustained reflection on the citizen-soldier tradition. The film is based on the novel of the same name by prominent 1950s science-fiction author Robert A. Heinlein, whose outlook was a mishmash of Cold War paranoia and high-tech fantasy, with a dash of civic republicanism thrown in. The story's major character is Johnny Rico, who is headed for service in a futuristic mobile infantry. Before that, he endures a "History and Moral Philosophy" course where the teacher rants to the impressionable class about the glories of personal sacrifice. The flashbacks to this class are reminiscent of the patriotic lectures in *All Quiet on the Western Front* except that Heinlein believed every word of it. Citizenship is linked to soldiering; there are numerous references to "civic virtue." But the democratic dimension has been lost. Only former soldiers can vote or run for public office, and only the elite few can become soldiers. As the class teacher puts it, "The franchise is today limited to discharged veterans," unlike the old days when anyone could vote who was eighteen years old and "had a body temperature near 37°C." This system followed the democracies of the twentieth century, which according to the novel collapsed because "people had been led to believe that they could simply vote for whatever they wanted . . . and get it, without toil, without sweat, without tears."

The film appropriates this material with a relentless tone of irony. Johnny Rico's parents are portrayed as typical of privileged parents today. They cannot comprehend why their son would join the military rather than go to Harvard, even though the latter choice would mean less-than-full citizenship. The military he joins is staffed by soldiers who increasingly look like Nazis in the cut of their uniforms. The story unfolds into a war with giant bugs from another planet that, the film makes clear, had no quarrel with Earth until the earthlings started bugging them. Endless scenes portray the high-tech capacities of the starship troopers to be as lumbering and ineffective as ED-209's. But Johnny Rico comes into his own after he is transformed into a cyborg. In the end, the toothy youngsters prevail in battle and decide to make the military a career—meaning that they will never become full citizens since only former soldiers have those rights.

Starship Troopers captures every contemporary fantasy about an all-volunteer, high-tech strike force. The book is apparently recommended reading within the U.S. Army and Marine Corps because of its emphasis on small unit cohesion, the fraternity of service, and its focus on the forward-serving elite mobile infantry. Heinlein's only quarrel with the Cold War was in his adamant opposition to conscription, which he regarded as a form of slavery. He saw a moral of his book to be that a nation that could not find volunteers to fight for it did not deserve to endure.

TRIUMPH OF THE CHICKENHAWKS

No one knew what George W. Bush would do in foreign policy when he ascended to the presidency in 2000. His campaign had called for a more humble approach to military actions and nation building especially. The triumph of the chickenhawk was the triumph of the neoconservative in particular. Some of their policies have been addressed in my remarks on corporate warfare. Some final comments on this strange phenomenon are appropriate.

The neoconservatives that achieved dominance after 9/11 were figures who had been obsessed with the "decline" of American power for decades. It is interesting to reflect on what they have in mind by "power." The United States was defeated in Vietnam, but there are different kinds of defeats. The defeat of Hitler destroyed his military capacity. Nothing of the sort happened in Vietnam. America's defeat was political, impacting its legitimacy. To "restore" American "power" would have meant restoring that legitimacy. This is not what neoconservatives worried about, except insofar as restoring legitimacy meant restoring a blind faith in the American people in the president's right to do whatever he wanted.

You would think that any doubts about sheer military power had been laid to rest by the end of the Cold War and the emergence of American military power as the largest and best financed several times over. Consider a parallel. If, in the midst of their fabulous string of World Series victories in the 1950s and 1960s, the owner of the New York Yankees had become obsessed with the decline in his team, some might have questioned his sanity. Yet the Bush neoconservatives rose to prominence in government (and, in some instances, higher education) by bemoaning American weakness when its military capabilities were without equal. They remain without equal. The failures in Iraq speak not to America's inadequate military power but rather to the inadequacies of military power per se as a form of power. You cannot prevail by military means alone.

Some have contrasted the neoconservative "New Vulcans" with those who created the post–World War II world order.[68] The latter tended to be businessman lawyers interested in creating international economic, legal, and diplomatic institutions rather than creating new military ones. The military institutions they did create, like NATO, followed the form of transnational institutions. These were men comfortable with negotiation and treaty making and saw the military struggle in the context of larger economic, legal, and diplomatic issues. They reflected a confident Northeast elite culture that, for all its faults, was not given to hysteria. Although they did not come from the military, many of them had military experience.

Today's neoconservative is typically a lifetime Pentagon bureaucrat, meaning that while his or her background is military related, he or she has little experience serving in the armed forces and none with actual fighting. The Bush administration marked the first time in American history that military policy was made principally by chickenhawks. The neoconservative foreign policy is sometimes termed "Wilsonian" for its stress on "ideals," especially "democracy," but this is a new development. Until the 1980s, championing democracy was the province of liberals. During the Cold War, the issue was not democracy so much as anticommunism. This began to change with the overthrow of Marcos in the Philippines, where Reagan, after first supporting Marcos, came around to support the democratic wave. Conservatism now portrays itself as highly idealistic, chastising its liberal opponents for failing to take values seriously.

The 2008 presidential election appeared to confirm the death of the citizen-soldier tradition. Despite the nomination of a former military officer for president and two vice-presidential candidates with children in the military, the larger questions raised by alienated war were not touched. The renunciation of the Bush legacy from all sides was noticeably silent on the question of war and sacrifice. Both sides called for aggressive military action though in different places. The Democrats criticize the Republicans for their failure to wage war aggressively enough in Afghanistan, but they did not address where the troops for this effort would come from. The Republicans championed the ongoing conflict in Iraq, insisting that only victory would suffice. They did not say where further troops would come from either. In the next chapter, I turn to a more detailed analysis of the chickenhawk phenomenon, sadly convinced that it remains a mirror to our times.

NOTES

1. W. Cabell Bruce, *John Randolph of Roanoke 1773–1833: A Biography Based Largely on New Material* (Whitefish, MT: Kessinger Publishing, 1922), 158.
2. Peter Guralnick, *Last Train to Memphis: The Rise of Elvis Presley* (Boston: Back Bay Books, 1995), 443.
3. Guralnick, *Last Train to Memphis*, 461.
4. Guralnick, *Last Train to Memphis*, 464.
5. The issue of standing armies and militias in the context of America's revolutionary ideology is addressed in Bernard Bailyn, *The Ideological Origins of the American Revolution* (Cambridge, MA: Belknap Press, 1992), 112 ff.
6. Political philosophers interested in civic republicanism have given short shrift to the citizen-soldier tradition, though. Michael Sandel says little about it in his otherwise excellent *Democracy's Discontent: America in Search of a Public Philosophy* (Cambridge, MA: Belknap Press, 1998). The same is generally true of Phillip Pettit's *Republicanism: A Theory of Freedom and Government* (Oxford: Oxford University Press, 2000), though he does mention the issue of standing armies (pp. 155–57). The most sophisticated work on republican security thinking is by Daniel Deudney. See his *Bounding Power: Republican Security Theory from the Polis to the Global Village* (Princeton, NJ: Princeton University Press, 2006).
7. Clare Snyder, "The Citizen-Soldier and the Tragedy of the Eighteenth Brumaire," *Strategies: Journal of Theory, Culture and Society* 16, no. 1 (May 2003): 23–37. See also her *Citizen-Soldiers and Manly Warriors: Military Service and Gender in the Civic Republican Tradition* (Lanham, MD: Rowman & Littlefield, 1999).
8. Cited in Charles Royster, *A Revolutionary People at War: The Continental Army and American Character, 1775–1783* (Chapel Hill: University of North Carolina Press, 1996), 49.
9. Niccolò Machiavelli, *The Chief Works and Others*, trans. A. Gilbert (Durham, NC: Duke University Press), 574, 578, cited in Snyder, "The Citizen-Soldier and the Tragedy of the Eighteenth Brumaire."

10. Max Farrand, ed., *The Records of the Federal Convention of 1787* (New Haven, CT: Yale University Press, 1911), I: 25.

11. On how the Revolution exhibited class divisions in who fought it, see Peter Karsten, "The US Citizen-Soldier's Past, Present, and Likely Future," *Parameters (Journal of the U.S. Army War College)*, summer 2001, 61–73. See also Gary B. Nash, *The Unknown American Revolution* (New York: Viking, 2005), 216–23.

12. See Anti-Federalist arguments in J. R. Pole, *The American Constitution For and Against: The Federalists and Anti-Federalist Papers* (New York: Hill and Wang, 1987).

13. See Bernard Bailyn, *The Ideological Origins of the American Revolution* (Cambridge, MA: Belknap Press, 1992), 36, 61 ff. (he speaks of the "obsessive concern in the colonies with standing armies"), and 112 ff.

14. Elaine Scarry, "War and the Social Contract: Nuclear Policy, Distribution, and the Right to Bear Arms," *University of Pennsylvania Law Review* 139 (1991): 1279.

15. John Brewer, *The Sinews of Power: War, Money and the English State, 1688–1783* (Cambridge, MA: Harvard University Press, 1990); Niall Ferguson, *The Cash Nexus: Money and Power in the Modern World, 1700–2000* (New York: Basic Books, 2002).

16. Immanuel Kant, *Perpetual Peace and Other Essays*, trans. Ted Humphrey (Indianapolis: Hackett, 1983), 108.

17. Kant, *Perpetual Peace*, 58.

18. Kant, *Perpetual Peace*, 88–89.

19. Daniel Deudney, "Publius before Kant: Federal-Republican Security and Democratic Peace," *European Journal of International Relations* 10, no. 3 (2004): 315–56.

20. Chalmers Johnson, *Nemesis: The Last Days of the American Republic* (New York: Metropolitan Books, 2006), chap. 2.

21. John Greville Agard Pocock, *The Machiavellian Moment: Florentine Political Thought and the Atlantic Republican Tradition* (Princeton, NJ: Princeton University Press, 2003).

22. Lois G. Schwoerer, *"No Standing Armies!" The Antiarmy Ideology in Seventeenth-Century England* (Baltimore: Johns Hopkins University Press, 1974), 193.

23. Clinton Rossiter, *Seed Time of the Republic* (New York: Harcourt, 1953), 331 and fn. 13; on the importance of the Boston Massacre, see Bernard Bailyn, *The Ideological Origins of the American Revolution* (Cambridge, MA: Belknap Press, 1992), 116, 129.

24. These are the words of Henry Knox, secretary of war, in Schwoerer, *"No Standing Armies!"* 199.

25. Federalist Paper No. 3 identified the providing of safety as the first concern of the government, and the next six are devoted to questions of external defense and protections against internal violence.

26. Walter Millis, *Arms and Men: A Study in America Military History* (New Brunswick, NJ: Rutgers University Press, 1981), 41.

27. There is a large literature on this topic, of exceptionally high quality. See Roy G. Weatherup, "Standing Armies and Armed Citizens: An Historical Analysis of the Second Amendment," *Hastings Constitutional Law Quarterly* 2, no. 4 (1975):

961–1001; David T. Hardy, "The Second Amendment and the Historiography of the Bill of Rights," *Journal of Law and Politics* 4 (1987): 1–62; Sanford Levinson, "The Embarrassing Second Amendment," *Yale Law Journal* 99 (1989): 637–59; and Glenn Harlan Reynolds, "A Critical Guide to the Second Amendment," *Tennessee Law Review* 62 (1995): 461–511.

28. See R. B. Sher, "Adam Ferguson, Adam Smith, and the Problem of National Defense," *Journal of Modern History* 61 (1989): 240–68; E. J. Harpham, "Liberalism, Civic Humanism, and the Case of Adam Smith," *American Political Science Review* 80 (1984): 764–74.

29. John Whiteclay Chambers II, *To Raise an Army: The Draft Comes to Modern America* (New York: Free Press, 1987), 37. See also George Q. Flynn, *Conscription and Democracy: The Draft in France, Great Britain, and the United States* (Westport, CT: Greenwood Press, 2001).

30. Leon Friedman, "Conscription and the Constitution: The Original Understanding," *Michigan Law Review* 67, no. 7 (1968): 1513.

31. Friedman, "Conscription and the Constitution," 1525.

32. Friedman, "Conscription and the Constitution," 1527.

33. Daniel Webster, Speech against Conscription, U.S. House of Representatives, December 9, 1814 (emphasis added); it can be found at http://www.duck daotsu.org/webster.html (accessed September 5, 2007).

34. Flynn, *Conscription and Democracy*, 251.

35. Chambers, *To Raise an Army*, 128. Dewey's views on the draft can be found in Dewey, "Conscience and Compulsion," in *The Political Writings*, ed. Debra Morris and Ian Shapiro (Indianapolis: Hackett, 1993), 192–95.

36. Chambers, *To Raise an Army*, 268–69.

37. Aaron L. Friedberg, *In the Shadow of the Garrison State: America's Anti-Statism and Its Cold War Grand Strategy* (Princeton, NJ: Princeton University Press, 2000), 167.

38. For an excellent discussion of the Vietnam experience, and the class bias of the draft, see Christian G. Appy, *Working-Class War* (Chapel Hill: University of North Carolina Press, 1993).

39. President Ford suspended draft registration in 1975, but President Carter reinstituted it in response to the Soviet invasion of Afghanistan.

40. Sol Tax, ed., *The Draft: A Handbook of Facts and Alternatives* (Chicago: University of Chicago Press, 1967), 482.

41. Tax, *The Draft*, 465.

42. Tax, *The Draft*, 466

43. Tax, *The Draft*, 475–76.

44. Friedberg, *In the Shadow of the Garrison State*, 194.

45. Milton Friedman, "Fair versus Free." This piece originally appeared in the July 4, 1977, issue of *Newsweek* and was reprinted in Friedman's *Bright Promises, Dismal Performances: An Economist's Protest*, a collection of his articles (San Diego, CA: Thomas Horton and Daughters, 1983).

46. Tax, *The Draft*, 366.

47. Robert Jay Lifton, *Home from the War: Vietnam Veterans Neither Victims nor Executioners* (New York: Simon & Schuster, 1973).

48. Opinion has not been unanimous, though. The best early discussion of the volunteer military's drawbacks, both militarily and ethically, is James Fallows, *National Defense* (New York: Vintage Books, 1981), chap. 5. Fallows points out the failings of the Gates Commission's predictions. Discussions of the draft versus volunteer approach based on subsequent experience include Charles Moscos and Frank Wood, eds., *The Military: More Than Just a Job?* (McLean, VA: International Defence Publishers, 1988); E. J. Dionne, Kayla Drogosz, and Robert Litan, eds., *United We Serve: National Service in the Future of Citizenship* (Washington, DC: Brookings Institution Press, 2003), especially the Moscos article, "Patriotism Lite Meets the Citizen Soldier"; and Peter Feaver and Richard Kohn, eds., *Soldiers and Civilians: The Civil Military Gap and American National Security* (Cambridge, MA: MIT Press, 2001), especially the article by William Bianco and Jamie Markham, "Vanishing Veterans: The Decline of Military Experience in the U.S. Congress."

49. P. W. Singer, *Corporate Warriors: The Rise of the Privatized Military Industry* (Ithaca, NY: Cornell University Press, 2007); Jeremy Scahill, *Blackwater: The Rise of the World's Most Powerful Mercenary Army* (New York: Nation Books, 2008); Deborah D. Avant, *The Market for Force: The Consequences of Privatizing Security* (Cambridge: Cambridge University Press, 2005); Sarah Percy, *Mercenaries: The History of a Norm in International Relations* (New York: Oxford University Press, 2007).

50. Singer, *Corporate Warriors*, 40.

51. Singer, *Corporate Warriors*, 525.

52. Singer, *Corporate Warriors*, 232.

53. Bruce D. Grant, *U.S. Military Expertise for Sale: Private Military Consultants as a Tool of Foreign Policy* (Washington, DC: National Defense University Press, 1998).

54. In December 2008, five Blackwater security guards involved in the incident were indicted by the Justice Department for manslaughter, attempt to commit manslaughter, and using and discharging a firearm during and in relation to a crime of violence.

55. James Risen, "Pentagon's Outsourcing in War Costs U.S. Billions," *New York Times*, August 12, 2008.

56. Singer, *Corporate Warriors*, 232.

57. Andrew J. Bacevich, *The New American Militarism: How Americans Are Seduced by War* (Oxford: Oxford University Press, 2006).

58. Bacevich, *The New American Militarism*, 42.

59. Bacevich, *The New American Militarism*, 102. Contrast Jimmy Carter's real calls for sacrifice—there's no way to avoid sacrifice, he said—with the politics of Ronald Reagan.

60. John Lucas, "Senseless Salute," *New York Times*, April 14, 2003.

61. Bacevich, *The New American Militarism*, 106.

62. Tom Brokaw, *The Greatest Generation* (New York: Random House, 2004), xxx (emphasis added).

63. Brokaw, *The Greatest Generation*, 25.

64. Brokaw, *The Greatest Generation*, xx.

65. Brokaw, *The Greatest Generation*, 276.

66. Combat veterans attest to how too much zealous patriotism was looked down on in wartime as something that could get people needlessly hurt.

67. See Ellen Goodman, "Getting the Picture," *Boston Globe*, April 29, 2004.

68. Bush's Advisors included two major groups—an "in-group" of hawks whose captain was Vice President Dick Cheney and which has had a decisive influence on Bush himself, and an "out-group" of "realists" headed by Secretary of State Colin Powell and his deputy, Richard Armitage. While the out-group, which ironically boasted men, including Powell, Armitage, retired Generals Anthony Zinni and Brent Scowcroft, with real war experience, the in-group was dominated by individuals, particularly Cheney and virtually the entire civilian leadership of the Pentagon, who had none at all. The sense of kinship that united the group was illustrated in part by a dinner hosted by Cheney shortly after U.S. troops took Baghdad. The guests included Wolfowitz, Libby, and Adelman; the atmosphere was warm and celebratory as they recounted their defeat of the "realists." "Someone mentioned Powell, and there were chuckles around the table," Woodward reported. Bob Woodward, *Plan of Attack* (New York: Simon & Schuster, 2004).

3

❧

Chickenhawk Variations

I am angry that so many of the sons of the powerful and well placed . . .
managed to wangle slots in Reserve and National Guard units. . . . Of
the many tragedies of Vietnam, this raw class discrimination strikes me
as the most damaging to the ideal that all Americans are created equal
and owe equal allegiance to their country.

—Colin Powell, *My American Journey*[1]

I first remember the chickenhawk charge being raised in the early 1980s
by the New York political commentator Jack Newfield in the pages of
the *Village Voice*.[2] These were days of heady Cold War rhetoric and bellicose pronuclear drumbeating by the newly installed Reagan administration. Newfield wrote several articles noting how many of the most vocal
hawks had avoided military service entirely or combat duty specifically
when given the chance. The issue emerged on a national level with the
designation of Dan Quayle as the elder Bush's running mate in 1988. It
began with evidence that Quayle had benefited from family influence in
gaining a position in the Indiana National Guard to avoid Vietnam service. It was fueled by Quayle's admission that he would have acted differently had he known that his political future would hold him accountable
for it. "I did not know in 1969 that I would be in this room today, I'll con-
fess," he admitted in one of his first press conferences. Reading Quayle's
statements now, there is something refreshing in his candor compared
with the evasions of today's leaders. "I [did] what any normal person
would do at that age. You call home. You call home to mother and father
and say, 'I'd like to get into the National Guard,'" he stated. Although he

insisted that "yes, I supported my president and I supported the goal of fighting communism in Vietnam,"[3] he acknowledged that "obviously, if you join the National Guard, you have less of a chance of going to Vietnam. I mean it goes without saying."[4]

The issue had previously emerged in the 1988 primaries. Conservative Christian and television host Pat Robertson was a candidate in the Republican primaries against two war heroes, Bob Dole and George Bush Sr. Early on, Robertson's campaign literature described him as having been a "combat marine" in Korea. Some were alerted by the fact that real marines never used such a phrase. He was challenged by former Republican Congressman Paul N. (Pete) McCloskey, who had seen combat in Korea and had known Robertson then. McCloskey charged that Robertson's father, U.S. Senator William Robertson, had persuaded the secretary of defense to keep his son out of combat. He had arranged for him to be assigned to Okinawa, where he served as liquor officer. Other allegations followed—that young Pat drank heavily at the time, provided party favors to his officers, and so on. The charge of war avoidance was enough to sink him in his race with Dole and the elder Bush.[5]

The 1980s also drew attention to the military pasts (or lack thereof) of prominent hawks in the entertainment industry. The most publicized case was actor Sylvester Stallone, who, following *Rocky*, achieved worldwide success as an embittered superpatriotic Vietnam veteran in the film *Rambo*. The role propelled him into a high-profile alliance with President Reagan, then at the height of his Cold War posturing. Stallone claimed to speak for the forgotten veterans of wars past. "If you don't have men willing to die for their country, you don't have a country," he proclaimed. "I love my country. I stand for ordinary Americans, losers a lot of them. The country tells them to fight in Vietnam? They fight."[6] He was subjected to criticism or ridicule for the fact that he himself had not answered his country's call to fight. He had avoided service via an "educational" deferment gained as a chaperone in an elite all-girls' school in Switzerland. "I was the fox guarding the hen-house," he later joked. (By contrast, the only major Hollywood figure to have seen combat in Vietnam, Oliver Stone, became the industry's leading antiwar voice.)

The lives of celebrities are a source of fascination to Americans. But there are more substantive reasons for focusing on the entertainment industry. A distinctive feature of modern warfare is the powerful role of media in motivating young men to fight. In World War I, President Woodrow Wilson went so far as to appear in a Hollywood feature supporting the war effort. The head of his office of public information charged with promoting war films went on to become a founder of modern advertising. During World War II, the Pentagon itself got into the filmmaking business with the Frank Capra series *Why We Fight*. Many of America's most famous film and sports stars not only volunteered for service but also sought out combat service. Both actor James Stewart and Major League Baseball slugger Ted Williams flew dangerous missions as pilots. Up through the Vietnam War, firsthand testimonies of soldiers documented the profound impact in getting them to enlist stars like John Wayne in films like *The Sands of Iwo Jima*. If impressionable young men are so influenced by Hollywood actors, one would hope that these actors would feel some obligation to abide by their own pronouncements.

In 1992, Bill Clinton's avoidance of military service in Vietnam was a subject of intense scrutiny by his adversaries. Critics charge him with having agreed to join an ROTC program to avoid service while studying at Oxford, then reneging on that agreement when the draft lottery left him unlikely to be called. Clinton's failure to serve was seen by conservatives as exemplifying his general disdain for "traditional" American values. In *House of War*, James Carroll describes how the Pentagon's disdain for Clinton weakened him in ways that left him often helpless before the Pentagon's demands. "Perhaps military people would not have held his avoidance of Vietnam against him if only he had forthrightly taken responsibility for his choices. But he never did—not during the election and not in the early months of his presidency." The military, Carroll writes, found his "obfuscations" on the service issue "infuriating."[7] As they should. But keep in mind that Clinton's resistance to serving in Vietnam was grounded in his *opposition* to that war, an opposition he consistently voiced at the time. He may have been a draft dodger, but he was not a chickenhawk, one who endorses a war but still refuses to serve. One would think that the military would be more contemptuous of the chickenhawk than the simple antiwar draft evader given its deep commitment to standing up for what you believe.

BUSH AND THE NEOCONS

The chickenhawk issue reemerged with the 2000 nomination of George W. Bush, who, unlike his opponent, Al Gore, had evaded Vietnam service. The issue was muted during the campaign by the fact that Bush was the more peace oriented of the candidates (he voiced doubts about nation building and urged a more humble foreign policy). It reemerged dramatically with the president's War on Terror and invasion of Iraq.

The Revenge of the 1960s

Debate around Bush's military past tended to focus on whether he acted illegally or blatantly violated military policy. There was consensus around the following facts.

Twelve days before losing his student deferment, the young George W. Bush was admitted to the National Guard for training to be a pilot. There was a waiting list of 100,000 wanting to get into the Guard and 150 in Texas seeking entrance to flight school. Bush was admitted immediately despite scoring the lowest acceptable grade on the pilot aptitude test. In contrast to his sharp memory of other events in his life (e.g., his religious conversion), Bush's recollections of his Guard service were hazy and often strange. He told the *Houston Chronicle* that they took him because they "needed pilots" and "they could sense that I would be one of the great pilots of all time."[8] In fact, Bush was the beneficiary of a Texas wheeler-dealer, Speaker of the House Ben Barnes, who ran an "underground railroad" for getting the sons of the privileged into the National Guard. Others to benefit from Barnes's largesse were the sons of Lloyd Bentsen and John Connally.[9]

As a contemporary of Bush's and someone who spent several years advising others about the draft, what I find the most striking in the Bush story is that on admission to the National Guard, he was given a form asking if he wanted to serve overseas.[10] He indicated that he did not. It was common knowledge at the time that one joined the National Guard to avoid service in Vietnam. It was common knowledge that the National Guard and Reserves were avenues by which the privileged did this. In 1969–1970, 28,000 more college-trained men entered the National Guard or Reserves than were enlisted or inducted into all the active forces combined. Only about 1 percent of all guardsmen were African American.[11] But I never heard of new enlistees given the official option of avoiding Vietnam (or any overseas service). What was the point of the large investment in flight education if not to serve overseas if needed?

Controversy continues to surround whether Bush violated National Guard policies when he took time off from his Guard service to campaign for a Louisiana Republican congressional candidate and friend of his father's. The candidate was a self-proclaimed opponent of "mixing the races" whose campaign's central theme was attacking draft dodgers and those too "cowardly" to serve in Vietnam.[12] The preoccupation with whether Bush violated official policy or otherwise acted illegally strikes me as misplaced. If a strong proponent of higher taxes does everything he can to avoid paying taxes himself, does it matter if his actions are legal or illegal? Illegality augments the problem. Bush's actions would have been more questionable if they had violated laws or formal policies. But shouldn't the question begin with why—if Bush was prowar—he did not *want* to serve his country but instead avoided such service (legally or illegally)?

Bush's behavior differed little from Dan Quayle's, yet he showed none of Quayle's candor. On the contrary, he went out of his way to voice intense dislike of the "guilt" he saw many of his college classmates still feeling over their privileged avoidance of Vietnam.[13] Bush prided himself, in fact, on his indifference to the moral dilemmas of his generation. This is another respect in which he was the first true alienated war president. Past presidents agonized over such matters. Our second president, John Adams, bemoaned the fact that he had not fought against the British. Past presidents who lacked military experience went out of their way to praise those who served. Abraham Lincoln poked fun at his own lack of combat experience and lavished praise on the service of his opponents, often to his own detriment.[14] By contrast, Bush attacked the patriotism of opponents like John McCain and John Kerry. And he reveled in the accoutrements of battle. In the Oval Office, he enjoyed bringing out military mementos for visitors and friends, a favorite being the pistol that Saddam Hussein carried. When he visited wounded Iraqi veterans, as at a Texas rehabilitation center, he enjoyed playing video games with disabled veterans in which he shot the "bad guys" in simulated Baghdad battles.[15]

In *Fiasco*, Thomas Ricks mused that Bush's actions as president were most like those of a 1960s counterculture veteran. Ricks spoke of him as a product of the "free-wheeling 1960s," a time "more in sync with the attitudes of '60s radical Jerry Rubin than with those of Winston Churchill." Ricks even ascribed the Iraq War to this. Describing that debacle, he wrote, "A less charitable way of putting it was that they were willing, a bit like Jerry Rubin, to take a chance and then groove on the ensuing rubble."[16] Bush and his conservative allies prided themselves on rejecting the "do-your-own-thing" ideology of the 1960s. Bush said, "I got into politics initially because I wanted to help change a culture. I wanted to banish the old '60s 'If it feels good, do it' culture, and help usher in an era of personal responsibility."[17] In truth, his orientation exemplified the worst aspects of the 1960s generation pattern of political irresponsibility.

Other Priorities

The issue of personal pasts was heightened by the nature of the Bush administration's leadership. Several websites detailed the relentlessness with which top Republican figures avoided serving themselves.[18] This prompted the flinty Chicago columnist Mike Royko to coin the phrase "as rare as a Republican war veteran." One could not help but be impressed with the curious and often exotic deferments gained. The Republican leaders included a striking number of serious athletes who claimed physical disabilities (Dennis Hastert, a champion wrestler deferred for "bad knees," or 1996 vice-presidential candidate Jack Kemp, excused for a "bad back" while playing in the National Football League). There were a striking number of skin problems (Ken Starr excused for psoriasis and war hawk Kenneth Adelman for skin rash). Republican leader Thomas DeLay claimed that he "tried" to volunteer for Vietnam, but all the spots were "taken" by minorities. Former Attorney General John Ashcroft said that he would have served "if asked." Instead, he received six student deferments and an occupational deferment for a job that was deemed by his draft board to be of an "essential nature" to society: teaching business law at Southwest Missouri State University.

After Bush, Vice President Cheney was the most publicized chicken-hawk. During his confirmation hearings as secretary of defense, he told an interviewer, "I think those who did in fact serve deserve to be honored for their service. . . . Was it a noble cause? Yes, indeed, I think it was." After John Kerry said of Cheney that he "got every deferment in the world and decided he had better things to do," Cheney insisted that he "would have obviously been happy to serve had I been called."

He did everything he could to avoid that call. Cheney did not ask for a student deferment on turning eighteen in 1959, assuming (correctly) that only older men were being drafted. He began aggressively seeking deferments once the Vietnam conflict began heating up in 1963. Between March 1963 and January 1966, he received four student deferments. He then applied for and was granted "hardship" exemption on the grounds that his wife was pregnant. Cynics have suggested that the Cheneys' pregnancy was motivated by draft avoidance. His biographies state that on turning twenty-six, he was "no longer eligible" for the draft. In fact, one remained eligible into one's thirties if one had received a deferment prior to age twenty-six. "I don't regret the decisions I made," he stated. "I complied fully with all the requirements of the statutes, registered with the draft when I turned 18." Some find his success at gaining deferments remarkable. "Five deferments seems incredible to me," says David Curry, author of the 1985 book *Sunshine Patriots: Punishment and the Vietnam Offender*. "That's a lot of times for the draft board to say O.K.," Curry said.[19]

The run-up to the Iraq War brought new attention to the issue with the widespread perception that support or opposition to the invasion related to past combat experience. Articles like "Hawks, Doves, and Dubya" drew attention to divisions along these grounds.[20] The only Bush cabinet member with combat experience was Colin Powell. The most persistent voices for attacking Iraq included Vice President Cheney, Defense Policy Board chairman Richard Perle, and Deputy Defense Secretary Paul Wolfowitz, all of whom had avoided service in Vietnam. Cheney's hawkish chief of staff, I. Lewis "Scooter" Libby, Elliott Abrams of Iran-Contra fame and the National Security Council member in charge of democratizing the Middle East, and former UN Ambassador John Bolton all avoided military service during the height of the Vietnam War. Other chickenhawks included *National Review* commentator Michael Ledeen, proponent of the "Ledeen Doctrine," according to which (in his words) "every ten years or so, the United States needs to pick up some small crappy little country and throw it against the wall, just to show the world we mean business."[21] Ledeen stated that the word "stability" gave him the "heebie-jeebies." Finally, there was Kenneth Adelman, who claimed that a military campaign in Iraq would be a "cakewalk."

In an interview with *Newsweek*, Senator Chuck Hagel said, "It is interesting to me that many of those who want to rush this country into war and think it would be so quick and easy don't know anything about war."[22] "They come at it from an intellectual perspective versus having sat in jungles or foxholes and watched their friends get their heads blown off. I try to speak for those ghosts of the past a little bit," added Hagel, a Vietnam War army infantryman with two Purple Hearts. Retired General Anthony Zinni, a White House special envoy to the Middle East, observed to the Economic Club of Florida that most of those urging caution on Iraq were people who knew war firsthand, like former generals Colin Powell, Brent Scowcroft, and Norman Schwarzkopf. "It's pretty interesting that all the generals see it the same way," Zinni said. "And all the others who have never fired a shot and are hot to go to war see it another way." "Do we really want to occupy Iraq for the next 30 years?" asked former navy secretary, Vietnam veteran, and later senator from Virginia James Webb.

As the Iraq conflict dragged on, criticism of hawks for their lack of combat experience increased. Most remarkable were the public pronouncements by military figures appalled by the leadership of Donald Rumsfeld. This culminated in the calls for his resignation by the four newspapers catering to armed services members and Rumsfeld's departure immediately afterward. One of the dissenting generals was quoted as saying that the decisions of Rumsfeld evidenced "all the casualness and swagger that are the special provenance of those who have never had to execute these missions—or bury the results."[23] The most consistent voice was thirty-seven-year marine veteran and Congressman Jack Murtha, long a staunch supporter of the military. Congressman Murtha retired from the Marine Corps Reserves as a colonel in 1990 after receiving the Bronze Star and two Purple Hearts. This did not spare him from being subjected to the politics of chickenhawk abuse. After stating his commitment to quick withdrawal from Iraq in a much-publicized speech, he was strongly attacked by the Republican leadership, none of whom had served in the military. Speaker of the House Dennis Hastert branded him a "coward," Representative David Dreier (R-CA) deemed his speech "an insult to the lives that have been lost," and Majority Leader Roy Blunt (R-MS) said that Murtha's words would "only embolden our enemies."

Murtha's response was to challenge the credentials of those who hurled such charges. "I like guys who've never been there that criticize us who've been there. I like that. I like guys who got five deferments and never been there and send people to war, and then don't like to hear suggestions about what needs to be done." (He was referring here to Vice President Cheney.) He continued to mock such figures as Karl Rove for championing war while "sitting in his air-conditioned office on his big, fat backside."[24]

A curious fact about the chickenhawk phenomenon was how consistently the histories of the Republican leadership were ones of military avoidance while those of the Democratic leadership were ones of military service. This had not always been so. Barry Goldwater, the man most responsible for pointing the Republican Party in its current promilitary direction, had a distinguished active-duty record as a pilot and rose to the rank of general in the Reserves. The funeral services for President Gerald Ford noted that he had volunteered for the navy in World War II rather than wait to be drafted. Then he volunteered for dangerous sea duty rather than spend the war as an instructor and athletic coach. Nearly losing his life in combat, he was awarded numerous decorations for his services. The 1996 Republican presidential candidate Bob Dole sustained lifetime injuries in combat.

Consider the contrast between the recent Republicans' pattern of war avoidance and Democrats' history of service. Both John Kerry and former Senator Bob Kerrey were decorated war heroes, the latter winning the Congressional Medal of Honor. Former Senate Leader Tom Daschle served in the air force in the Vietnam years (as did Representative David Bonior), Senator Tom Harkin served in the U.S. Navy from 1962 to 1967 and remained in the Reserves until 1974, and Al Gore served in Vietnam in 1969, and though he worked as a journalist, he was often in areas of danger. The pattern was a consistent one, though some have noted that one Democratic leader who avoided military service, Senator Joe Lieberman of Connecticut, was also one of the more vocal supporters of the president's Iraq policy. I have no idea what explains this difference between Democrats and Republicans. Not all Republicans who avoided Vietnam service were privileged like Bush, and not all Democrats who served in Vietnam did so because they had no other options.

The 2008 Republican nomination was won by John McCain after a drawn-out primary fight. McCain was the only candidate with a record of military service. His two main opponents, Mitt Romney and Rudolph

Giuliani, had avoided Vietnam service for reasons that the press found questionable.[25] McCain's nomination reflected Americans' admiration for those who have served, consistent with the "Support the Troops" ethic, but it hardly reflected a return to the citizen-soldier tradition. McCain was no more inclined than Bush to encourage young people to enlist or to criticize the failure of privileged youth, especially prowar youth, to serve. His campaign was conducted around a robust outsider image. Yet he did not say a word about the mind-set of alienated war and its aversion of shared sacrifice. If anything, McCain embodied the modern ideal of professional soldiering. He was not a child of wealth who left the civilian world to fulfill his civic duty. He was a third-generation military officer who embodied what the military had become in its professional form, not what it had been.

THE CHILDREN

> If the war in Iraq is worth fighting—if it's a noble venture, as the hawks insist it is—then it's worth fighting with the children of the privileged classes. They should be added to the combat mix. If it's not worth their blood, then we should bring the other troops home.
>
> —Bob Herbert[26]

A further aspect of the chickenhawk syndrome involves the children of those who took us to war. Filmmaker Michael Moore raised the issue on numerous occasions, notably in *Fahrenheit 9/11* when he offered Congressmen brochures for their children on how to enlist. What the Michael Moore case illustrated, though, was the fact that when the issue of children serving was raised at all, it was often as a source of humor. The exception was when mothers of fallen soldiers raised it, as they did consistently or tried to do, from the start of the Iraq conflict.

During the 2004 campaign, Sue Niederer, a fifty-five-year-old homemaker from Hopewell, New Jersey, attempted to raise the issue at a pro-Bush rally. Her son, Seth, had been killed in Iraq in February 2004 while trying to disarm a bomb. Although Seth had been happy in his first few weeks in Iraq, believing that he was helping rebuild the country, he became convinced that he had not been properly trained or equipped for combat. He was killed after being ordered to leave his platoon to search for homemade bombs on the roadside. After his death, Mrs. Niederer ran into a wall of military bureaucracy. An observant Jew, she asked that her son not be embalmed or undergo an autopsy. Both requests were denied.[27]

During a standard speech by First Lady Laura Bush praising the War on Terror, Mrs. Niederer attempted to ask the question, "If it's such a justified war," why weren't the First Lady's *daughters* serving in it?

Mrs. Bush looked "stunned," according to news reports. Bush supporters yelling "Four more years" and wielding "Bush/Cheney" signs quickly boxed in Mrs. Niederer. Although she left voluntarily, she was quickly arrested, handcuffed, thrown in a paddy wagon, and charged with trespassing. Only one person in the crowd came to her aid, a man whose own son had known her boy in Iraq.

What's astonishing is that even after all this commotion, not a single reporter was inspired to ask Mrs. Bush how she would have answered Mrs. Niederer's question—"Why aren't your daughters serving?" The event offered a great opportunity for the question. The fact that the Bush twins were women did not preclude raising it. When the Niederer incident occurred, there were about 8,000 female military members in Iraq. As I write this, in the fall of 2008, more than one hundred women have died in Iraq of various causes. More servicewomen have died in Iraq of hostile causes than in all of America's previous wars combined.

Two women died in Iraq the month that Niederer challenged the First Lady. Sergeant Tatjana Reed, age thirty-four, of Fort Campbell, Kentucky, died in Samarra, Iraq, when an improvised explosive device detonated near her convoy vehicle. She had been in the military for more than a decade. She left a ten-year-old daughter, Genevieve. Sergeant First Class Linda Ann Tarango-Griess, age thirty-three, of Sutton, Nebraska, also died from an improvised explosive device. In addition to her parents, she was survived by her husband, Nebraska Army National Guard Staff Sergeant Douglas L. Griess, who remarked, "Hearing that she's gone is kind of hard to believe right now. I e-mailed her and told her to contact me. She called me right after midnight," he said. "We talked about her getting some leave time."

In tandem with their appearance at the Republican National Convention, Barbara and Jenna Bush, the Bush twins, were the subjects of a puff piece in *Vogue* magazine marking their twenty-first birthdays and their entrance into "public life."[28] The excerpts from the article on the Internet carried the title "Dad Is a Controversial Wartime President. They Look Like Cupcakes." The article was not a story so much as a photo shoot, conducted while they were celebrating Mother's Day in New York with their mother, a photo shoot, "their first ever," for which they were "trying on clothes" in the Central Park South hotel room where they were staying.

Barbara had college papers to finish, the article explained. "Still, she manages to find a shimmery fitted Zac Posen to step into, while Jenna goes straight for a pair of Joe's jeans and a white jacket that accentuates her tan." "But then they get to a flotilla of enormous debutante-style ball gowns. Jenna looks at her sister, whose tight-bodiced white satin number boasts a skirt better suited to a Velasquez infanta."

"'Mom,' she asks, 'do we look like cupcakes?'

"'Yes, you do.'"

(If you're like me, you may not know what a "shimmery fitted Zack Posen" is. Zack Posen is the name of a hot young New York fashion designer whose life goal is to bring "couture" back to America. He was a favorite of Barbara Bush, who had been seated in the front row of his shows and was pictured beaming alongside him in the *Vogue* article.)

The article went on to recount how the country was about to get its first real glimpse of the first daughters. "Until now," it acknowledged, they were better known for their "tabloid appearances and the much-mentioned reports of their 2001 run-in with the law for underage drinking." But now they had the opportunity to "define themselves." In the process, Bush's handlers hoped that the "unjaded" first daughters would help "humanize and soften the image of a controversial wartime president."

"I'm just not political," Jenna confessed. "There's nothing about the process that has ever interested me." But they were happy to help out their dad—and grateful that they weathered the "college experience" "unscathed."

Mother's Day has its origins in a proposal of Julia Ward Howe, author of "The Battle Hymn of the Republic," to rename July 4 "Mother's Day" and make it a day dedicated to peace. A similar proposal was advanced by Anna Reeves Jarvis, whose daughter's diligent efforts eventually led to its official affirmation by President Woodrow Wilson in 1914. From the start, the day was associated with peace and the special burden that war places on mothers. In his 2004 proclamation of Mother's Day, President Bush stated,

> We take time to recognize the many mothers who are supporting their brave sons and daughters in the armed forces and the many others who are themselves serving proudly in defense of America's freedom and security. The service and sacrifice of these women reflect the best of our nation. They and their loved ones are in our thoughts and prayers.

In the three days it took to photograph the Bush twins in their "shimmery fitted Zac Posens," six Americans were killed in Iraq, eight coalition soldiers totally. Sergeant Rodney Murray was typical of them. He was a member of the Reserves who was a teacher of history and English at Ayden-Griffin high school in Ayden, North Carolina, where he lived with his wife of three years, Amanda. He had been slated to come home that spring, but the military had extended his stay into the fall. He was killed when his Humvee collided with a Bradley Fighting Vehicle, throwing him to the ground and breaking his neck. He was twenty-eight years old.

As the twins were celebrating Mother's Day in the Plaza, Specialist Isela Rubalcava, twenty-five, of El Paso, Texas, died in Mosul, Iraq, when a mortar round hit near her. She was the first woman from El Paso ever killed in combat. She was the only daughter of Maria Isela Rubalcava, whose husband, Ramon Rubalva, told the *El Paso Times* that "they took a piece of my heart. I only hope this war ends soon because I don't wish this pain on anyone else." A lifelong friend and neighbor, Thomas Sandoval, a Korean War veteran, told the newspaper, "It made me feel very sad. We should have pulled out every American soldier a long time ago. We shouldn't have gone to Iraq in the first place."[29] The Bush twins told reporters that they were grateful to have come through the "college experience" "unscathed."

The following year, a revolt of war mothers raised the question of who served and who didn't—though newspaper and magazine reporters remained wary of posing the issue to the nation's leaders and their children. The most prominent was Cindy Sheehan, who rocketed to public attention by her futile attempts to engage President Bush in a dialogue in front of his Texas ranch. She consistently challenged those who supported the war to walk their talk. "If you fall on the side that is pro-George and pro-war, you get your ass over to Iraq, and take the place of somebody who wants to come home. And if you fall on the side that is against this war and against George Bush, stand up and speak out." She put the matter in terms of what I shall call the "reciprocity" issue in the next chapter: prowar people should not ask antiwar people to die for them. Of her vigil in front of the Bush ranch at "Camp Casey," named for her fallen son, she said,

> One thing I haven't noticed or become aware of though is an increased number of pro-war, pro-Bush people on the other side of the fence enlisting to go and fight George Bush's war for imperialism and insatiable greed. The pro-peace side has gotten off their apathetic butts to be warriors for peace and justice. Where are the pro-war people? Everyday at Camp Casey we have a couple of anti-peace people on the other side of the road holding up signs that remind me that "Freedom isn't Free" but I don't see them putting their money where their mouths are. I don't think they are willing to pay even a small down payment for freedom by sacrificing their own blood or the flesh of their children. I still challenge them to go to Iraq and let another soldier come home. Perhaps a soldier that is on his/her third tour of duty, or one that has been stop-lossed after serving his/her country nobly and selflessly, only to be held hostage in Iraq by power mad hypocrites who have a long history of avoiding putting their own skin in the game.[30]

"I think they seriously 'misunderestimated' all mothers," she stated. "I wonder if any of them had authentic mother-child relationships and if they are surprised that there are so many mothers in this country who are bear-like when it comes to wanting the truth and who want to make meaning of their child's needless and seemingly meaningless deaths?"

Another to speak out was Patricia Roberts, whose son Jamaal Addison was the first soldier from Georgia to be killed in Iraq in 2003. In fact, her son was with the 507th Maintenance Company, which also included Jessica Lynch, except he was one of the eleven killed in the event that came to be called "Bloody Sunday." Roberts, an African American, spoke of how "it's very important for the African Americans and the minorities to support [the protests] going on here and all over, statewide, worldwide. I think they should support it, because I believe that this is a poor man's war." She drew attention to the hypocrisy of the privileged sending other people's children to die. "They have solicited the minorities to go in, and if you look at all of the rates and you look at all the statistics, you have more minorities die in this war than you have had anything else, and between the ages of 18 and 25, you have wiped out generations of minorities."[31]

One of the more eloquent comments on Cindy Sheehan was by Ralph Nader, writing in August 2005.[32] He began by citing the problem of alienated war. "While George W. Bush keeps saying that the United States is at war, for most of the United States, apart from the soldiers and military families, the people seem detached from the daily devastation in Iraq." The emergence of Cindy Sheehan and other mothers meant that "the times may be changing." "Mother Cindy has personalized this automated war and its scripted Presidential promoter who lowballs U.S. casualties and prevents families and reporters from going to Dover, Delaware, where the deceased are returned from Iraq." In conjunction with others, Nader hoped that Sheehan would be the spark that, in the words of one military mother, would force "the architects of this war, who have no children at risk, to start listening to those families who do."

The response of the Bush twins to the challenge posed by Cindy Sheehan, Patricia Roberts, and others was to laugh about it. During the 2004 campaign as they were leaving an event at the University of Wisconsin–Oshkosh, a protester held up a sign saying, "Send the Bush Twins to Iraq!" A male student yelled out, "No way, don't send them to Iraq. Send them to my room!" The Bush twins started laughing and applauding along with their supporters in the audience.[33] That same day, my hometown newspaper carried a story about a man with thirteen children being sent to Iraq.

The issue of children serving was raised across the Atlantic as well. Unlike Prince Harry, who sought Iraq service, the son of British war architect Tony Blair chose not to fight in the Middle East. Euan Blair, the prime minister's eldest son, headed off to Washington, D.C., to work as an intern for Republican politicians. In his last campaign for office, Blair was hounded by another candidate who ran against all the odds to hold Blair accountable for his war policies. Reg Keys was a fifty-two-year-old retired ambulance training manager from the West Midlands whose son, Lance Corporal Tom Keys, was a British military policeman killed by a 500-strong mob of Iraqis in June 2003. Keys believed that his son went to Iraq trusting the false case for war that Blair set before the House of Commons. Of his son and the others that died with him, he stated,

> There were no medals or honor for them. There was no letter from Tony Blair. Instead, he managed to find time to write a letter of condolence for Ozzy Osbourne when he fell off his quad bike. But not to my son, who was shot 31 times. I can't help but think angrily about that, and about Tom's beautiful green eyes. He was four days short of his 21st birthday.[34]

George W. Bush, his three brothers, and his sister combined had ten children who were military age. None of them served in the global War on Terror or showed any interest in doing so.

Chickenhawks, Chickee-Hawks, Etcetera

We see that there are different aspects to the chickenhawk issue, though all of them bear on the problem of alienated war. The first (and most discussed) involves the *prowar draft-dodging baby boomer*. What is the significance for a prowar leader today that his or her past is one of avoiding sacrifices in wars he or she endorsed? The focus here is on individuals, but the pervasiveness of military avoidance in the Vietnam era links it to our unresolved relation to the Vietnam legacy generally. Viewed thus, the chickenhawk problem is a prism through which America's relation to its past can be approached. Henceforth, the chickenhawk problem will refer to the prowar draft-dodging baby-boomer problem specifically.

What about prowar young people today and their responsibility to step forward and serve? I say "young person," but a more accurate phrase would be "of military age" since the maximum age is now forty-two. I've raised this issue about the Bush twins. Critics of the Bush administration started what they call the "Yellow Elephant Campaign" seeking to enlist young conservatives for Iraq. "Yellow Elephant" might be an apt name for a prowar military-eligible person today who is not serving.

There is a final aspect to the young person issue that pertains to their *parents* if they are prowar. What is the obligation of prowar parents today to urge their children to serve? In the past it was assumed that parents played a crucial role in encouraging the patriotism of their children. What is the obligation of prowar parents to promote "Just Say Yes" campaigns? I'll call these problems pertaining to the children and their parents the *chickee-hawk* problem. I speak to them in chapter 5.

TOWARD A DEFINITION

Analyzing exactly what's wrong with the chickenhawk begins with agreeing on a definition. One of the better discussions of the chickenhawk syndrome occurred on February 24, 2004, on the floor of the U.S. Senate.[35] The speaker was New Jersey Democrat Frank Lautenberg, a World War II veteran, who made a long speech, with visual aids, titled "An Illustrated Guide to Chickenhawks." He offered this definition:

> Chickenhawks: they shriek like a hawk but they have the backbone of a chicken. We know who the chickenhawks are. They talk tough on national defense and military issues and cast aspersions on others. When it was their turn to serve, where were they? A-W-O-L, that's where. A-W-O-L.

This definition is notable for stressing how chickenhawks avoid sacrifice while casting aspersions on the patriotism of others. It raises the issue of shamelessness central to the chickenhawk syndrome, discussed in the next chapter.

The Chickenhawk Database, a leading online source, defines the chickenhawk as "public persons—generally males—who

> (1) tend to advocate, or are fervent supporters of those who advocate, military solutions to political problems, and
> (2) personally declined to take advantage of a *significant* opportunity to serve in uniform during wartime.

"Some individuals," it continues, "may qualify more for their political associations than for any demonstrated personal tendency towards bellicosity. Some women may be included for exceptional bellicosity." The first point about preferring military solutions over political ones evokes the preference for such solutions of the Bush administration's "New Vulcans."

The database provides a further variation on points 1 and 2. A chickenhawk is

> a person enthusiastic about war, provided someone else fights it; particularly when that enthusiasm is undimmed by personal experience with war; most emphatically when that lack of experience came in spite of ample opportunity in that person's youth.

A chickenhawk is not just someone who supports war but also one who has avoided fighting in a war himself. He is someone whose support for war *rests* on his ability to avoid sacrifice himself; if he knew he'd be compelled to sacrifice he'd be a peacenick.

People mean different things by the term. Our concern is to fashion a definition that does not construct a straw person and that allows us to focus on the issues of political principle involved. Here is my definition of the baby-boomer chickenhawk: someone who vigorously and publicly endorses a war and its sacrifices while diligently and successfully *avoiding* such sacrifices himself.

Let me unpack the components of this definition, with commentary.

Chickenhawk Essentials

1. *Endorses a war vigorously and publicly*: This captures a key feature of draft-dodging baby boomers: they went on record at the time as favoring the Vietnam War. As noted, Bush spent months campaigning for a candidate who attacked Vietnam War opponents as un-American. This element is essential because, in a democracy, a citizen who endorses a war in this manner is not only saying something by his actions. He is also *doing* something. He acts to commit his country to the war in ways that have implications for his fellow citizens.

The point is illustrated by contrasting endorsing a war of one's own country with endorsing the war of another country. As a citizen of the United States, my support for a war like the Iraq War is quite a different matter than, say, my support for Georgia in its conflict with Russia. This is partly a matter of its practical impact. Citizens' opinions do not always matter much, but the Vietnam War case (and the Iraq case, apparently) show that they sometimes do. Someone who endorses a war of another country while rejecting any thought of sacrifice would not be a chickenhawk because the circumstances preclude any talk of "avoiding" those sacrifices. It's like the difference between saying that the program of one's own department should be better and saying that the program of someone else's department should be better: saying this about your own department commits you to *doing* something about it; saying it of another department does not. What if someone was in favor of the Vietnam War (or Iraq today) but kept his opinion entirely to himself, to the point of not even voting? Does silent support of a war, linked with diligent avoidance of its sacrifices, constitute a chickenhawk behavior? I think this is less egregious; the silent chickenhawk is less shameless. The issue revolves around whether silent support for a war implicates you in the way vocal support does.

2. *Diligently avoids service*: The definition stipulates that the chicken-hawk is someone who avoids sacrifice as distinct from one who is willing to sacrifice but, for reasons beyond his control, is not asked or given the opportunity—like those who had legitimate medical deferments. But there are gray areas. In the Vietnam years, certain factors like fatherhood got you out of service if you wanted to get out. They did not prevent you from serving if you wanted to serve. The databases do not show many instances of alleged chickenhawks who had conclusive reasons for not serving. Medical excuses like Rush Limbaugh's "anal cysts" were the sort you could ask the military to ignore if you wished or could hide. The story of war is replete with people whose patriotism led them to hide factors that would have kept them out. Audie Murphy, the most decorated soldier of World War II, was too short for the military but still got in.

What about a high draft number? The fact that you got a high number did not prevent you from serving. It meant only that you could not be compelled to serve. If I believed firmly in the war, I wouldn't think a high draft number would have been a good reason for not serving, especially when I knew that many of those who got lower numbers and were being forced to serve did *not* believe in the war. Since these are gray areas, my definition speaks of diligently avoiding service—to specify those who went to a good deal of time and effort to ensure that they would avoid the sacrifices imposed on others. A bogus medical deferment or a place in the National Guard took effort. Questions can be raised about the other cases.

3. *Does the law matter?* To say that a chickenhawk avoided military service need not imply that he violated the law in so doing. If someone vigorously and publicly supports using tax money for a certain project and then seeks out exotic deductions to avoid paying taxes for it, he can be faulted even though he acts legally. For the draft-dodging baby boomer, the problem was compounded by the fact that the laws *themselves* were unfair, and everyone knew it. This is another reason why the whole debate about whether Bush violated the law or military policies to avoid Vietnam service strikes me as beside the point. The Civil War parallel holds: someone who loudly supported the war and then used his wealth to buy himself out of service was not breaking the law but could still be faulted since the laws were so obviously unfair.

But how can someone be faulted for acting within the rules? If the rules are unfair, doesn't the fault lie with *them* and not the chickenhawk—who was just looking out for himself? Isn't it perfectly understandable that any young man would avoid service if he could do so within the law? This is not a standard we have applied to earlier wars. In World War II, we did not regard all war avoidance as "understandable" if it was legal. If the rules are unfair and someone takes advantage of this, the fault lies in *both* places. Given human nature, self-interested behavior is always understandable, especially in young men. This doesn't exempt it from moral appraisal. It was understandable for a passenger on the *Titanic* to do everything he could to save himself. But this would not excuse actions that caused the needless loss of others' lives. The chickenhawk is like one who saved his life on the *Titanic* at the expense of others and then built a career around the importance of heroism in sea catastrophes.[36]

Draft-dodging baby boomers were shirkers, but shirking was easier for some than others. Some mechanisms were open to all. A prowar college classmate of mine who went on to work for the Reagan administration created a deferrable medical condition by sitting on the toilet for five straight days. This took no special privileges, only willpower. Others exploited class advantages. Another prowar classmate of mine got an expensive set of braces for his teeth as he was finishing college (braces got you a medical deferment). This was not an option for the less affluent. All chickenhawks can be faulted for their behavior, but chickenhawks who exploit class advantages can be doubly faulted.

In a strange piece, "Hunting Chickenhawks," Eliot Cohen, speaking of the chickenhawk pasts of Bush and others, wrote that "a terrible curse lies on the Vietnam generation."[37] The "curse" is that the draft system of the time made it "easy" for "young men" to "behave badly and evade their duty as citizens." Rather than be condemned for their acts, chickenhawks should be pitied for the fact that society made it too "easy" for them to behave "badly." First of all, it wasn't that easy for everyone to behave "badly." Only the privileged had such an easy time. More to the point, this is a strange argument from the mouth of a conservative: I thought conservatives wanted to hold young people to *higher* standards of responsibility. Are welfare cheaters to be pitied because the system makes it "easy" for them to cheat? If anything, shouldn't the ease of shirking responsibilities make the wrong of doing so *worse*?

Many people are inclined to cut draft-dodging baby boomers more slack than they deserve because they don't understand how the draft system worked. No one was forced to take a student deferment, for example. A popular song of the first Gulf War, resurrected after 9/11, was Lee Greenwood's "God Bless the USA." It proclaimed that he would "stand and fight" for his country today, if needed. But Greenwood avoided the chance to "stand" and "fight" as a young man. He has explained this by the fact that he received a draft deferment for being a parent. But no one was forced to take such a deferment; many men with children were killed in Vietnam.

Since the issue of military service does not arise for young people today, it is easy for them to presume that no one thought about it very much during Vietnam; hence, the choices they made were casual ones.

But a young man of my generation who attended college had four long years to think about what he would do about serving. Throughout that time he was surrounded by constant debates about the legitimacy of war and what to do about serving. For someone of my generation—and Bush's—the military decision may have been the first truly serious moral decision they made in their lives. For anyone who took moral account-ability seriously, it involved much reflection. Many chose easy ways out, but many did not. Taking the issue seriously was an option.

Wars, Police Actions, Etcetera

Does the *nature* of the war matter? The problem I have in mind is raised by Ben Tripp in a piece in *Counterpunch*:

> George W. Bush couldn't cement the handle back on a shaving mug. He served some of a tour of duty defending Alabama from the Viet Cong, but the only scalp he ever saw was firmly affixed to George McGovern's head. Yet Bush has a hunger for war (or at least Karl Rumsfeld [*sic*] does, which amounts to the same thing, as Rumsfeld rents the basement apartment in Bush's head). The war in Afghanistan doesn't count as a chickenhawk action, because we didn't pick the fight, it picked us. It was a defensive action, like burning a forest down because there's a beehive in it. But this war on Iraq is a chickenhawk's war, through-and-through. It's all about rattling sabers and being a Big Man.[38]

The author is claiming that the chickenhawk issue does not arise when the war is one that is truly *needed* for self-defense, when it is a fight that "picked us" rather than us it, and when it's like "burning a forest down" to get the beehive.

Few wars "pick us." Consider the Afghanistan case Tripp mentions. Everyone agreed on the right of the United States to respond to 9/11. Outside the United States there was substantial disagreement in Europe on the wisdom of going to *war*. Noted war scholar Michael Howard doubted its efficacy; he said that going after terrorists in this manner was like going after ants with a blowtorch. Tripp likens the Afghanistan action to burning down a forest to get a beehive. I wonder if this is the analogy he wants. Does getting a beehive really warrant burning down the whole forest? Won't the bees take off at the first smell of smoke, leaving the forest's other inhabitants to their fate?

The notion that a war can pick us rather than us pick it is one that the founding fathers viewed with skepticism. Immediate threats could be met with immediate force that the president could initiate on his own. But the Constitution's thrust is to distinguish this sort of action from war proper. War is a *political* act. Constitutionally, the decision to go to war requires

maximum democratic input (and the willingness of citizen-soldiers) because the decision to go to war is an inherently controversial one. It is
not like the decision to fight a fire. In the twentieth century, presidents
anxious to avoid democratic deliberation have urged us to envision war
on the firefighting model. Truman characterized the Korean War as a
"police action" to *de*politicize it.[39] Attempts to characterize every war as
a form of necessary "self-defense" is a variation of this. What if the war
is completely unavoidable? Does this make chickenhawk behavior unob-
jectionable? I don't see why. Suppose I vigorously and publicly endorse a
new sewer system in my town on the grounds (valid, in this case) that the
current one is making everyone sick. After the town votes for it, I do all I
can to avoid paying my fair share of the taxes. Does the fact that the new
sewer system is necessary make my behavior less objectionable? I would
think it makes it worse.

Yet chickenhawk behavior seems especially repugnant when the war is
not necessary. Consider this remark by *Washington Post* columnist David
Ignatius, a supporter of the Iraq War. In an editorial, "A War of Choice,
and One Who Chose It," he wrote,

> The reality is that this [the Iraq War] may be the most idealistic war fought
> in modern times—a war whose only coherent rationale . . . is that it toppled
> a tyrant and created the possibility of a democratic future. It was a war of
> choice, not necessity, and one driven by ideas, not merely interests. In that
> sense, the paradigmatic figure of the war is Wolfowitz, deputy secretary of
> defense and the Bush administration's idealist in chief. (November 2, 2003)

This description is accurate insofar as the Iraq War was entirely op-
tional. When the war lacks *any* necessity the chickenhawk's behavior
seems especially vile in that it vigorously endorses actions that require altruism on everyone's part but shirks altruism itself. Altruism is a precious
if not sacred capacity of persons. Chickenhawks degrade it by exploiting
other people's altruism.

Ignatius later voiced regret over his prowar missives but in a manner
that, typical of alienated war, evaded much personal responsibility. In
April 2006 he explained his earlier position thus:

> In a sense, the media were victims of their own professionalism. Because
> there was little criticism of the war from prominent Democrats and foreign
> policy analysts, journalistic rules meant we shouldn't create a debate on our
> own.

This is an interesting view of the media coming from a lead columnist of
the *Washington Post*. "Journalistic rules" require that you don't challenge
presidential actions if "prominent" politicians are not already doing so;

you do not "create a debate" on your own. The implication is that Bob Woodward and Carl Bernstein should have kept their mouths shut about the Watergate affair until Congress investigated it fully, which never would have happened without their initiative.

DOES COMBAT EXPERIENCE MATTER?

Contemporary politics suggests that Americans simply don't know what they think of combat experience. In the 2004 election, voters apparently didn't regard John Kerry's combat experience as making him a more qualified commander in chief. But when Democrats made the same point about John McCain in the 2008 election, they were attacked. Wesley Clark, former NATO commander under President Clinton, was quoted as saying, "I don't think riding in a fighter plane and getting shot down is a qualification to be president." He was quickly denounced by members of both parties. Supporters of McCain charged that he should be ashamed of himself and demanded that he apologize. Senator McCain characterized it as an attack on his military service and pressed Illinois Senator Barack Obama to remove Clark from any role in his campaign. Clark responded that he would never discredit anyone who chose to wear the uniform and was careful to distance himself from Obama on this matter.

The Republican position was inconsistent. I am not simply thinking of how Republicans could get so upset about these remarks about McCain while they did nothing to stop the attacks on Kerry in 2004. More to the point, how could they insist that McCain be praised for his Vietnam service while also insisting that Bush could not be *criticized* for his avoidance of the same? If character counts in one case, why doesn't it count in the other? This harkens to the larger point, though—that Americans don't know what to think about combat experience. As the draft era recedes, fewer and fewer Americans will have any military experience. If corporate war triumphs, we may face a future in which hardly any Americans have experience with the military they send to foreign lands. Americans who've experienced war will be viewed as curiosities, like survivors of the Holocaust or of shipwrecks like the *Titanic*. Reflection on the dangers of alienated war means considering the potential impact of this for military policy.

The founders of the United States were more concerned about the future than about the past. It was imperative that citizens face the prospect of fighting the wars they endorsed so that they would take the decision seriously. Those who shirked their responsibilities were condemned for violating this principle; in the next chapter, I explore questions that can be raised about the leadership potential of someone who acted this way in the past. It is difficult to glean a position from the nation's founders, though, on the importance of military experience generally. If anything, they were suspicious of military heroes as part of their worry about the threat of standing armies. Let us consider what recent experience suggests.

Civilians, Soldiers, and Iraq Policy

I have noted the conflict that arose between Bush and his own military on the wisdom of his war policies, raising the issue of Bush's lack of combat experience. Conflict between a president and the military did not begin with Bush. George Washington constantly quarreled with civilian leaders in the American Revolution. Abraham Lincoln fired his chief general George McClellan more than once. Truman's dismissal of Douglas MacArthur over Korea had an impact on the military that lingered for decades.

Truman dumped MacArthur for being overly bellicose. But it would be simplistic to conclude, as some often have, that military figures are generally more prowar then others. The matter is more complex. Eisenhower was generally skeptical of the military's orientation, mainly for being so self-serving. His administration was characterized by a reluctance to use troops, though this reflected his reliance on nuclear weapons and a policy of massive retaliation. Civilians, like Robert McNamara, that John F. Kennedy recruited to his administration regarded military leaders as old-fashioned in their ignorance of tools like modern statistical analysis, and they generally discounted the importance of actual combat experience. The behavior of the military in the Cuban missile crisis, General Curtis LeMay in particular, convinced Kennedy that military advice was of little value. Except for General Maxwell Taylor, whom he called back from retirement, Kennedy gave no weight to the views of the armed forces.

Some have seen a pattern of hawkish civilians and reluctant military originating with Kennedy and Johnson. This does not withstand analysis. During Vietnam, senior military advisers were unenthusiastic about committing ground troops to Asia, but in some cases this was because they preferred massive bombing, as with LeMay. Once the commitment was made, the military's general complaint was that it was not aggressive *enough*. The so-called Powell Doctrine later captured this ambiguous legacy. Military force should be used only in special circumstances, as when the national interest is at stake. But when used, it should be used massively and decisively.

Another key legacy of the Vietnam experience was self-criticism on the military's part for not speaking up. This was a central theme of Colonel H. R. McMaster's *Dereliction of Duty*, a book that had a profound impact on post-Vietnam military culture.[40] As Colin Powell wrote in his memoirs, during Vietnam, "as a corporate entity, the military failed to talk straight to its political superiors or itself. The top leadership never went to the secretary of defense or the President and said, 'This war is unwinnable the way we are fighting it.'" The message was that the unquestioned allegiance to the commander in chief needed to be rethought. Powell said that he and his post-Vietnam military colleagues "vowed that when [their] time came to call the shots, [they] would not quietly acquiesce in halfhearted warfare for half-baked reasons." The Bush presidency witnessed an unprecedented amount of public criticism and second-guessing of its policies by members of the military and former members—though, ironically, not by Powell himself.

The criticism of Bush policies began before the Iraq invasion. From the start, his critics linked it with the chickenhawk issue. One State Department skeptic quipped to a room full of senior military advisers that "there's more combat experience on the seventh floor of the State Department than in the entire Office of the Secretary of Defense." The list of former generals that doubted the wisdom of the invasion included Bush Sr.'s national security adviser, Brent Scowcroft; Gulf War commander Norman Schwarzkopf; and his logistics chief and later successor at Central Command, Anthony Zinni. The main point of dispute became the size of the military force needed. It began with Paul Wolfowitz's cavalier rejection of troop requirement estimates by General Eric Shinseki, the army chief of staff. Wolfowitz dismissed Shinseki's assessment that the United States would need in excess of "several hundred thousand troops" for postwar stability operations as "wildly off the mark." Wolfowitz prevailed, but as the postinvasion debacle in Iraq began to materialize, the conflict between Bush administration figures and former military men became pronounced. Lieutenant General Gregory Newbold, former director of operations for the Joint Chiefs of Staff, wrote in *Time* magazine that it was his "sincere view . . . that the commitment of [U.S.] forces to this fight was done with a casualness and swagger that are the special province of those who have never had to execute these missions—or bury the results."

The conflict between Bush and the military continued. Bush often voiced disdain for civilian meddling in military policy. "It's important to trust the judgment of the military when they're making military plans," he remarked. "I'm a strict adherer to the command structure." He said this as he prepared to launch a surge of troops in Iraq that military commanders overwhelmingly opposed. The Joint Chiefs of Staff opposed the increase in troops and grudgingly went along only because they were promised that the military escalation would be matched by renewed political and economic efforts. General John P. Abizaid, former head of Central Command, said on leaving that adding U.S. troops was not the answer for Iraq. In 2006 a *Military Times* poll reported that almost 60 percent of servicemen and servicewomen did not believe that civilians in the Pentagon had their "best interests at heart."

There is a historical question here of how much the Iraq debacle can be ascribed to an orientation of Bush leaders that is due to their lack of military experience. This will be answered only by empirical inquiry. Our interest is what follows (or does not follow) from this for the chickenhawk issue generally.

Combat Experience as Essential

One conclusion one might draw—and the strongest to be drawn—is that no one should ever make policy on war if he has not served in combat himself. This is how conservative critics of the chickenhawk charge typically construe it. In their eyes, it is akin to saying that one can take a stand on gender oppression only if one is a woman.

The conservative regards both claims as absurd. Construed this way, the chickenhawk argument *is* absurd.

For starters, it would exclude almost every American from making war policy or even having opinions on the matter since such a small number of Americans have ever seen combat or even been in the military. It would exclude all those who have been excluded from combat in the past, like women of a certain age; ironically, it would prevent homosexuals from ever making war policy or having opinions on the matter since they are legally excluded from the military. Moreover, if making war policy required combat experience, Dennis Kucinich's opposition to Iraq is just as dubious as Cheney's endorsement of it since neither served. In addition, the general principle here leads to obvious reductios: should only those who have children make family policy, or should only those with farms make farm policy?

But this is a straw person. In all my research, I have never encountered a critic of chickenhawk behavior who has endorsed this view. If someone truly held this view, they would be equally critical of Condoleezza Rice (or, before her, Madeleine Albright) making policy as Bush since she never served in combat either. But you don't encounter this claim. Whatever the chickenhawk charge is, it's clearly not this.

Combat Experience as Valuable

We can distinguish the question of whether lack of combat experience excludes you from making war policy from the question of whether such experience is a prerequisite of being a *good* policymaker on these matters. A parallel is with priests and sex: no one says celibacy should exclude you from having opinions on sex (how much experience would you need to have a voice on these matters?). But it's natural to assume that some experience is valuable if you are to make wise policy. In general, we take people's past experiences to be a crucial factor in determining their competence to serve in important positions. It's hard to see why past military experience should be any different, especially in the case of the president—who has exceptional power over matters of war. We expect the secretary of housing to have experience with housing. We expect the secretary of the treasury to have financial experience. Why not expect the commander in chief of the armed forces to have military experience?

John McCain pressed this point in the primary campaigns. He argued that his Republican rivals were not qualified to deal with issues like torture or to be president in wartime because they never served in the military.[41] He was quoted as saying, "There's a clear division between those who have a military background and experience in these issues and people like Giuliani, Romney, and Thompson who don't—who chose to do other things when this nation was fighting its wars." "I don't think there's any greater indication of experience and knowledge of how wars should be fought and how crisis should be handled."

Yet there are several different ways to construe the claim that combat experience is valuable that still need to be sorted out.

1. One construal says that prior combat experience is desirable because combat veterans are likely to be more *dovelike* in their approach to war. (World War II correspondent Bill Mauldin once said, "The surest way to become a pacifist is to join the infantry."[42])

There are notable examples of leaders whose wartime experience seems to have pushed them in a more peacelike direction. Ulysses S. Grant, for example, resisted employing the same tactics against Native Americans as president that he applied against southerners as general of the Union army. Grant's "peace policy," as it is termed by historians, eschewed the genocidal policies of others. Grant resisted loud voices that clamored for war with Great Britain because of sour relations between the two countries growing out of the Civil War and continuing disputes around fishing rights, boundary issues, and the like. Instead, Grant worked with the Gladstone government to submit the issues to arbitration, a landmark instance of this approach being used to preserve the peace. Grant also resisted calls for war with Spain around the issue of Cuba and employed the American navy to prevent American freebooters from joining that conflict.

The first problem with this general line of thought, though, involves the alleged general link between past military experience and dovelike attitudes. John McCain regarded his experience as contributing to his distain of torture, but it also made him more hawklike on the Iraq War generally, in his own mind. Grant, the former general, resisted war with Spain. Civil War combat veteran William McKinley declared war on Spain. The examples of Winston Churchill and Theodore Roosevelt show that experience with war can engender a love of war. Scholarly analysis of the matter is inconclusive. Christopher Gelpi, a professor of political science at Duke University and coauthor of *Choosing Your Battles*, says that his 1998–1999 research shows that "veterans are very skeptical of the kind of mission that Iraq is: nation-building, a long commitment where our goals are really political more than military." But once the decision is made to intervene, he reports, veterans, like military officers, lean toward using overwhelming force, an attitude of "let's do it right and do it large scale, or let's get out." Others have argued that the importance of military background in such judgments pales next to things like partisan affiliations. William Bianco, professor of political science at Indiana University, reports that his research on voting patterns reveals that, "in the main, veterans look like non-veterans in Congress, on any dimension we can measure."[43]

A further problem is that, even if there were a link between combat experience and dovelike attitudes, it would not be an *argument* for much of anything; rather, it would be only an argument for choosing veterans if one assumed that our leaders should always be dovelike. Most people won't want to assume this, though. On reflection, they would probably say that sometimes they want our leaders to be dovelike but sometimes not; for example, many have bemoaned the dovelike approach of Great Britain's leadership prior to World War II and applauded the ascension of the arch-hawk Churchill.

2. There is another variation on the combat experience argument that is easily confused with the first but is distinct. This is the claim that such experience renders one more *prudent* in matters of war, though not necessarily more dovelike in the judgments one ultimately reaches. This was the issue raised by the extreme haste with which the Bush administration went to war in Iraq and its indifference to alternative peaceful solutions. Not just liberals have advanced this point. Senator Chuck Hagel remarked of superhawk chickenhawk Richard Perle, "Maybe Mr. Perle would like to be in the first wave of those who go into Baghdad." (Hagel also stated on the occasion of Cheney accidentally shooting his duck-hunting partner that if Cheney had served in the military, he might have learned how use a gun safely.) As noted, General Anthony Zinni observed that many who were most skeptical of invading Iraq were former generals like Norman Schwarzkopf. In Jim Mann's *Rise of the Vulcans: The History of Bush's War Cabinet*, widely regarded as the best account of the Bush neoconservative foreign policy team, Colin

Powell is reported to have remarked informally to acquaintances on the lack of military experience of Bush's advisers.

Combat veterans attest to the profound impact the experience can have. "The world is a lot bigger after you've been in a war," said Bob Kerrey, the former Democratic senator from Nebraska who lost a leg in Vietnam and won the Medal of Honor. "There's a lot less black and white, and a lot more gray." Senator Hagel added that combat experience "doesn't mean we're right, but we do bring a frame of reference when it comes to war." "When you've never experienced war, it's a little easier to be more cavalier about committing troops and not understanding the consequences of war." *If* combat experience rendered people more prudent, this would count in favor of choosing them as our leaders according to our civic republican tradition, which felt so strongly that the decision for war should be made cautiously.

But *are* combat veterans more prudent? Again, the matter is ambiguous. When John F. Kennedy the combat veteran ran in 1960 against Richard Nixon, who had seen no combat, he was clearly the more bellicose of the two. But the defining event of his presidency, the Cuban missile crisis, was one where his prudence and good sense prevailed over that of experienced combat figures like Curtis LeMay. Congressman Murtha's Republican colleague on the Armed Services Committee, Duncan Hunter, is also a decorated Vietnam veteran yet led the charge for the Bush position. Scholarly studies are inconclusive. Writing in the *Journal of Conflict Resolution*, Todd S. Sechser of Stanford University suggests that this sobriety of former soldiers is more a matter of our system of civilian control than anything else.[44]

Opponents of the chickenhawk charge counter it with what might be termed the *Chicken Little* problem: whether people who have seen combat might not be too afraid to wage war when necessary. This thought may be present in Thomas Friedman's previously cited remark arguing for the desirability of leaders who are slightly insane. It has also been voiced by right-wing television personality Dennis Miller. Miller said of John Kerry in the 2004 campaign that while he admired Kerry's combat record, he worried that it had left him gun-shy. If combat veterans were more cautious in their actions, as the Chicken Little argument bemoans, this would be a count in their *favor* according to our founding civic republican ideology. But we have seen that the connection remains to be established.

It is crucial to keep in mind one distinction. The focus has been on whether one's own past experiences make one more prudent. This is different from the issue of whether knowing that one's own *children* will be fighting a war makes one more prudent. The citizen-soldier model most definitely assumes that it does and assumes that prudence is desirable here.

Civilian Control

A familiar claim in countering the chickenhawk charge is that privileging past combat experience conflicts with the principle of civilian control over the military. *Boston Globe* columnist Jeff Jacoby writes,

> The founders of the American republic were unambiguous in rejecting any hint of military supremacy. Under the Constitution, military leaders take their orders from civilian leaders, who are subject in turn to the judgment of ordinary voters. Those who wear the uniform in wartime are entitled to their countrymen's esteem and lasting gratitude. But for well over two centuries, Americans have insisted that when it comes to security and defense policy, soldiers and veterans get no more of a say than anyone else ("Are You a Chicken Hawk?," July 23, 2006)

Former Republican National Committee communications director Cliff May calls the chickenhawk charge a "wrong and rather cheap argument":

> In the United States, we have civilian control of the military and that's probably [!] a good idea. If you make the case that unless you have served you have no standing on this issue, then you could also argue that if you're not a police officer you have no standing on law enforcement issues.

Prowar *Vanity Fair* columnist Christopher Hitchens has also charged that the concern with chickenhawk behavior would undermine civilian control.

The issue of civilian control assumed an odd dimension in the Bush administration. The perception of civilian leaders as more prowar than the military led some to argue that civil control was valuable in promoting a more aggressive foreign policy. A key text here was *Supreme Command* by Eliot Cohen, subsequently named by Secretary of State Condoleezza Rice as counselor for the State Department. It argued for the importance of civilian supremacy in wartime on the grounds that military leaders tended to be habitually overcautious. President Bush counted himself among the admirers of this book. The argument rested on an empirical claim that I have already questioned, namely, that military leaders were generally more dovish in matters of war making.

The issue of civilian control has never had much to do with the desirability of past military experience. The founders of this country who enshrined civilian control in the Constitution had no feelings one way or another about whether the political leadership of the nation should have experience in war. George Washington had military experience, of course, and his authority drew on that fact. But Thomas Jefferson, the next most significant president, did not. More important and in keeping with the chickenhawk charge, the principal mechanism that the authors of the

Constitution devised for ensuring continued civilian oversight over matters of war and peace was that wars, when fought, would be fought by ordinary civilians. The way to prevent irresponsible war making was to ensure that its sacrifices would be born by everyone.

RETURNING TO PRINCIPLES

The issue of past military experience, its bearing on leadership, and its bearing on political judgment generally is a legitimate one. It is certainly worth exploring as we increasingly move toward a society where, because military service is increasingly for the marginalized, the pool of political leaders may include fewer and fewer people with past combat experience.

For our purposes, though, the major problem with this line of thought is that it does not really speak to the chickenhawk issue. For a chickenhawk is not just someone who lacks military experience. He is defined by the fact that he diligently *avoided* such experience while endorsing the war in question. If the claim is that chickenhawks are especially bad policymakers in matters of war, the argument must show how this follows from a history of avoiding wars that one endorsed in the past. If the claim is that chickenhawks are excessively imprudent, that imprudence must be traced to a history of *avoiding* war, not only the lack of war experience.

Up to now, the focus has been on questions of policy—whether chickenhawks make good decisions. I think the focus should be on matters of principle: does the chickenhawk possess a flawed moral character? These questions may be related: people with flawed moral characters may make bad policy decisions. But the relation needs to be spelled out. Many people who disagreed with Bill Clinton's politics traced them to his flawed moral character in personal matters. Others granted the latter but did not see any relation to his political decisions. It will depend in part on the nature of the flaw in question.

In the next chapter, we turn to the chickenhawk's character flaws.

NOTES

1. Colin L. Powell and Joseph Persico, *My American Journey* (New York: Ballantine Books, 1996), 148.

2. Jack Newfield, "Reagan's War Hawks without Wings," *Village Voice*, June 11, 1985. The first discussion of it seems to have been Jane Mayer, "Vietnam Service Isn't on the Resumes of Some Vocal Middle Aged Hawks," *Wall Street Journal*, January 11, 1985. See also Arthur M. Schlesinger Jr., *The Cycles of American History* (Boston: Houghton Mifflin, 1999), 294–95.

3. Senator Dan Quayle (speaking August 19, 1988) reported in *Esquire*, August 1992.

4. Calvin Trillin, "Quayle, Reconsidered," *New York Times*, February 23, 2004; see also "After the Convention; Excerpts from Questioning of Quayle about Guard Role in Vietnam War," *New York Times*, August 20, 1988.

5. The charges are discussed in Paul N. McCloskey Jr., *The Taking of Hill 610 and Other Essays on Friendship* (Woodside, CA: Eaglet Books, 1992).

6. Andrew J. Bacevich, *The New American Militarism: How Americans Are Seduced by War* (Oxford: Oxford University Press, 2006), 112.

7. James Carroll, *House of War: The Pentagon and the Disastrous Rise of American Power* (Boston: Mariner Books, 2007), 456.

8. R. G. Ratliffe, "Bush War Record," *Houston Chronicle*, August 19, 1988.

9. Molly Ivins, *Shrub: The Short but Happy Political Life of George W. Bush* (New York: Vintage Books, 2000), 4–5.

10. Sara Rimer, Ralph Blumenthal, and Raymond Bonner, "Portrait of George Bush in '72: Unanchored in Turbulent Time," *New York Times*, September 20, 2004. He was trained on F-102 fighters, which were already being phased out of frontline service.

11. Lawrence Baskir and William Strauss, *Chance and Circumstance: The Draft, the War, and the Vietnam Generation* (New York: Alfred A. Knopf, 1978), 49.

12. Rimer et al., "Portrait of George Bush in '72."

13. Ivins, *Shrub*, 11.

14. David Herbert Donald, *Lincoln* (New York: Simon & Schuster, 1995), 44.

15. "Bush Plays Video Games with Recovering War Veterans," *American Free Press*, November 9, 2007.

16. Thomas E. Ricks, *Fiasco: The American Military Adventure in Iraq, 2003 to 2005* (New York: Penguin, 2007), 47–48.

17. Maureen Dowd, "Awake and Scream," *New York Times*, September 16, 2006.

18. See, for example, http://www.sourcewatch.org/index.php?title=Chickenhawk#SourceWatch:_.22Chickenhawks.22, http://www.awolbush.com/whoserved.html, and http://www.nhgazette.com/chickenhawks.html.

19. Katherine Seelye, "Cheney's Five Draft Deferments during the Vietnam Era Emerge as a Campaign Issue," *New York Times*, May 1, 2004.

20. Michael Hirsch, "Hawks, Doves, and Dubya," *Newsweek*, September 2, 2002.

21. Cited in Jonah Goldberg, "Baghdad Delenda Est, Part Two," *National Review Online*, April 23, 2002.

22. James Bamford, "Untested Administration Hawks Clamor for War," *USA Today*, September 16, 2002.

23. Greg Newbold, "Why Iraq Was a Mistake," *Time*, April 9, 2006.

24. Robin Toner, "Who's This 'We,' Non-Soldier Boy?" *New York Times*, June 25, 2006.

25. On Giuliani's avoidance of the draft, see Cathy Burke, "Rudy Is Chilled by the Draft—He's a Dodger: Vets," *New York Post*, April 15, 2007, and Geoffrey Gray, "Rudy and 'Nam: He's No War Hero. Will It Matter?" *New York Magazine*, April 16, 2007. On Romney, see Michael Kranish, "Mormon Church Obtained

Vietnam Draft Deferrals for Romney, Other Missionaries," *Boston Globe*, June 24, 2007.

26. Bob Hebert, "Blood Runs Red, Not Blue," *New York Times*, August 18, 2005.

27. "Grieving Mom Heckles Laura Bush—Woman Whose Son Died in Iraq Interrupts N.J. Speech, Is Arrested," *CBS News*, September 17, 2004; Chris Hedges, "Mourning the Warrior, and Questioning the War," *New York Times*, September 22, 2004.

28. Julia Reed, "Sister Act," *Vogue*, August 2004.

29. Laura Cruz, "El Paso Soldier's Death Rattles Neighbors, School," *El Paso Times*, May 19, 2004.

30. Cindy Sheehan, "Hypocrites and Liars," *Common Dreams*, August 20, 2005.

31. "Mother of First Soldier from Georgia Killed in Iraq Also Demands to Speak with Bush," *Democracy Now*, August 22, 2005.

32. Ralph Nader, "American Detachment—It's Time to Make the Iraq War Personal," *Common Dreams*, August 25, 2005.

33. Evan Thomas and Eleanor Clift, "All in the Family," *Newsweek*, November 15, 2004.

34. Stuart Jeffries, "'I'll Hold Blair to Account," *The Guardian*, March 22, 2005.

35. "Senator Lautenberg Blasts Republicans as 'Chicken Hawks,'" press release, February 24, 2004.

36. An interesting problem is raised by those who avoided a war in the past because they disagreed with it but now agree with the war in retrospect and urge the prosecution of similar wars. I think this is the case with right-wing radio commentator Michael Medved. Such a person would not be a chickenhawk on my definition, which requires that they avoided a war they endorsed at the time. But it does raise the question of whether they tailor their beliefs about war to the likelihood of their having to fight it. This harkens back to the issue of whether the chickenhawk supports a war *only* because he is able to avoid its sacrifices.

37. Eliot Cohen, "Hunting Chickenhawks," *Washington Post*, September 5, 2002.

38. Ben Tripp, "A Bird Lover's Guide to Chickenhawks or Chickenhawk a la Mode," *Counterpunch*, October 15, 2002.

39. See John Hart Ely, *War and Responsibility* (Princeton, NJ: Princeton University Press, 1995), chap. 1.

40. H. R. McMaster, *Dereliction of Duty: Johnson, McNamara, the Joint Chiefs of Staff, and the Lies That Led to Vietnam* (New York: HarperPerennial, 1998).

41. "McCain Slams Rivals on Military Service," *CBS News*, November 2, 2007.

42. John Morton Blum, *V Was for Victory: Politics and American Culture during World War II* (San Diego, CA: Harvest/HBJ Book, 1977), 69.

43. Cited in Toner, "Who's This 'We,' Non-Soldier Boy?"

44. Todd S. Sechser, "Are Soldiers Less War-Prone Than Statesmen?" *Journal of Conflict Resolution* 48, no. 5 (2004): 746–74. See also Peter D. Feaver and Richard H. Kohn, eds., *Soldiers and Civilians: The Civil-Military Gap and American National Security* (Cambridge, MA: MIT Press, 2001), especially William Bianco and Jamie Markham, "Last Post for 'The Greatest Generation': The Decline of Military Experience in the US Congress," Peter Feaver, *Armed Servants: Agency, Oversight, and Civil-Military Relations* (Cambridge, MA: Harvard University Press, 2005).

4

~~~

Integrity, Reciprocity, and the Murtha Test

Ultimately a nation must pay the price for using troops in war, and it will be more attentive to the price from the start if all its members think they must pay.

—James Fallows, *National Defense*[1]

The chickenhawk's problem is not that the wars he supports are necessarily good or bad ones. The chickenhawk's main problem is *himself*: his flawed moral character. This flaw has two dimensions. The chickenhawk lacks personal integrity. And, because of this, he stands in a "nonreciprocal" relation to his fellow citizens. Put simply, the chickenhawk is a hypocrite and a freeloader. Not every moral failing has unsavory political consequences. But these do. They warrant our moral censure of chickenhawks and our doubts about them as leaders as well as a deep concern about the soul of the republic if the chickenhawk orientation prevails among the citizenry.

This chapter is devoted to unpacking these claims. Doing so will raise many specific questions along the way (e.g., should a leader's chickenhawk youth be held against him?). It will also raise larger philosophical issues about our social responsibilities, the meaning of citizenship, and the moral fabric of a democratic polity. Issues like these warrant much more attention than I can give them here, though I hope to show how central the issue of military service is to the most fundamental questions of politics. What follows from our critique for how we *should* think and act in these matters? My answer is the Murtha test, which I discuss in the second part of this chapter. I conclude with some words on the obligation to resist wars we oppose.

PERSONAL INTEGRITY AND HYPOCRISY

> I find war detestable. Even more detestable are those who praise war without participating in it.
>
> —Romain Rolland

Like all basic moral values, personal integrity is complex. One of its core meanings involves a consistency between word and deed—captured in the phrase "walking one's talk." Integrity means having the courage of your convictions, putting your money where your mouth is, and standing by your words—walking your talk. The chickenhawk lacks integrity of this sort. He is happy to talk the talk when he endorses a war but is unwilling to walk the walk that this implies. He is like the preacher who rants against pornography while sneaking out to watch *Teenage Milkmaids Go Wild!* except the chickenhawk's behavior pertains to the most public of matters, war and peace. He is a hypocrite and a fitting object of our moral distaste.

Not all moral failings are politically relevant. But our political culture puts great emphasis on personal integrity. In his important study of integrity, Stephen Carter notes how much integrity is invoked in the praise and self-praise of politicians.[2] Bill Clinton praised Al Gore as "a leader of great strength, integrity and stature." The senior George Bush, running against Michael Dukakis, called on Americans to elect someone with "the integrity and the stability to get the job done." More recently, Edward Kennedy endorsed Barack Obama by citing his integrity as his greatest virtue. In 1972, writing of Nixon's reelection, the *New York Times* opined that "the most important virtue in politics is integrity."[3] Nixon is regarded as one of the worst presidents ever because he was so lacking in that virtue.

Integrity is not just a central virtue of leaders. A healthy democracy rests on the integrity of its individual citizens. This was implicit in our civic republican heritage's stress on civic virtue. The term "virtue" derives from the term for strength, or power. Civic virtue involved the sober responsibility of integrity applied to public matters. Our political culture focuses on the integrity of leaders because they are a mirror to ourselves—to our better selves, we hope. Why should integrity possess such importance in leaders and the citizenry, and why should its absence be cause for such concern?

Some may doubt its importance. If integrity means sticking by your convictions, it would seem to be good or bad, depending on the nature of the convictions. If people's convictions are hateful, we don't want them to walk their talk. Furthermore, while we admire people who walk their talk, we don't admire people who are pigheaded. Indeed, no one exemplified the danger of pigheadedness better than George W. Bush or, before him, Lyndon Johnson, who were so fixed in their convictions that they were willing to drag everyone down with them. Weren't they living proof of what can go wrong when people are obsessed with "sticking by their guns"?

These are good questions. Answering them requires a more nuanced account of integrity.

Steadfastness

Let us turn to Steven Carter's analysis. He suggests that integrity has three elements, each of which is crucial. The first is acting on your convictions even at great personal cost, "walking your talk" in my parlance. I'll call this *steadfastness*.

The political importance of this aspect of integrity rests in its relation to trustworthiness. The steadfast person is someone you can trust. This is essential in leaders. In choosing our leaders, we want to assume that they will do what they say, even at cost to themselves. Once they are in office, their steadfastness provides a degree of predictability to public affairs that can be valuable even if we disagree with specific policies. Ronald Reagan was popular with many who disagreed with him because they felt they knew where he stood and could count on how he would act. But its importance extends beyond leaders to the citizenry generally. In *Democracy and Disagreement*, Amy Gutmann and Dennis Thompson provide an account of what they term "civic integrity" as crucial to a democratic culture. One of its key features is "consistency between speech and action." They give examples of the prochoice advocate that prohibits his own daughter from having an abortion or the antiabortion advocate who helps his daughter attain one.[4] Such behavior dilutes the respect of citizens for one another by weakening the bonds of civic trust. It undermines the capacity for collective decision making insofar as that capacity requires that citizens trust their fellow citizens to abide by the view they advocate. Alexis de Tocqueville stressed that democracy rests on civic trust. Totalitarian societies manifest a culture of mistrust: no one believes that people's words have any relation to their deeds.

The premium we place on steadfastness points to its role as the precondition of other virtues. To say of someone that he or she possesses some virtue X is to say that he or she will continue to manifest it, even when the going gets tough. A compassionate person who ceases to be compassionate the moment it is inconvenient is not truly compassionate; the same holds for other virtues. We seek integrity in our leaders because it is the precondition of any other virtues we admire in them. Nixon's flawed integrity made people wonder if he was capable of virtue at all. So too with our fellow citizens. A certain steadfastness is the precondition of any other civic virtues. Some philosophers have suggested that a minimal integrity is a precondition of social life itself. The late Peter Winch wrote,

> To lack integrity is to act with the appearance of fulfilling a certain role but without the intention of shouldering the responsibilities to which the role commits one. If that, per absurdum, were to become the rule, the whole concept of a social role would thereby collapse.[5]

And, with it, society itself. This too was a component of civic republican ideas of civic virtue. If such virtue became sufficiently corroded, that is, if the society became sufficiently corrupt, the very possibility of a political order would be undermined. Society would return to something like the war of all against all envisioned in Hobbes's state of nature.

How does steadfastness bear on matters of war and peace? If the war is just, we admire the leader who sticks by his convictions in the face of adversity. This is why Winston Churchill was so admired as a war leader; he seemed to be committed to the cause regardless of the personal cost. Steadfastness is also important in the opposite direction. If a war is unjust, we want leaders who stick to their opposition. One of my heroes is William Jennings Bryan, who remained steadfast in his opposition to World War I, even at the cost of his position as secretary of state. Contrast this with the pathetic behavior of Democratic Party leaders facing the Iraq War. Or contrast it with another secretary of state, Colin Powell, who championed the Iraq conflict despite his own alleged doubts.

The integrity of leaders is always a crucial issue in wartime, but it is especially crucial when the military is a volunteer one like ours. This is because of the special role of leaders in inspiring people to enlist in the first place. If you believed in promoting voluntary abstinence among the young, you would not choose Bill Clinton to lead your campaign given his problems in this realm. If you believe in promoting military enlistment, you would not choose someone to lead that campaign with a history of war shirking. This should be enough, I would think, to explain the relevance of Bush's chickenhawk past to his standing as commander in chief. The volunteer approach places extraordinary weight on the credibility of those who lead the volunteer effort; a flawed leader is one who lacks such credibility. I find it significant that, for all the studies of the military recruitment problem, no one thought to explore the impact of Bush's chickenhawk past on the reluctance of young people in joining the armed forces. Volunteerism also requires people being inspired by one another, hence the importance of steadfastness among the citizenry generally in a society committed to a volunteer military. It requires what Gutmann and Thompson term "civic integrity." A campaign for donating blood would not last long if most people who championed it ran away at the first sight of a needle and then denied having done so. The same holds for military service, though I would stress again that my aim is not to champion an unthinking patriotism. Society needs blood; its need for war is another matter.

Talk of steadfastness in the face of sacrifice presumes some agreement about the meaning of "sacrifice." What if people have drastically different ideas about what "sacrifice" means? In the spring of 2008, President Bush boasted that his support for combat efforts in Iraq had led him to give up golf. He claimed that he made the decision after the August 2003 bombing of the UN headquarters in Baghdad, whose victims included Sergio Vieira de Mello, the top UN official in Iraq and its high commissioner for human rights. "I remember when de Mello, who was at the U.N., got killed in Baghdad as a result of these murderers taking this good man's life," he stated. "I was playing golf—I think I was in central Texas—and they pulled me off the golf course and I said, 'It's just not worth it anymore to do.'"[6] Like much about the surreal Bush/Iraq years, the challenge is to capture the full strangeness of this position. It reminds us that talk of steadfastness in the face of sacrifice presumes some agreement about the meaning of "sacrifice." What can we say of someone who likens a UN official's dying in the course of duty to his own giving up golf? Has alienated war so disconnected war and sacrifice that the latter has lost all meaning? Is this the moral cluelessness of corruption? One is reminded of another incident in the Bush presidency. In the early days of 2006, in his first official act of that year, Bush met privately with veterans of Iraq and Afghanistan and their family members at the Brooke Army Medical Center. The president joked about his "own injury in combat" incurred at his Crawford, Texas, ranch—from his encounter with a tree. "As you can possibly see, I have an injury myself—not here at the hospital, but in combat with a cedar. I eventually won," he was quoted as saying. "The cedar gave me a little scratch. As a matter of fact, a colonel asked if I needed first aid when she first saw me. I was able to avoid any major surgical operations here, but thanks for your compassion, colonel." President Bush was joking about his "combat with a tree" with soldiers who had recently lost arms or legs in battle.[7] If integrity means the willingness to endure sacrifices, this presumes the moral capacity to recognize what a real sacrifice is or is not.

Mindfulness

Steven Carter characterizes the second element of integrity as "discerning what is right and what is wrong" in formulating one's convictions.[8] To understand this, consider some exemplars of integrity like Abraham Lincoln or Martin Luther King Jr. A key part of their integrity was their thoughtfulness. They did not simply take responsibility for their convictions. They arrived at those convictions responsibly. Carter speaks of their "discerning what is right and wrong," but their capacity to do so reflected the fact that, as persons of integrity, they cared about right and wrong and the difference between them. Hence, they were attentive to these matters in fashioning their beliefs.

Let us call this element of integrity *mindfulness*. People of integrity stick by their convictions because they arrive at them thoughtfully. Hence, the first two elements of integrity are intimately related. Persons of integrity are both directed and deep, and they are directed because they are deep. The element of mindfulness serves to distinguish the steadfastness of integrity from mere pigheadedness. If someone arrives at her convictions mindfully, she will change her convictions if responsible thought requires it. Martin Luther King Jr. changed his mind on many things, most notably in coming to view the Vietnam War as a great evil. He came to this position in the face of opposition from his own cohorts. His own organization, the Southern Christian Leadership Council, disagreed with him. But King remained steadfast in going where deliberation took him. This is why integrity is not a purely "formal" virtue, as some have maintained. It is manifested in how one arrives at one's convictions as well as how one sticks to them.

Many of the doubts about George W. Bush as a leader pertained to his mindfulness. Perhaps this is why many regarded him as stupid. But a lack of mindfulness is a *moral* failing, not a cognitive one. It is irresponsibility in how one fashions one's beliefs. Consider Bush's attitude to the Vietnam War. When queried about his past actions, Bush claimed that he never thought about Vietnam in college. He claimed that he never talked about it with friends or was even aware of antiwar activism on his campus. In our age of alienated war, a young person might find this credible. The Iraq War is an abstraction to most people. With little campus activism, one can imagine going through college without talking about it with friends or thinking about it much. But this is not a credible claim for the Vietnam era. Not surprisingly, Bush's classmates don't believe it. One has said, "God knows the guy did a lot of drinking in college, but he just couldn't have been that drunk." Another has remarked, "All we ever talked about at Yale then was school, sex, and the war in Vietnam, and not always in that order." There are questions about Bush's forthrightness, then. The issue of mindfulness is raised by the question, What if his remembrances are true?

A young man with a student deferment like Bush had four long years to think about what he would do when his deferment ran out. By the late 1960s, when Bush was in college, the Vietnam issue was omnipresent in American culture. Popular music addressed it and not always from the antiwar side. The number one hit song of 1965 was "The Ballad of the Green Berets" by Sergeant Berry Sadler. For the average male baby boomer, Vietnam posed the first significant political choice of his life. Bush was a student at Yale, the site of numerous antiwar demonstrations; in addition, he was from a prominent political family with a history of diplomatic service. For Bush *not* to have thought about Vietnam at all suggests an astonishing lack of what I have termed "mindfulness."

A striking example of lack of mindfulness on the collective level was the previously mentioned behavior of the Senate, especially the Democrats, in the run-up to the Iraq War. Which is the greater failure in responsible thought: Bush's failure as a young man to think about the Vietnam War or the comportment of those Democrats, faced with the Iraq conflict, who spent their time thinking about the hundredth anniversary of the 4-H Club or the Future Farmers of America chapter in Caldwell County, Kentucky? One would have to say the latter, given the senators' positions of power.

Notions like "mindfulness" or "responsible thought" are very abstract, though. Are they purely subjective: is mindful, responsible thinking simply thinking we agree with? It would be difficult to give an account of what "mindfulness" means in general, though a central component would seem to be thinking through the consequences of your beliefs and actions and asking if you are willing to accept them. Consider Clinton in the Monica Lewinsky affair. One aspect of his flawed integrity was his apparent obliviousness to the consequences of his actions for his family and political supporters. There was something shortsighted in such behavior, bespeaking of a certain narcissism. A concern for the consequences of one's beliefs and actions is especially important in the public realm, which is why the mindfulness of integrity is a crucial political virtue. Nowhere is this truer than in matters of war and peace. Lincoln's greatness as a war president lay in how he brooded over the upshot of his decisions. Statues of war heroes traditionally depicted men on horseback, charging ahead brazenly. The Lincoln Memorial portrays a thoughtful, even pained figure whose face reflects his agony at the human cost of his decisions. Bush bragged that he never lost sleep over his war decisions, suggesting that the lack of mindfulness he exhibited as a young man persisted into adulthood. What of mindfulness as a feature of the public culture generally?

The U.S. Constitution was designed to require responsible deliberation in the decision to go to war. It was, we might say, an instrument of
mindfulness on the most momentous question a sovereign state could
confront. The Senate's behavior leading up to Iraq flouted the spirit of
the Constitution. Taking time in such matters allows for more discussion
among the citizenry, leading, it is hoped, to wiser outcomes. Ideally, the
president's role is one of deliberator, leader of the public dialogue that
gives democracy its meaning. This distinguishes the president's role from
a general's. None of this is sufficient if it is not grounded in a citizenry
that has the integrity to reflect on the consequences of their beliefs and actions. The citizen-soldier model aimed to institutionalize this mindfulness
by ensuring that the citizenry bore the cost of its policies. At numerous
points in this book, I have dwelled on the lack of mindfulness in alienated
war. I argue later in this chapter that mindfulness is promoted by something like the Murtha test.

Forthrightness

Forthrightness is the third element in Carter's account, "saying openly
that you are acting on your understanding of right and wrong" once you
have acted on your convictions.[9] Integrity is not just walking your talk; it
is talking your walk: being candid with others and yourself about your
reasons for acting as you do. I have commended former Vice President
Dan Quayle for acknowledging his avoidance of Vietnam service. If that
avoidance showed a lack of integrity, there was integrity in his later
forthrightness.

Forthrightness, in leaders and in the citizenry, is a precondition of
meaningful public dialogue. Such dialogue is both prohibited and pointless in a totalitarian culture because no one acknowledges their real reasons for their actions. By contrast, forthrightness in a democratic culture
allows for the critical assessment of positions of a kind that can correct
them should those positions prove wrong. This capacity for self-correction is crucial in matters of war. A government's reasons for going to war
can be assessed only if the government is transparent about its reasons;
only then can its policies be corrected. The issue of self-correction has
special bearing on the chickenhawk syndrome.

The chickenhawk syndrome involves the contradiction between waging war and refusing to bear its sacrifices. There are two ways this contradiction can be resolved. One can continue to wage war and accept its
sacrifices, or one can cease waging war. If we endorse the latter course, as
I do, we must consider the factors that stand in its way. One of them, I'd
suggest, is that citizens are not forthright with themselves about their own
reasons for acting as they do. The next chapter explores the kinds of rea-

sons that prowar young people today give for their failure to enlist, and it will find these reasons seriously wanting. In some cases, the problem may be a failure in logic. But in others, it may be that the young people are not being candid with themselves about why they do not serve. Their real reasons may be that they do not actually regard the Iraq War as worth fighting, even dying in. Candor of this sort can be a spur to deliberate reflection of a kind that may have been absent in the initial formulation of positions. The upshot of such self-correction may be determining that the war is one that cannot be supported with full integrity.

Further Elements of Integrity (or the Lack Thereof)

I've been to war. I've raised twins. If I had a choice, I'd rather go to war.

—President Bush (*Houston Chronicle*, January 2002)

Comparing the cases of George W. Bush and Bill Clinton illuminates further aspects of integrity.

1. *Shame*: A major similarity between Clinton and Bush is their lack of *shame*. By his own account, Clinton assumed that Monica Lewinsky would eventually tell the world about their affair. How could he have pursued the affair if he had any sense of shame in such matters? Bush's shamelessness seems to have been a pattern throughout his life. By his own admission, Bush had a serious substance abuse problem when young. Yet this did not prevent him from becoming the National Guard poster boy for opposing substance abuse. In 1969, a Guard press release proclaimed, "George Walker Bush is one member of the younger generation who doesn't get his kicks from pot or hashish or speed. Oh, he gets high, all right, but not from narcotics." His act of dressing up like a fighter pilot to proclaim "mission accomplished" in the early days of the Iraq conflict drew the attention it did because it exemplified a certain shamelessness. The issue of shamelessness is implicit in the chickenhawk syndrome. Discussions of the chickenhawk phenomenon have stressed how the chickenhawk often casts aspersions on the patriotism of others while avoiding sacrifice himself.

Some philosophers have challenged the value of the shame as a moral emotion. They view it as entirely negative in its import. My own view is that shame and integrity are closely linked insofar as both involve a sense of *limits*. Persons of integrity have a strong moral identity that sustains their sense of what they can or cannot do ethically; they find certain acts inconceivable. By contrast, the shameless person is capable of anything; hence, nothing he ever does surprises us. Nothing about Bill Clinton's sexual behavior would surprise us, nor would anything about George W. Bush's behavior in matters of war.[10]

Shame concerns how others perceive us.[11] Our capacity to feel shame reflects the value that we place on others' views. Clinton's shamelessness suggested that he placed no importance on how his wife and family viewed him. Bush's reflected a similar indifference. The concern with how you are viewed can be exaggerated, of course. It can make you pander to others or have no convictions at all. In its proper place, though, shame awakens us to the existence of others; it is conducive to moral dialogue in compelling us to attend to the judgments of others.

This explains the importance of shame to the political realm. Leaders in a democracy must be attentive to the judgment of others. They should be capable of saying to the American people, "I'm ashamed of myself," to mark the fact that they do have a moral core, which they have betrayed in this case. Shame is essential to the moral core of the country, too. In the eyes of its critics, America's endorsement of torture was not just wrong but shameful, raising questions about the importance it gave to anyone's views but its own. A proponent of shame as a political factor was Martin Luther King Jr. His nonviolent tactics sought to transform the segregationist power structure by provoking a sense of shame. "Non-violent resistance does not seek to defeat or humiliate the opponent," he wrote. The nonviolent resister "realizes that non-co-operation and boycotts are not ends themselves; they are merely means to awaken a sense of moral shame in the opponent."[12] Provoking shame is a means to moral dialogue and, it is hoped, ultimate reconciliation. Cindy Sheehan attempted the same tactics outside of Bush's Crawford ranch when she camped out there for several months bearing witness to the needless death of her son in Iraq.

Both Clinton and Bush were shameless. They differed in that Clinton never claimed to be a paragon of sexual virtue. He did not lecture the nation on sexual probity as Bush lectured us on war's sacrifices. He did not claim to be an "abstinence president." Most important, Clinton's flawed integrity involved private matters, while Bush's pertained to matters of war and peace. Clinton's critics charged that his sexual escapades were not peripheral to his public office since they were symptomatic of a flawed integrity generally. Richard Land, president of the Ethics and Religious Liberty Commission of the Southern Baptist Convention, invoked Harry Truman's remark that he would never hire someone who cheated on his wife because a person who broke his marriage oath could also break his oath of office. I think this is a reasonable view. It's logical that flawed integrity in one key area of life will extend to others. But this holds for the chickenhawk, too. If someone like Bush evidenced such flawed integrity with respect to military service, his first political act, it's reasonable to presume that his integrity is flawed generally.

2. *Youth and privilege*: At this point, someone may object that there is one huge difference between Clinton and Bush, one that bears on the criticism of draft-dodging baby boomers generally. Clinton was a grown man when he consorted with Monica Lewinsky. Draft-dodging baby boomers like Bush were youths. Doesn't this place far too much weight on actions taken long ago?

Youthful lapses in integrity need not reflect on the mature adult; we are inclined to cut people slack for their actions at that age. As a defense of the draft-dodging baby boomer, though, this would be a strange excuse coming from conservatives. Conservatives consistently argue for *lowering* the age of responsibility in many legal matters, especially criminal ones. They argue for longer prison terms for crimes committed when young. They endorse executing children (those under age eighteen) who have been convicted of murder. If an adolescent can be held accountable for such acts, why should we discount the acts of young men like George W. Bush because they were committed in their mid-twenties? Conservatives are adamant about the responsibility of young people for sexual matters. If a sixteen-year-old girl can be held accountable for premarital sex, why can't a George W. Bush be held accountable for avoiding his civic responsibilities when he was ten years older?

This is especially true in military matters. During the Vietnam War, a young man could enlist at age eighteen. Society assumed that he was old enough to make this decision responsibly. The military gives soldiers responsibility over life-and-death matters before the age of twenty. The history of our nation is one of *crediting* soldiers for acts they performed at a young age. One of the most decorated soldiers of World War II, Audie Murphy, was celebrated throughout his life for acts he performed when he was seventeen years old. Others have built political careers on acts of youthful heroism. If we celebrate soldiers for doing their duty while in their teens, why shouldn't we condemn the draft-dodging baby boomer for shirking his duty at the same age or older?

The question of whether youthful acts reflect on the adult returns us to the issue of forthrightness. Someone who acknowledges his youthful failings seems more likely to have rectified them as an adult. In general, the prominent draft-dodging baby boomers have not done this. Quite the contrary, they have followed Bush's pattern of denial. Forthrightness, I've suggested, is important to rectifying wrong behavior. Hypocrisy will persist into adulthood if the hypocrite does not recognize his acts for what they are.

Finally, there is the question of *privilege*. Not all baby-boomer chickenhawks were privileged. Nothing about chickenhawk behavior presumes an element of privilege. But with Bush and other political leaders, not just conservatives, the class issue is unavoidable. It is hard not to view their lack of mindfulness, their failure to think through their views, as reflecting a standpoint of privilege from which one is never obliged to think through the costs of mistake or failure. Daddy will take care of it. This privileged orientation may have impacted many middle-class youths less dramatically.

At the close of the Bush presidency, Secretary of State Condoleezza Rice leveled the chickenhawk charge against one of the administration's adversaries. Responding to anti-American cleric Muqtada al-Sadr, hours after the radical leader threatened to declare war unless U.S. and Iraqi forces ended a crackdown on his followers, Rice observed, "I know he's sitting in Iran. I guess it's all-out war for anybody but him. I guess that's the message; his followers can go to their deaths and he's in Iran." She was speaking of the privileges of position rather than wealth, but the implication was the same: leaders should not impose costs on others that their privileges allow them to avoid.

3. *Cowardice*: Is the chickenhawk a *coward*? The name suggests as much. This makes for effective rhetoric, especially when the target is a swaggering chief executive. But the matter is more complex—in intriguing ways.

Cowardice *might* be the basis of chickenhawk behavior. One can imagine a cowardly chickenhawk who arrives at support for a war via sober reflection but who becomes uncontrollably frozen with fright at the thought of physical danger, rendering him incapable of carrying through on his views. He fails to serve because he literally cannot do it; in Harry Frankfurt's words, he cannot will to will it, in ways he might privately regret.[13] He is like a pornography-watching minister who has a psychological problem that rendered him incapable of *not* watching pornography.

I think that the chickenhawk who is truly chicken is a more sympathetic figure. People who cannot control themselves are certainly viewed more sympathetically in today's therapy-oriented culture. Public figures caught in grossly hypocritical behavior typically plead an addiction problem or some other psychological compulsion. Think of the Congressman who led the fight against child pornography while sex-talking young male pages. Fear of death, like sexual attraction, is a perfectly human trait. We can understand fearing combat no matter how much one believes in the cause. At the same time, we can understand why an aspiring politician leader might not explain his past chickenhawk behavior by appealing to his uncontrollable cowardice.

Is the cowardly chickenhawk still a hypocrite? I think so. He is certainly a hypocrite if, while too cowardly to serve himself, he condemns other people for cowardice in not serving. At the same time, I think it would be a mistake to lump Bush and other privileged baby boomers in the cowardice category for reasons that pertain to the issue of corruption. Explaining Bush's Vietnam War avoidance by cowardice presumes that

Bush had reason to believe that if he went to Vietnam, he had a high likelihood of being injured or even killed. This was a reasonable presumption for a working-class boy but not for someone like Bush. Just as privilege got you out of serving entirely, it could get you out of being in harm's way once you were in Vietnam. Few truly privileged youth went to Vietnam at all. Of those who did, even fewer got injured or killed.

I'd suggest that Bush and other beneficiaries of privilege were *worse* than the cowardly chickenhawk. Their actions suggest not someone psychologically incapable of serving in Vietnam but rather someone who felt that it was not *worth* their time to serve. Cheney said so explicitly in remarking that he had other priorities. Both felt that the war was worth other people's serving, even dying, but they could not be bothered with it. The problem here was not a psychological malady but moral casualness.

A Note on the Jacksonian Tradition

Here and throughout, my discussion has drawn on the civic republican tradition. My account of integrity draws on its notion of civic virtue, my critique of flawed integrity on its notion of corruption. But this is not the only American political tradition. Many have argued that it has been substantially displaced by the tradition of market liberalism, which would reduce the political realm to just another realm of market exchange. The replacement of the citizen-soldier model by the hired professional model is one expression of this, heartily endorsed by free-market theorists like Milton Friedman. The market liberal tradition does not ascribe central importance to personal integrity except insofar as it counsels honesty in commercial relations. Steadfastness, mindfulness, and forthrightness are important only insofar as they promote efficient results for individuals and groups.

A third American tradition does ascribe great importance to personal integrity, especially in relation to military service. Walter Russell Mead has termed it the "Jacksonian tradition" after its greatest exemplar, Andrew Jackson. It gets less attention from political theorists because its primary home is popular culture, like movies or television; indeed, it may be the dominant strain in our popular political culture. It has always stood in an angular relation to the Constitution; hence, it is not a major presence in the nation's legal culture, which today's political philosophers draw on. The best study of this tradition is *Gunfighter Nation: The Myth of the Frontier in Twentieth-Century America*, by cultural theorist Richard Slotkin.[14] After him, I term it the "frontier tradition."

This is the political perspective found in the classical cowboy-and-Indian movies, starring figures like John Wayne, or urban cop movies, like *Dirty Harry*, starring Clint Eastwood. Its perspective could not be more different than civic republicanism in many ways. It has little regard for the Constitution's constraints on military or police violence, which it regards mainly as a source of annoyance. Indeed, it has little regard for politics at all as a shared endeavor. Its mind-set is that of the loner, or the "rugged individual" of frontier lore. The importance it gives to personal integrity is an expression of this individualism. More than anything else, individuals—male individuals, in particular—must "stick to their guns." A true man "keeps his word" (entire westerns are built around this theme, like the classic *The Wild Bunch*), and that is all that a "true man" asks of another. Hence, the other elements of integrity matter little. Mindfulness is for sissies; the true man makes decisions in a flash since good and evil are transparent. He is direct with others but feels no need to apologize or explain; he is a man of few words. Hence, the forthrightness of shared dialogue holds nothing for him.

Bush's success as a political leader rested on placing himself in this frontier tradition. He trumpeted himself as the "decider." He proclaimed that he did not have to explain anything to anybody. These resonated with many Americans, especially white males. But the realities of alienated war are such that even its Jacksonianism is fraudulent. Summarizing this tradition, Walter Russell Mead writes that for the Jacksonian, "Americans are people who make their own way in the world"; "they don't slide by on welfare, and they don't rely on inherited wealth or connections." "Courage is the crowning and indispensable part of [their] code" since "Americans believe that they ought to stick up for what they believe." Hence,

> Jacksonian America views military service as a sacred duty; when [others] dodged the draft in Vietnam or purchased exemptions and substitutes in earlier wars, Jacksonians soldiered on, if sometimes bitterly and resentfully. Failure to defend the country in its hour of need is to the Jacksonian mind evidence of at best distorted values and more probably contemptible cowardice. An honorable person is ready to kill or to die for family and flag.[15]

Alienated war poses the question of whatever happened to civic republicanism and its citizen-soldier tradition. George W. Bush poses the question of whatever happened to the frontier tradition since Bush would seem to exemplify the "distorted values" that Jacksonianism has traditionally scorned.

RECIPROCITY

The discussion thus far has made assumptions about what "walking your talk" means. Discussions of personal integrity always make such assumptions. And there is always room for disagreement. One can imagine an objection of the following sort.

Personal integrity *is* a virtue. But your critique of the chickenhawk presumes that endorsing a war necessarily commits him to serving in it himself. This is surely false. There are always many who are incapable of serving for reasons of age, health, and so on; in addition, the military never needs that many soldiers. In a war of even the most minimal popularity, there will always be more people endorsing it than can serve in it.

Are they *all* corrupt? No, they aren't. But "walking their talk" does not in fact mean that every prowar person serves. What does it mean? This partly depends on the military system in place. I'll argue in the next chapter that, with a volunteer military like ours, endorsing a war commits you to volunteering yourself or having a good reason not to. (The fact that you volunteer does not mean that the military will take you, only that you offer your services.) Figures like the Bush twins or the Romney sons are clearly chickee-hawks on this view: they fail to walk their talk.

The draft-dodging baby boomer is even clearer. My critique of their chickenhawk behavior has not presumed that endorsing the war means serving. It has presumed that endorsing a war means *not* diligently *avoiding* service. Consider the parallel with taxes. Endorsing a costly public project, such as a new school, need not commit me to paying taxes for it myself—a property tax, say. I may not be eligible because I am a renter and not a home owner. But endorsing such a project means that I cannot diligently *avoid* paying the taxes for it. That would be failing to walk one's talk. The same holds for military service. Note that this bears on what "deliberating responsibly" means in such matters. In the school case, it would be irresponsible of me to support the construction of a new facility because I knew I wouldn't be taxed myself. Integrity requires that I support the project only if I would be willing to pay the taxes, if my circumstances were different. Indeed, if I knew ahead of time that I would not have to pay for it, it strikes me that I would be especially beholden to ask if I would pay my fair share if circumstances were different. This would ensure that my judgment is not biased.

Such responsible thinking stands behind the *Murtha test:* support only a war that you would be willing to fight in or even die in.

I have already remarked on the importance of whether the avoidance involves breaking the law. Doing the right thing is not just a matter of doing the legal thing. If the school supporter diligently sets out to avoid paying taxes for it, I don't see why it should matter if all his methods fit within the income-tax code. Obviously, it is worse if he violates the law. But it's enough that he attempts to avoid paying his fair share. The same holds for the war avoider. Men who avoided military service in the Civil War by buying their way out were not excused from moral blame by the fact that their actions were legal. Then, as in Vietnam, the laws themselves were so patently flawed that they provided little moral respite.

Doing Your Fair Share

The issue of doing one's fair share raises a key difference between the chickenhawk and the preacher who runs off to watch *Teenage Milkmaids Go Wild!* The preacher's act of watching pornography does not impose a burden on anyone else. By contrast, the chickenhawk's avoiding military service does impact others: because he does not serve, someone *else* will have to serve. Both the chickenhawk and the preacher fail to walk their talk. But the chickenhawk does more than this. He makes others walk his talk *for* him. The chickenhawk, unlike the preacher, is a freeloader: he endorses a war because he sees it as bringing great benefits, yet he imposes the *burdens* that those benefits involve on someone else.

The issue here—of shared benefits and burdens—is one of what political philosophers term *reciprocity*. The leading political philosopher of our day, John Rawls, holds that reciprocity lies at the heart of a just society. My claim is that the chickenhawk violates this value; indeed, alienated war violates it insofar as some expect others to do their fighting for them. What is the nature of this reciprocity?

Rawls encourages us to think of society as involving both benefits and burdens. Justice exists when the burdens of the society are fairly shared by citizens in return for society's benefits, fairly shared. Then no one stands in an exploitative relation to others. This model can be extended to the social projects that society as a whole pursues, like war. War is an endeavor to which the whole society commits itself, involving great benefits and burdens. War's benefits accrue to all citizens. Reciprocity requires that the burdens be fairly shared as well: "Equality of obligation . . . is the essence of democracy," in the words I have cited from the preamble to the Universal Military Training Act.

War has many burdens. Consider how people have approached another one of those burdens, paying for war, and what it reveals about the importance of reciprocity.

Throughout our history (or until recently), a national ideal has been that the paying for war should be fairly shared. In the nineteenth century, this was most evident in debates around paying for war through deficit spending. Many saw deficit spending as immoral because it imposed one generation's costs on another. In the twentieth century, presidents stressed the importance of sharing financial cost. At the start of World War II, Franklin Roosevelt chose to raise taxes before it was needed so that the average citizen would appreciate war's sacrifices in all its dimensions. He made a special fireside chat explaining to the American people that going to war meant the willingness to bear the sacrifice. Later presidents followed suit. In his televised speech of July 1961 responding to Russian pressure on Berlin, John F. Kennedy announced the need for new taxes to pay for the military buildup along with increased draft calls. He was concerned that the buildup not increase the federal deficit. He said of such measures,

> I realize that no public revenue measure is welcomed by everyone. But I am certain that every American wants to pay his fair share, and not leave the burden of defending freedom entirely to those who bear arms. For we have mortgaged our very future on this defense—and we cannot fail to meet our responsibilities.

He concluded with the reminder that Americans had willingly born sacrifices before in the name of freedom and that they should not flinch from that task now.[16]

On financial matters, Roosevelt and Kennedy invoked a financial version of the Murtha test. If you endorse a war, you should be willing to pay for it—today. In the past, *anti*war figures invoked the same principle. Prior to our entrance into World War I, mainstream opponents of that war proposed that if President Wilson wanted to go to war, he should immediately estimate the total cost of the conflict, divide it by the number of taxpayers, and then send everyone a bill—payable on receipt. Again, the thinking was, don't go to war if you're not willing to pay for it. Our federal income tax system originated in such thinking. First introduced in the Civil War and then expanded to its current form in World War I, a principal argument for it was to ensure that in times of war everyone would pay his or her fair share.[17] Our federal estate tax had similar origins. As we moved toward World War I, Congress passed the emergency Revenue Act of 1916, taxing large inheritances. It was concerned about loss of tariff revenue. It also believed that the most privileged members of society should help pay for the nation's military effort. (By contrast, House Leader Tom DeLay stated that "nothing is more important in the face of a war than cutting taxes.")

How we pay for war is a matter of values as well as efficiency. If a people want war, then they should be willing to pay for it. In the first Gulf War, Saudi Arabia picked up much of the bill. This was explained by the fact that the war was presumably defending Saudi Arabia. But what if a country like Saudi Arabia offered to pay for *all* of America's wars, perhaps in return for protection when they needed it? This might be a great deal financially; it might substantially lower our taxes. Still, many of us would find it weird. It would render us beholden to Saudi Arabia in unacceptable ways. And it would grate against the notion that people should fight their own fights and pay for their own wars. If fairness is important in paying for war, why should the burden of fighting a war be any different?[18]

My talk of sharing the benefits and burdens of war requires an important qualification. I have said that the chickenhawk wants to share in the benefits of war without assuming any of the burdens. One might conclude that he is a "free rider," or *parasite*. The problem, though, is that the war may not bring any benefits in reality; its benefits may be an illusion. This was the case of the Vietnam War, in my view. So it would be a mistake to say that the draft-dodging baby boomer shares its benefits but not its burdens if there were no benefits. To mark this fact, I term the chickenhawk a freeloader, not a parasite. As I understand it, the freeloader is someone who diligently avoids the costs of activities he regards as benefiting him, whether or not those activities really do benefit him.

Reciprocity, Iraq, and Democracy

The citizen-soldier model was committed to the ideal of sharing the burden of fighting. This ideal remained strong for much of the twentieth century. Prior to Pearl Harbor, in one of his most dramatic acts of 1940, President Roosevelt pushed through legislation mandating a major enlargement of the army's ground forces. At first, even the War Department and its head, George C. Marshall, opposed this. Roosevelt's motives were military but also political. He wanted to awaken the public to the possibility of war and to affirm the principle that if war came, the burden of fighting would be shared by the public generally and not by a select few. No one should count on sitting by and letting others do their fighting for them.[19] He spoke not of reciprocity but of democracy and its elementary principles of fairness. But the thinking was same.

The issue of reciprocity has been prominent from the start of the Iraq conflict. It is an issue that other voices have raised as one of fairness. One of the more courageous was Nebraska Republican Senator Chuck Hagel. Hagel bemoaned the fact that "we have more than 300 million people in this country, but less than 1 percent of our population has to bear all of the burden, to make all of the sacrifices, to do all the fighting and all the dying for the rest of us":

> There are people serving in Iraq for the third time, in Afghanistan for the third time. They're ruining their families, suffering post-traumatic stress disorder and significant injuries. They're not going to bear that burden any longer.[20]

Another eloquent voice on the fairness issue has been former officer Andrew J. Bacevich. He writes,

It is not "we" who are fighting, and it is not "we" who are in Iraq. Rather, 160,000 U.S. troops along with several thousand other government employees are there. Many of the soldiers currently serving in Iraq are back for their second, third, or even fourth combat tours. "We," that is, have assigned to a tiny fragment of our overall population the burden of discharging whatever moral responsibility the nation as a whole has accrued in Iraq. The vast majority of Americans have opted out of the war, preferring instead to go about their daily lives as if the war did not exist. In practical terms, we have never cared a fig about Iraq; the exertions of our military sustain the pretense that we really do. The inevitable consequence of continuing the war is to perpetuate this odious arrangement.[21]

Bacevich identifies a further dimension of fraudulence with Iraq: claiming credit for caring about the well-being of the Iraqi people while refusing the sacrifices that go with it. He argues that America's war on Iraq imposes a shared responsibility for its consequences. He lists several possibilities: we could create programs for Iraqis injured or displaced by the war, we could issue a public apology for having collaborated with Saddam Hussein in the 1980s and for having abandoned the Kurds and Shiites who rose up against him at our behest, we could offer them monetary compensation, and so on. What are the chances of this? Bacevich continues,

> Somehow, of course, the money to fund a continuation of the war is easily found. Which makes the crucial point: "We" care about moral consequences that derive from U.S. policy only as long as addressing them doesn't require us to make any sacrifice, shoulder any burden, or assume any risk. If addressing the nation's moral obligation entails something other than sending someone else's kid to fight a misbegotten war, then we are not especially interested. That's the dirty little secret embedded in the argument of those who say we should continue on our current course.

Finally, the principle of shared burdens is implicit in one of the most revered principles of liberal political thought: the "democratic peace thesis." It holds that democracies are less inclined to wage war than other political forms. They are certainly disinclined to wage war against each other. This thesis has its roots in the civic republican tradition; Thomas Paine was one of its originators.[22] Why are democracies more peacelike? In democracies, it is claimed, the burden of fighting and paying for war is spread among the citizenry as a whole, rendering them more prudent. Both Clinton and Bush touted the democratic peace thesis in arguing for aggressively spreading democracy to the rest of the world. Ironically, they championed this thesis at the same time that they were undoing the principle of shared sacrifice that underlay it.

Fairness

The fact remains, though, that many Americans do not regard the current situation as unfair. Quite the contrary. What explains the difference between today's attitudes and those that prevailed for much of America's history?

Let's distinguish two notions of fairness: procedural fairness and distributive fairness. In the case of soldiering, procedural fairness involves the question of whether the procedure by which individuals become soldiers is an equitable one. In our post–civil rights movement era, we tend to focus on discrimination. Does our "volunteer" approach discriminate against some groups (e.g., poor and minorities) in favor of others (e.g., whites and the well-off)? I think it does, in ways that raise questions about how "voluntary" it really is. The poor may be compelled by circumstances to enlist. My point now is that there is a second way of thinking about fairness.

I call this *distributive* fairness: is the burden shared equally? To see how different this is from procedural fairness, consider this example. Suppose a fraternity house must clean itself up. One way to do this would be to draw lots to identify one fraternity member who would do all the cleaning. Such a procedure would not discriminate against anyone; that is, it would be procedurally fair. But it would not ensure that the burden of cleaning the house was shared equally; quite the contrary. It is not distributively fair.

Historically, America believed that war making should be distributively fair, not only procedurally fair. Ideally, the burdens of war should be shared equally; there have been disagreements about what this means, but they have assumed this common ideal. If our sole concern were procedural fairness, we could meet this goal with an all-mercenary military as long as the mercenaries were hired fairly. The draft was instituted in the name of distributive fairness, but there are other ways of realizing it. If everyone who favored war took their responsibility for fighting it seriously, distributive fairness could be achieved through volunteer means. But they don't. Many who bemoan the inequities in who fights our wars argue for augmenting the volunteer military with other forms of volunteer service and requiring some form of service from every young person. This doesn't address the problem. If war means everybody doing their fair share, this is not achieved by some volunteering for poverty programs in Appalachia. My endorsing a war commits me to sharing the burden of fighting it if I am able. It does not commit me to performing community service of some other kind.

THE MURTHA TEST

> Look around and ask yourself if you believe that stability or democracy in Iraq—or whatever goal you choose to assert as the reason for this war—is worth the life of your son or your daughter, or your husband or wife, or the co-worker who rides to the office with you in the morning, or your friendly neighbor next door. Before you gather up the hot dogs and head out to the barbecue this afternoon, look in a mirror and ask yourself honestly if Iraq is something you would be willing to die for.
>
> —Bob Herbert, "Consider the Living," *New York Times*, May 29, 2006

How should we think about the decision to endorse a war? My answer is the Murtha test. Exploring it will further illuminate the ideals of personal integrity and reciprocity.

Before I begin, a note to the reader: if you are someone who finds the Murtha test obvious, you could skip this section since unpacking the argument may be a bit tedious.

The Murtha test states the following: endorse a war only if you would be willing to fight and die in it yourself, tomorrow. Thus stated, this test is not unlike what has been termed the "Dover test," first proposed by former Chairman of the Joint Chiefs of Staff General Hugh Shelton. "Dover" refers to the Dover Air Force Base in Delaware, home to the Defense Department's Center for Mortuary Affairs, where the bodies of American soldiers are returned. In 1999 and again in 2000, General Shelton stated that military actions

> must be subjected to what I call the "Dover test." Is the American public prepared for the sight of our most precious resource coming home in flag-draped caskets into Dover Air Force Base in Delaware—which is a point entry for our Armed Forces?

"When bodies are brought back," Shelton has also stated, "will we still feel it is in U.S. interests?"[23]

Presidents have avidly sought to avoid this test in recent years. The first President Bush prohibited media coverage of returning casualties from the invasion of Panama. He was provoked by a split screen showing a government news briefing on one side and returning caskets on the other. He banned any photos of the returning deceased at Dover during the first Iraq War. Such photos have been banned from the start of the War on Terror. When Tami Silicio, an employee of a military contractor in Kuwait, took photos of coffins that made their way to the front pages, she and her husband were fired from their jobs. In August 2008, the *New York Times* self-critically noted that although 221 Americans had been killed in Iraq that year, not a single photo of a dead body had appeared in their pages until that month.[24] Gail Buckland, a professor of photo history at Cooper Union in New York, was quoted as saying that, because of the lack of a comprehensive photographic record of the Iraq War, we are "more impoverished today than Americans were in the 19th century," when battlefield photographs by Timothy O'Sullivan and others documented the Civil War. [25]

In contrast to the Murtha/Dover tests, the chickenhawk logic of today seems to be the following:

1. My endorsing a war has *no* implications for my sacrificing for it or even thinking about the matter.
2. If society goes to war and imposes burdens on its members to fight it, I can endorse the war while doing everything I possibly can to avoid those burdens.

Such thinking strikes me as absurd. But it obviously does not strike everyone so; thus, more must be said about the Murtha test.

War and the Division of Labor

Endorsing war means accepting the sacrifices. One objection to the Murtha test involves how it characterizes those sacrifices. I may be willing to fight myself, but must I be willing to *die* myself? This is an important question, but let me return to it after other aspects of the test have been explored.[26] As I consider it here, the Murtha test speaks of fighting and dying *oneself*. One might add the willingness to have one's children or loved ones fight and die in a conflict one endorses (as I did in the introduction to this book). There are, in fact, good reasons for adding this further element. War is a matter of society's sending its children to fight and die. For every soldier who sacrifices him- or herself in war, there are many more parents and family members who are touched by that sacrifice. Many people would prefer fighting and dying themselves to having a loved one do so. Still, I want to begin with the question of fighting and dying oneself. If one is *not* willing to do this, it's hard to see how one could be willing to have one's loved ones do so. I speak to the issue of children and loved ones in the next chapter.

By far, the biggest objection I've encountered to the Murtha test appeals to the division-of-labor issue. "I am in favor of garbage collecting but have no intention of collecting garbage myself. I am in favor of fighting fires but have no intention of becoming a fireman myself. Why should my favoring a war have anything to do with my becoming a soldier myself?" When the distinguished philosopher I noted in the introduction to this book said that my reasoning would undermine civilization itself, his thinking was that the whole point of society is that we rely on others to do what we don't want to do. Garbage men and firemen (and soldiers) don't want to be professors of philosophy either. That's why we have a division of labor.

I'm not convinced that something like the Murtha test doesn't hold for garbagemen and firemen too. Part of the problem involves distinguishing what we "want" to do from what we are "willing" to do. I don't "want" to be a garbageman or fireman, but the importance of these endeavors means I'd be "willing" to do them if needed. No one "wants" to die in a war, and most people don't "want" to fight in one. The Murtha tests speaks of being "willing" to fight and die if needed. In general, we speak of our "willingness" to do X to contrast it from something we "want" to do.

A more substantive response to the division-of-labor objection questions whether garbage collecting/firefighting and waging war are parallel endeavors. War is a *political* act. This is how our Constitution treats it. This is why it seeks to ensure that going to war is done prudently with the maximum popular input. To say that war is political is to say that it is inherently controversial; hence, our system allows for ongoing debate and criticism around the question, Is this war worth it? Garbage collecting and firefighting do not require ongoing popular input because they are not inherently controversial. They are not political acts. But isn't war *sometimes* like fighting fires—an apolitical act of self-defense?

I have spoken to the notion that wars sometimes "pick us." Our Constitution allows for the president to respond to immediate attacks. But as soon as that response threatens to become a full-fledged war, the Constitution—in theory at least—insists that the political process be respected to allow for deliberation and debate.[27] The distinction between immediate acts of self-defense and war has been drawn in other ways. In the eighteenth and nineteenth centuries, resident aliens were expected to participate in the immediate defense of the country on the assumption that everyone within its borders had an interest in its physical security. But only citizens were expected to fight in formal wars, which were political acts engaging members of the political community.[28]

It was the political nature of war that led the civic republican tradition to *reject* the applicability of the division-of-labor principle to war. War is a social project, pursued in the collective name, a project in which all are implicated so that one cannot be hired out to others. The philosopher who charged me with undermining society itself assumed that every social endeavor is properly pursued via the division of labor. But we do not assume this as a society. Consider the constitution of juries. We do not have a professional jury system; we do not constitute juries by having a select group of people who do nothing else but serve on juries for pay. Why not? If the point of juries is to be judged by a group of your peers, we might get a more representative sample of people by having people who serve on juries as a profession. Would professional jurors be less impartial? Judges are judges by profession, but that does not make them less impartial. Quite the contrary. We assume that their doing it as a profession will make them more informed about the kinds of issues they're likely to encounter. The same might hold for jurors.

Yet we do not employ the division of labor when it comes to constituting juries. Why not? One reason has been explored by political philosopher Michael Sandel.[29] A system in which every citizen is expected to serve on juries cultivates civic virtue among the populace as a whole in ways that a division-of-labor approach would not. If civic virtue is promoted by everybody's doing their fair share of jury duty, the same should hold for military duty. I asked, Why not have Saudi Arabia pay for all our wars if they were willing? Why not hire Canadians to serve as jurors in our criminal trials? They might be more impartial, being from Canada. If one believes in the division-of-labor approach to soldiering, why limit it to other Americans? Why not enlist foreigners to do our fighting for us? This is exactly what we are doing, of course. True believers in division of labor endorse it wholeheartedly. The answer, in both cases, is that both trials and wars are endeavors done in our name. They define who we are as a polity.

Another problem people have with the Murtha test is its hypothetical character: endorse a war only if you would be willing to fight and die in it yourself, tomorrow. Talk of whether one "would" be willing to fight can be confusing. Yet it's important to put the matter in hypothetical terms. There may be good reasons why one is not in fact willing to serve in a war one endorses. A veteran friend of mine has said to me that he was not willing to serve in any war regardless of what he thinks of it since he has already served. Or one may be too old, an invalid, and so on. A full account of the thinking behind the Murtha test would spell out the legitimate grounds for not serving in a war that one endorses. In theory, this was what the Selective Service System's system of deferments sought to do. At best, the question of what constitutes a good reason for not serving is a complex matter involving large issues of political philosophy.

The Selective Service System precedent suggests that there will be no single factor determining who is exempt and who is not. There are good reasons why people may not in fact be willing to serve in a war they endorse, and no single factor seems to stand behind such reasons. But whatever those reasons are, they must be *fair*. For example, they cannot exploit arbitrary social advantages, as the system of draft deferments seemed to do. But what is "fair" and "unfair" in these matters? Doesn't the hypothetical nature of the Murtha test lead to an endless debate on this matter?

Here is another formulation of the Murtha test that might avoid some of these problems: do not endorse a war if there are no conceivable circumstances in which you would be willing to serve in it yourself. The baby-boomer chickenhawk failed this insofar as his acts suggest that there were no conceivable circumstances in which he would have walked his talk. The next chapter explores the kinds of reasons given by today's chickee-hawks for not volunteering.

War and Dying

A final concern with the Murtha test involves its stress on *dying*. In the critique of alienated war, this part of the test may not be necessary. Chickenhawks are unwilling to serve, much less die. Why get hung up on the latter? I think there are good reasons for stressing it, but first some clarifications.

As noted, to speak (as the test does) of being "willing" to die does not mean that one wants to die. Quite the contrary. But talk of willingness does imply acceptance. Soldiers are willing to die insofar as they accept death as part of what they are doing because they regard the cause as worth their dying for. This is why we honor them if they perish. They gave their lives for their country—meaning that they did so willingly if reluctantly. Perhaps we could restate the Murtha test to say that one should endorse a war only if one regards it as worth one's dying for. There still might be chickenhawks who regard a war as worth their dying for in theory but are unwilling to do so in practice.

The Murtha test's stress on dying strikes me as important for several reasons:

1. By raising the bar on the question of endorsing war, it promotes the mindfulness required by integrity. This is especially important in thinking about wars that we endorse as well as oppose. In the 1990s, many progressives supported military actions in Eastern Europe and elsewhere in the name of "humanitarian intervention." As war actions, progressives should have asked the question, "If I believe my government should intervene in country X [Kosovo, say], am I willing to fight and even die there—tomorrow?" The prominent war theorist Mary Kaldor has raised this question for new forms of war generally.[30] Those who call for a global security force to intervene in troubled areas must address the problem of why people should give their lives in such endeavors.

2. Adding the dying condition provides a response to the penchant of governments to *obscure* the dying in war. World War I did not allow

publication of a single photograph of a dead soldier; World War II was not much better. We've seen how recent administrations have gone to extraordinary lengths to prevent photographs of returning coffins. Many said that the events of 9/11 brought the "reality of death" home to us. But U.S. policy since has sought to hide that reality from us. This is what the mothers of deceased soldiers like Cindy Sheehan have sought to protest. The president's mother, Barbara Bush, stated on *Good Morning America* on the eve of the Iraq invasion, "Why should we hear about body bags and deaths. Oh, I mean, it's not relevant. So why should I waste my beautiful mind on something like that?"[31] Beautiful mind, indeed.

Lurking here is the possibility that if people truly appreciated the connection between war and death, no one would ever want to be part of it. Almost 200 years ago, the Roman writer Vegetius said that no great weight should be placed in the eagerness of young men for action "for the prospect of fighting is agreeable only to those who are strangers to it."

3. Finally, it stresses the intimacy of death and war that is obscured by viewing it as just an occupational hazard. Here is another difference between war and other dangerous endeavors, like firefighting or policing. Soldiers, firemen, and policemen all risk death in what they do. But war does not just involve a lot of dying. It *requires* dying—in ways firefighting and policing do not. For firemen or policemen, dying is an unfortunate thing that can happen on the job. For soldiers, dying can be part of the job. This is why soldiers, unlike policeman or firemen, can be ordered to die. I've found that many people are upset by the claim that soldiers can be "ordered to die." It grates against our notions of individual autonomy.[32] People envision suicide bombers, with explosives strapped to their chests, and respond, American soldiers can't be ordered to do *that*!

My point still stands if we reformulate it as something like this: soldiers can be ordered to do acts that carry an absolute certainty of death. A policeman or fireman who refuses to carry out an obviously suicidal command faces no sanctions. But a soldier who so refuses can be charged with cowardice under the Uniform Code of Military Justice. Indeed, some soldiers in Iraq have been charged for disobeying orders they saw as suicidal. If there is doubt about whether officers can order their soldiers to die, it is not shared by officers themselves. The correspondence of Generals Marshall and Eisenhower in World War II is replete with talk of ordering men to die. When General Marshall ordered American troops to defend the Philippines at all costs, he remarked to his colleagues on the burdens posed by a "command to other men to die."[33]

4. Still, some have objected to me that none of this shows that soldiers must be willing to die, only that they must be willing to risk death. One need not follow from the other. I willingly risk death when I drive on the

highway. It does not follow that I am willing to die. Why should the one imply the other in the case of soldiers?

Because sometimes the willingness to risk death *does* presume the willingness to die. Consider this case. You and six others are in a lifeboat stranded in the ocean. The boat threatens to sink from excess weight. Two options are proposed. One is to do nothing and hope that the boat stays afloat long enough to be saved. The other is for one person to sacrifice him- or herself for the others by jumping out of the boat. Drawing lots will choose the unlucky person.

What is involved in endorsing the second approach? Clearly, someone who endorsed drawing lots must be willing to risk his or her own death. But I would claim that their willingness extend beyond this. If you endorse the lottery, you must be willing not only to risk death but also to die if you choose the short stick. Someone who said, after drawing the short stick, "I was willing to endorse such a lottery but am not willing to pay the ultimate cost now that I have been chosen," would be guilty of not understanding what they committed themselves to by endorsing the lottery. Risking your life on a highway or risking it in the lifeboat lottery—which is the better analogy to war? I would claim the lifeboat case because someone's dying is intrinsic to the end being achieved, not an accidental side effect of the endeavor.

Only a very small percentage of society actually fights in a war, much less dies in it. To focus only on the willingness to risk death makes war easier insofar as one knows in one's gut that the risk of dying is really very low, even for many involved in fighting. I would argue that the fact that war imposes such an enormous cost on such a few people makes it all the more *imperative* that we attend to the ultimate sacrifice involved and ask if we would accept it. What if there were six people in the lifeboat but one of them could not be thrown over? Perhaps he is the only one who knows how to read the stars and keep the lifeboat on course. If *you* are that one person, and the question is posed to everyone—"Should we do a lottery or just take our chances?"—how should you think about whether to endorse the lottery? I would claim that the fact that you know that you are *not* going to be the one thrown over, if people choose the lottery, makes it all the more important for you to ask if you would be willing to go overboard were it not for your safe position. Otherwise, your decision is biased by your special circumstances.

This is quite close to the war case. War involves a life-and-death lottery of sorts. Most people know that if they endorse war, they will not get the short end of the stick. They will not have to serve, much less die, because of their age, infirmities, or other circumstances. For them, the decision to go to war is like the decision to choose a lottery, where one knows that one cannot possibly be the one whose life is lost. This makes it all the more essential, in considering the war "lottery," to ask if one would hold the same position if one were not so confident about being among those spared.

There is a classic World War II film titled *Twelve O'Clock High*. Gregory Peck stars as General Frank Savage, the no-nonsense commander of an American bomber group. The inspiration for his character was Frank A. Armstrong, leader of the 306th Bomber Group. The film is now widely used in both the military and the civilian worlds to teach the principles of leadership. It is required viewing at all the American service academies and at the U.S. Air Force's Squadron Officer School for junior officers, where it is used as a teaching example for the Situational Leadership Model. The most famous moment in the film, based on the real-life character's speeches, is where Peck/Savage instructs his bomber crews, "Don't worry about dying. Because you are already dead." That is, you've already accepted death in becoming what you are. This is an unromantic view of war but one that must be kept in mind in assessing that endeavor.

INTEGRITY AND OPPOSING WAR

This book is about what it means to endorse a war. Political thinkers starting with Henry David Thoreau have reflected on what it means to *oppose* a war. The questions are similar enough that it's worth considering how our discussion impacts this issue.

Thoreau's discussion focused on personal integrity. A difference between his discussion and mine is that he did not address the issue of reciprocity. Thoreau's political vision was a highly individualistic one that didn't give a lot of weight to shared benefits and burdens. In *A Theory of Justice*, John Rawls discussed civil disobedience in ways that draw on the importance of reciprocity in a democratic society. Conscientious refusal is not only an act of personal integrity but also a way that responsible citizens contribute to society's ongoing deliberative dialogue.[34]

Endorsing a war commits you to sharing in its sacrifices. Refusal to do the latter commits you to not endorsing the war. Does it commit you to *opposing* the war? To begin with, this would depend on why you refuse to share in its sacrifices. I have noted that some people may refuse to share in the sacrifices of war because they are cowards. It seems to me that if your basis is cowardice, your refusal to serve does not commit you to opposing a war since your refusal does not embody the judgment that the war is not worth fighting. You may feel that it is worth fighting, but you just can't bring yourself to do it. I don't think the cowardly chickenhawk can ask others to do his fighting for him, but that is not the same as saying that he must encourage others not to fight—which opposing the war amounts to. Someone who refuses to serve because he regards the war as not worth his fighting or even dying for *is* committed to opposing the war in my view. If it's not worth his fighting or even dying for, it cannot be worth any of his fellow citizens' doing so either, which is simply to say that the war is bad and needs opposing. The question then becomes, What does "opposing" a war mean?

A notable fact about Thoreau was that he equated opposing a war with not supporting it in the form of things like paying taxes for it. This partly reflected his conception of personal integrity as requiring that you not identify yourself with bad things, which was not the same thing as aggressively opposing them. It also reflected political facts of his day, rooted in the civic republican tradition. If war is being financed by income tax revenues and is not being paid for by borrowing against the future, then refusing to pay those taxes does materially countermand the war effort. But when borrowing finances war, as with alienated war, refusal to pay one's taxes may be a noble symbolic gesture, but it is only that—since the link between the cost of war and the average citizen's paying it has been severed. Opposing a war cannot be a matter simply of not supporting it since, as Randolph Bourne observed, alienated war does not require the support of its citizens.

More generally, a citizen today may credibly argue that little he or she does support our war efforts, like that in Iraq. But it does not follow that the citizen's actions are in opposition to our war efforts since those efforts do not require the support of average citizens. Passive opposition is no longer opposition when the war is sustained by passivity.

In this sense, I think that alienated war increases the moral burden on those who oppose war. This is exactly what it aspired to do in making opposition to war more difficult. I have argued that endorsing a war implies the willingness to assume great sacrifices. Alienated war means that opposing war implies great sacrifices as well.

NOTES

1. James Fallows, *National Defense* (New York: Vintage Books, 1981), 136.

2. Stephen L. Carter, *Integrity* (New York: HarperPerennial, 1996). I have also benefited from Martin Benjamin's *Splitting the Difference: Compromise and Integrity in Ethics and Politics* (Lawrence: University Press of Kansas, 1990).

3. Carter, *Integrity*, 16.

4. Amy Gutmann and Dennis Thompson, *Democracy and Disagreement* (Cambridge, MA: Belknap Press, 1998), 81.

5. Peter Winch, *Ethics and Action* (London: Routledge and Kegan Paul, 1972), 71.

6. Nineteen U.S. soldiers were killed in Iraq the month that Bush made this statement. The day that he boasted about renouncing golf, Army Sergeant Victor M. Cota, age thirty-three, was killed when his vehicle struck an explosive device. He was described by his commanding officer as a man who "wanted to make the world a better place with his life, and he saw being a soldier as a way to do that." Known to his friends as Chico, he was described by a boyhood friend, Aaron Valencia, as someone who loved to sing and dance and make people laugh. He left behind a wife and two young children. Cota was assigned to a special troops battalion based in Texas, not far from the golf course where President Bush had his epiphany.

7. Michael Hedges, "Bush's Focus Is on Iraq as '06 Begins," *Houston Chronicle*, January 7, 2006.

8. Carter, *Integrity*, 7.

9. Carter, *Integrity*, 7.

10. Both integrity and shame are related to *forgiveness*. The shameless person is capable of forgiving himself for anything, while the person of integrity finds certain acts inconceivable because they could never be forgiven.

11. The philosophical literature on shame is excellent, but it does not explore its political importance. James David Velleman, "The Genesis of Shame," *Philosophy and Public Affairs* 30, no. 1 (Winter 2001): 27–52; John Deigh, "Shame and Self-Esteem: A Critique," *Ethics* 93 (1983): 225–45; Gabrielle Taylor, *Pride, Shame, and Guilt: Emotions of Self-Assessment* (Oxford: Clarendon Press, 1985), chap. 3; Simon Blackburn, *Ruling Passions* (Oxford: Clarendon Press, 1998), 17–19; Richard Wollheim, *On the Emotions* (New Haven, CT: Yale University Press, 1999), chap. 3; John Rawls, *A Theory of Justice* (Cambridge, MA: Harvard University Press, 1971).

12. Martin Luther King Jr., "Non-Violence and Racial Justice," *Christian Century* 6 (February 6, 1957).

13. Harry Frankfurt, *The Importance of What We Care About: Philosophical Essays* (Cambridge: Cambridge University Press, 1988), chap. 13.

14. Richard Slotkin, *Gunfighter Nation: The Myth of the Frontier in Twentieth-Century America* (Norman: University of Oklahoma Press, 1998).

15. Walter Russell Mead, *Special Providence: American Foreign Policy and How It Changed the World* (New York: Alfred A. Knopf, 2001), 231, 235. Chapter 7 is essential on this topic.

16. "Radio and Television Report to the American People on the Berlin Crisis President John F. Kennedy," White House, July 25, 1961.

17. Steven R. Weisman, *The Great Tax Wars: Lincoln—Teddy Roosevelt—Wilson: How the Income Tax Transformed America* (New York: Simon & Schuster, 2004); Steven A. Bank, Kirk J. Stark, and Joseph J. Thorndike, *War and Taxes* (Washington, DC: Urban Institute Press, 2008).

18. One contrast is that the burden of paying for war can be spread over a large number of people through taxation, while the burden of fighting a war will invariably be born by a relative few. Reciprocity, then, does not mean that every citizen actually shares the burden of fighting the wars that he or she endorses. It does mean that every citizen be *willing* to share in that burden.

19. Allan Millet and Peter Maslowski, *For the Common Defense* (New York: Free Press, 1994), 396.

20. Leslie Reed, "Sen. Hagel Says U.S. Draft May Be Unavoidable," *World Herald*, November 6, 2007.

21. Andrew J. Bacevich, "No Exit from Iraq?" *Commonweal* 134, no. 17 (October 2007): 21.

22. M. W. Doyle, "Kant, Liberal Legacies, and Foreign Affairs," *Philosophy and Public Affairs* 12 (summer and fall) (1983): 205–35, 323–53; Thomas C. Walker, "The Forgotten Prophet: Tom Paine's Cosmopolitanism and International Relations," *International Studies Quarterly* 44 (2000): 219–38.

23. Mark Shields, "Time to Take the Dover Test," *CNN.com*, November 3, 2003; Robert C. Byrd, *Losing America: Confronting a Reckless and Arrogant Presidency* (New York: Norton, 2004), 144 ff.

24. Clark Hoyt, "The Painful Images of War," *New York Times*, August 3, 2008.

25. Hal Bernton and Ray Rivera, "How Two Women, One Photo Stirred National Debate," *Seattle Times*, April 26, 2004.

26. In *The Rebel*, Albert Camus claimed that you should kill another only if you yourself would be willing to be killed.

27. Arthur Schlesinger Jr., *The Imperial Presidency* (Boston: Mariner Books, 2004), chap. 1.

28. Michael Walzer, *Obligations: Essays on Disobedience, War, and Citizenship* (Cambridge, MA: Harvard University Press, 2005), 102–3.

29. Michael J. Sandel, "What Money Can't Buy: The Moral Limits of Markets," *Tanner Lectures on Human Values*, Brasenose College, Oxford (1998), 89–122.

30. Mary Kaldor, "Cosmopolitanism and Organized Violence," paper presented at the "Conceiving Cosmopolitanism" conference, Warwick, United Kingdom, April 27–29, 2000.

31. Joyce Marcel, "Her Beautiful Mind," *CommonDreams.org*, April 29, 2004.

32. Michael Walzer and George Kateb have noted that the obligation to die that soldiers possess is difficult to square with a certain liberal individualist picture in which the ultimate basis of all political arrangements is a basic regard for oneself. Reflecting on the "absolute obedience" required by the military, John Locke, in his *Second Treatise of Government*, notes that the anomaly is in the fact that while a superior officer can command a soldier "to march up to the mouth of a cannon . . . where he is almost sure to perish," that same officer is prohibited from demanding "one penny of his money."

33. Thomas Parrish, *Roosevelt and Marshall: Partners in Politics and War* (New York: Quill, 1991).

34. Rawls, *A Theory of Justice*, 363–94.

5

❧

"Invisible in War, Invincible in Peace": Chickee-Hawk Variations[1]

We have people serving today—God bless them—because they volunteered.

—Donald Rumsfeld, January 2003

The political leadership of the country needs to expend political capital to make clear that support for the global war on terrorism must come from all sectors of society. Then they need to put their money where their mouth is and encourage their children to join. If this is such a great cause, let us see one of the Bush daughters in uniform. That would send a powerful message. But it's considered in bad taste even to suggest such a thing.

—Andrew J. Bacevich, *The New American Militarism*[2]

What is the responsibility of a prowar youth today to volunteer for service? What is the responsibility of prowar parents to encourage their children to do so? Do prowar political leaders have a special obligation to encourage their children to serve? Do the prowar children of the privileged have a special obligation to do so? Critics of the Iraq War, like Michael Moore in Fahrenheit 9/11, Rosie O'Donnell, and parents of fallen soldiers like Cindy Sheehan have answered yes to these questions. Defenders of the Iraq War reject such talk of responsibility in the harshest terms.

The Murtha test holds that support for a war means the willingness to serve and even die. This chapter endorses the stronger claim that supporting a war means the *readiness* to serve in it if one is able. The prowar youth of today are obliged to volunteer for it or have good reasons for not doing so. The prowar parent is obliged to encourage his or her children or loved ones to volunteer or have good reasons for not doing so. Young people who violate this principle are chickee-hawks. Their parents are the parents of chickee-hawks (rooster-hawks, or hen-hawks?).

These issues of personal responsibility are posed by the country's shift from a compulsory approach to military service to a volunteer one. Questions can be raised about whether our current approach is truly a "volunteer" one, but I will not explore them here. Instead, my focus is on what it *means* to adopt a volunteer approach to a problem like fighting war. American political culture has always evidenced a strong commitment to volunteerism. Yet political philosophers have not said much about the logic of volunteerism. What obligations does adopting a volunteer approach impose on the average citizen to volunteer him- or herself or to encourage others to do so? I've remarked on the striking lack of discussion of these issues with the turn to a volunteer military. Our survey of current attitudes will find them strange, to the point of bizarre, all of which argues for more substantial reflection on these matters. I offer some reflections on how the chickee-hawk problem might be addressed in practical terms. I conclude with some skeptical remarks on reconciling liberty and fairness in our approach to fighting wars.

"WE'RE THE BIG GUYS"

Citizens accept hardship only when their elites are viewed as self-sacrificing.

—Charles Moskos[3]

Critics of the Iraq War have focused on the responsibility of children of the privileged to volunteer. Their thinking is supported by attitudes of the past. Consider the Plattsburgh movement of the World War I era. The years preceding America's entrance into the war saw establishment figures like former President Roosevelt arguing for programs to prepare the country for war, especially for the nation's elites. In 1913, Army Chief of Staff General Leonard Wood conducted two experimental camps for privileged young college men with an eye to training new officers. At the same time, the navy came up with the idea of offering college students a two-month summer cruise aboard battleships to train them as officers. General Wood eventually developed a plan for an all-volunteer summer camp for young men interested in serving and identified two officers to be in charge, one of them Captain Douglas MacArthur.

With the Wilson administration's backing, General Wood sent a circular to presidents of universities and colleges stating that the purpose of the camps was to increase the officers corps "by a class of men from whom, in time of national emergency, a large proportion of the commissioned officers will probably be drawn, and upon whose military judgment at such time, the lives of many other men will in a measure depend." Concern for military preparedness was especially strong among the northeastern elites, anxious to maintain their position as the nation's leaders. General Wood's proposal inspired a group of influential young executives and politicians to create what came to be known as the Plattsburgh movement.

The movement was an all-volunteer effort. Hundreds of men from elite backgrounds in their thirties and forties rushed to sign up for a summer training program in Plattsburgh, New York. They included the thirty-six-year-old mayor of New York City, John Mitchell, as well as two Roosevelt sons, and Julius Ochs Adler, general manager of the *New York Times* and nephew of Adolph Ochs, the newspaper's publisher. It was officially known as the "Business Men's Camp" and inspired the West Coast version under the guidance of George C. Marshall. The West Coast Camp was held on the plush grounds of the Del Monte Hotel in Monterey, California. Marshall's boss would later write that its members included all the blue bloods of San Francisco. "I saw more Rolls-Royces and other fine cars around there than I [had] ever seen collected," he wrote. At the conclusion of World War 1, Secretary of War Baker praised the program. "Thousands of our young men, he wrote, left positions of responsibility and profit, dropped their personal affairs and devoted themselves wholeheartedly to the new business of war."[4]

One of the most famous essays on war, William James's "The Moral Equivalent of War," echoed this idea. Claiming that there was a warlike impulse in young men, James argued for the establishment of alternatives to war, like summer camps for fighting forest fires, to satiate the "martial instinct" by replacing the war against others with the war against nature. The privileged would be especially attracted to such ventures, he maintained, because of their strong desire to sacrifice. James's thinking was typical of past times in holding that privileged young men had a special duty to serve to justify all the benefits they had been given in life. This sort of thinking has disappeared from our consumer elite-oriented society, which assumes that the special privileges of certain groups require no justification at all.

This speaks of the privileged. What of the ordinary, run-of-the-mill prowar youth?

The issue was raised in 2004 at the annual national gathering of Young Republicans.[5] It has since blossomed into the "Yellow Elephant Campaign," the title of which speaks for itself. Queried by reporter Adam Smeltz as to why they were not serving, many at the gathering responded that they would volunteer if there were a dire troop shortage. (In fact, there was a troop shortage at that time.) Some at the gathering insisted they could "do more here." "I physically probably couldn't do a whole lot" in Iraq, said one young woman while terming the war a "moral imperative." She insisted that she could be more useful engaging in political action to support the war and the troops. "We don't have to be there physically to fight it," she said. Others voiced similar sentiments.

The issue was revisited at the Young Republicans' 2005 gathering, when antiwar activists challenged them to walk their talk.[6] The convention's theme was "Supporting Our Troops, Honoring the Fallen." A few attendees agreed with the challenge posed. One Republican activist who had recently tried to sign up for the military but was turned down for being too old stated, "If our president cannot persuade his strongest supporters to serve when our country desperately needs them, then how will he ever be successful to persuade the entire country?" But the vast majority rejected the notion that supporting a war meant volunteering oneself.

One attendee stated, "Enlisting is a personal decision that you have to make. The military is about combat and it's about war. That's what you have to do, you have to search within yourself." No one would quarrel with the claim that the military is about combat and war; that's why it's the *military* and not the post office. This makes it a serious decision, to be sure. But concluding that it's a "personal" decision, of the sort that can be reached only by "searching within yourself," is strange, to say the least. It suggests that the decision to join the military is a moment in one's spiritual journey (it is just a matter of "lifestyle," as I've said). On the contrary, the fact that the military is about war, our most serious public endeavor, means that individual citizens are answerable to the public about it, not just to their inner selves. They are certainly answerable for whether their public positions are consistent with their personal actions. What will they discover by "searching within themselves"? Whether they will be a good soldier? Isn't the military best suited to determine that?

Endorsing a war does not oblige you to serve, but it does oblige you to offer your services or have good reasons for not doing so. My discussion of the Murtha test spoke to the question of what constitutes good reasons in these matters. Let's consider some of the reasons given by the Young Republicans:[7]

1. One senior at Washington State University stated he's "sick and tired of people saying our troops are dying in vain" and added, "This isn't an invasion of Iraq, it's a liberation—as David Horowitz said."

When asked why he was staying on campus rather than fighting the good fight, "he rubbed his shoulder and described a nagging football injury from high school. Plus, his parents didn't want him to go. 'They're old hippies,' he said."

The military is best equipped to determine if his old football injury would impact his military service. This young man's respect for his old hippie parents strikes me as admirable. It doesn't deter him from supporting the war, though, only serving in it himself. For those who support wars like Iraq, attitudes like these only reinforce the importance of prowar *non*hippie parents doing their utmost to encourage their children to serve.

2. Another young man, a senior at St. Edwards University in Austin, Texas, stated, "I support our country. I support our troops." So why wasn't he there?

"I know that I'm going to be better staying here and working to convince people why we're there [in Iraq]," he explained, pausing in thought. "I'm a fighter, but with words." Wouldn't he be more effective "fighting with words" if those words were backed up by actions and firsthand experience with the conflict he supported?

3. The vice chairman of the Georgia Association of College Republicans, America's largest chapter of College Republicans, stated, "The country is like a body and each part of the body has a different function. Certain people do certain things better than others." He said his "function" was planning a "Support Our Troops" day on campus this year in which students honored military recruiters from all four branches of the service.

This is the division-of-labor argument, with a dash of Plato's *Republic* thrown in: different people are naturally suited for different functions (e.g., rulers and guardians). Plato envisioned social mechanisms for deciding where people belonged. The Young Republican model is self-selection. I look into myself and decide if I am a ruler or guardian. This young man organized a day to "honor" military recruiters. Wouldn't he have honored them more by volunteering himself to help them fill their recruitment quotas?

4. A senior from the University of Pennsylvania's Wharton School of Business maintained, "The people opposed to the war aren't putting their asses on the line." Then why wasn't he putting his ass on the line? "I'm not putting my ass on the line because I had the opportunity to go to the number-one business school in the country," he declared, his voice rising in defensive anger, "and I wasn't going to pass that up."

He recounted the pride he and his buddies had felt walking through the center of campus waving a giant American flag and wearing cowboy boots and hats with the letters B-U-S-H painted on their bare chests.

"We're the big guys," he said. "We're the ones who stand up for what we believe in. The College Democrats just sit around talking about how much they hate Bush. We actually do shit."

5. Many others who were questioned as to why they were not serving simply responded, "I'd rather not answer that question."

The month of the Young Republican gathering, seventy-eight Americans died in Iraq. Seven Americans died the day these interviews were conducted. One of them, Lance Corporal Holly A. Charette, was a twenty-one-year-old former cheerleader from Providence, Rhode Island, who wanted to become a marine to "do something for her country." She was popular with her classmates, who saw her as always ready to help anyone out. Twenty-year-old Lance Corporal Veashna Muy, from Los Angeles, California, was the son of Cambodian refugees. He enlisted in the hope of obtaining a college education. Corporal Ramona M. Valdez, age twenty, of Bronx, New York, was killed like the others by an improvised explosive device. A motive for enlisting was to get away from the noise and crime of her neighborhood. On learning of her death, her mother collapsed on the floor screaming and did not speak to the officers bringing the news. Her sister, Fiorela Valdez, said that the family was bitter about the war, which it increasingly regarded as senseless, and blamed President Bush. "If he had a family member there, he'd end the war right now," she said.

Young conservatives do not have a monopoly on irresponsibility. There should be a "Yellow Donkey Campaign" for all the Young Democrats who support the war in Afghanistan but have not volunteered either. I suspect that their replies would be every bit as silly. These are young people whose thinking on these matters may reflect the naïveté of youth; perhaps we should not be too hard on them. Yet our society regards eighteen-year-olds as sufficiently mature to make the decision to *join* the military, with the life-and-death costs that can involve. Why is it unfair to challenge those who do *not* join the military, especially when their views require others to fight? Young people may not think about these issues much, but that is the problem. If we ask some young people to fight our wars, we should have a political culture in which every young person takes the question seriously in ways their thinking reflects. This argues further for the importance of parents raising the issues with their children.

Shooting Elephants

Volunteer systems rely on moral leadership more than compulsory systems. We are inspired by the example of famous and prominent figures to do that which we otherwise might not do. Movie stars, sports heroes, and other celebrities stepped forward in past wars. They helped in other ways, like fund-raising. I've noted that taxes were raised substantially to pay for war in the past, but the government also relied on the sale of war bonds. Roosevelt's secretary of the treasury, Henry Morgenthau, insisted that purchase of the bonds be totally voluntary to "make the country war-minded and give people an opportunity to do something." Campaigns to sell the bonds stressed the importance of average Americans having both a financial and a moral stake in the war, but celebrities also enlisted in the cause. Hollywood conducted a "bond blitz" involving 337 movie stars, many of whom worked eighteen-hour days before admiring fans. Free-movie days were held with the admission being a war bond. Hollywood stars made seven tours through 300 cities and towns during the war. Glamour girl Dorothy Lamour was credited with personally selling more than $350 million in bonds. Another glamorous star, Hedy Lamarr, gave kisses to buyers of $25,000 bonds. Film stars Greer Garsen, Bette Davis, and Rita Hayworth suffered physical and nervous exhaustion from their efforts. Ultimately, the War Finance Committee in charge of the loan drives sold $185.7 billion in bonds, a marketing achievement unmatched before or since. By the end of World War II, more than 85 million Americans had invested in war bonds.[8]

There are not many pro–Iraq War celebrities or ones who publicly identify themselves as such. The list reportedly includes Dennis Miller, Ted Nugent, Kid Rock, Britney Spears, Bruce Willis, Alice Cooper, and Jessica Simpson. Kid Rock wrote a song, "Warrior," to encourage enlistment and chastised other celebrities for thinking they knew better than the president. In contrast to patriotic celebrities of the past, none of these prowar figures have volunteered for the military or offered their services to support the war. Thus far, the most prominent person to interrupt his life for his principles has been Pat Tillman, who quit a lucrative professional football career to serve, a decision that cost him his life. Many were surprised to learn that Tillman was not politically conservative; far from it. I know of no conservative sports figure who has followed the lead of Tillman in sacrificing for his or her principles. Indeed, I know of no conservative public figures at all who have made that choice despite the positive impact it might have had in encouraging young people to enlist in the war they endorse.

Raising the age of enlistment has made this more of an option for prowar figures. Kid Rock is well below the maximum enlistment age, as are Britney Spears and Jessica Simpson. Consider the case of conservative pundit Tucker Carlson, who, as I write this, is still young enough to serve. Carlson is one of several prominent prowar news figures in this category. He has done the most to promote his own qualifications as a fighter.

In "Hired Guns," published in *Esquire* magazine in March 2004, Carlson described an incident while on journalistic assignment in Iraq.[9] Carlson had been invited by a private security firm to ride along on a mission. He was equipped with an AK-47, though he mentions no training in using it.

Somewhere south of Nasiriyah, his band stopped for gas. He noted that because of the chronic shortage of oil,

> every station has a gas line. Some are more than a mile long. People can wait for days, camped out in their cars, for a full tank. We had no intention of doing that. Instead, we commandeered the gas station.

As the first of the vehicles filled its tank, Carlson joined those who were using their guns to stop traffic and hold off others who needed gas:

> There was a large and growing crowd around us. It looked hostile. And no wonder. We'd swooped in and stolen their places in line, *reminding them*, as if they needed it, of the oldest rule there is: Armed people get to do exactly what they want; everyone else has to shut up and take it.

Carlson acknowledged that there were children present, "I'd seen them watching as we *forced their fathers* out of the way to get to the pumps." We had "neutered their dads," he admits but *"We'd had no choice."*

Carlson was apparently elated by the experience of holding a gun on a defenseless crowd, including "neutered" fathers and their children. Commandeering gas, he described his feelings as an angry crowd approached him:

> The groups of men were definitely walking toward me now, talking to one another and looking angry. The crowd behind them was getting larger and more agitated. In my peripheral vision I could see shapes, people darting in and out between cars parked in the gas line. I hoped someone else was watching them.
>
> At the center of the group advancing on me were two youngish men with tough-guy expressions on their faces. They were obviously leading whatever was about to happen. *I decided to shoot them first.* I'd start with the one on the right. I unfolded the AK's paratrooper stock and tucked it into my shoulder, raising the muzzle. Then I switched off the safety. I waited for one of them to make a quick movement.
>
> Neither one did. In fact, both stopped where they were and glared at me. I glared back. Five minutes later, our tanks were full and we left.

What does it say about our political culture that a respected journalist could write such things with so little self-awareness? He was unburdened by any moral qualms about shooting innocent people in the process of stealing their gas. This scene is reminiscent of George Orwell's "Shooting an Elephant," except that Orwell's encounter was meant to illustrate the utter cluelessness of British imperial presence in Southeast Asia. As a police officer in Lower Burma, Orwell wrote, "I was hated by large numbers of people—the only time in my life that I have been important enough for this to happen to me." He came to understand their hatred as a logical response to the callousness of their oppressors. Carlson, by contrast, revels in his self-confidence as a killer while leaving the real killing—and dying—to others. Imagine the boost his prowar cause might have gotten had he told this story on the air as a way of explaining why he was giving up his television position for military service in the War on Terror.

Again, liberals are as guilty as conservatives of hypocrisy on these matters, but the striking lack of self-awareness on the right side of the political spectrum requires an explanation all its own. Bill Kristol is a well-known pundit whose championing of the Iraq War has been vehement, even for a conservative. Kristol did not serve in Vietnam, though he has been harsh in his judgment of anti–Vietnam War protesters. Nor did he question the failure of the Bush administration to promote military enlistment. Yet in spring of 2006, in the pages of the *New York Times*, he devoted an entire editorial to attacking Barack Obama for failing to encourage military service in a commencement address.[10] Obama's theme was service to one's country, but, according to Kristol, there was "one obvious path of service Obama [didn't] recommend—or even mention: military service." Kristol attributed this to the fact that he was speaking at an "elite Northeastern college campus," where he "felt no need to remind students of a different kind of public service—one that entails more risks than community organizing. He felt no need to tell the graduating seniors in the lovely groves of Middletown that they should be grateful to their peers who were far away facing dangers on behalf of their country." Kristol concluded, "He certainly felt no impulse to wonder whether the nation wouldn't be better off if R.O.T.C. were more widely and easily available on elite college campuses."

THE LOGIC OF VOLUNTEERISM

What does it mean to adopt a volunteer approach to a problem? The view I endorse holds that adopting a volunteer approach to a crucial social problem requires that everyone take the problem of volunteering seriously. This does not mean that everyone volunteers, but it does mean that those who are eligible have good reasons for *not* doing so. Critics of the chickenhawk argument hold the contrary. They insist that endorsing a war has nothing to do with volunteering oneself. A prominent proponent of this view has been Christopher Hitchens. He wrote in June 2005,

> I resent the taunt that is latent in the anti-war stress on supposedly uneven sacrifice. Did I send my children to rescue the victims of the collapsing towers of the World Trade Center? No, I expected the police and fire departments to accept the risk of gruesome death on my behalf. All of them

were volunteers (many of them needlessly thrown away, as we now know, because of poor communications), and one knew that their depleted ranks would soon be filled by equally tough and heroic citizens who would volunteer in their turn. We would certainly face a grave societal crisis if that expectation turned out to be false.

This remark contains a number of claims about volunteerism worth distinguishing:

1. If others have already volunteered for a dangerous job, I need not volunteer myself or encourage my loved ones to do so, nor must I give any thought to volunteering.

2. If those who are doing a dangerous job volunteered for it, there can be no question of uneven sacrifice in who performs that dangerous job.

The same claim was at work in an exchange between antiwar activist Cindy Sheehan and prowar journalist Andrew Cline. Sheehan asked, "Why [are] Jenna and Barbara [Bush's twin daughters] and the other children of the architects of this disastrous war . . . not in harm's way, if the cause is so noble?" Cline responded, "The simple answer is: because they did not volunteer for military service."[11] This does not answer Sheehan's question; rather, it sharpens it: why *haven't* the Bush twins volunteered?

3. Hitchens claims that he "expected the police and fire departments to accept the risk of gruesome death on [his] behalf."

This is an odd remark. I might assume that policemen or firemen accept the risk of death on my behalf, but do I "expect" this of them? This sounds awfully entitled, or it regards their lives as rather expendable. One is reminded of Republican Senator Mitch McConnell's remark on the floor of the Senate: "Nobody is happy about losing lives but remember these are not draftees, these are full-time professional soldiers." The fact that our soldiers (or policemen or fireman) have chosen their profession means that we can expect them to give their lives for us. The point is not purely verbal; I suggest that it expresses an important fact about Hitchens's view of volunteerism.

4. We would face a "grave social crisis" if people did not volunteer to be policemen, firemen, or soldiers.

We currently face the shortage of volunteer soldiers that Hitchens feared and were already facing it when Hitchens wrote what he did. But what if Hitchens's assumption had been correct? Would his views on volunteerism be valid? For the purposes of argument, I distinguish two issues: what is my responsibility to volunteer for military service if there are already enough people volunteering, and what is my responsibility if there is a shortage of volunteers? Let me say something about each.

Volunteering and Military Needs

There doesn't seem much *point* to volunteering for something if there are already enough volunteers. But with military service, the matter does not rest there.

Many people believe that soldiers are the "nation's finest" and honor them as such. If you believe this and are eligible to serve yourself, wouldn't you want to become one of the nation's finest yourself—even if the military were meeting its volunteer quotas? I've never understood how leaders like Bush could wax so eloquently about the superior quality of the soldier and not want his own daughters to become one. It's like saying, "America's best minds go to college, but I'd never encourage my own children to do so."

A larger point, though, pertains to the fact that soldiering has a qualitative dimension as well as a quantitative one. If one believes in a war, one shouldn't want just any bunch of soldiers fighting it. One should want the best soldiers possible. The fact that there are "enough" volunteers does not guarantee this. This is best achieved if all those who endorse a war (and are eligible) offer themselves for service and let the military choose from them according to its needs. Given today's military's high-tech needs, all students in elite colleges who endorse the Afghanistan or Iraq conflicts should volunteer their services and let the military choose accordingly. The Plattsburgh movement could be a model for this.

Conservative attitudes are odd on this matter. Conservatives are exceedingly deferential toward the military in how wars should be fought. They assume that the military knows best and reject any second-guessing by critics of the military. But their thinking does not extend to *who* should fight our wars. Here, prowar conservatives maintain that *they* are the best ones to decide who should serve by "looking within themselves" and so on. Hitchens claims that there is no issue of fairness in who fights our wars if those who fight do so voluntarily. It depends on how you construe the issue of fairness. But this raises the important point that the unfairness issue is one that can be solved through volunteerism. This is a fact that liberal critics of today's military might take more seriously. Liberals who support the Afghanistan War but are also upset about the inordinate sacrifices of minorities and the poor could initiate their own "Just Say Yes!" campaign to encourage privileged youth to rectify the disparities by volunteering themselves. This would be in keeping with the Plattsburgh movement's precedent. If one believes in a volunteer military, as most liberals do, taking personal responsibility for the unfairness of that system logically follows.

Historical precedent suggests that the military will always need more and better volunteers. For a prowar young person to assume that he or she is not needed is highly unrealistic. Even when recruitment quotas are filled, it does not follow that there are enough volunteers, given the ongoing issues around terms of deployment. In the spring of 2008, the government reported that 20 percent of all suicides were current or former military personnel.[12] The statistics were from 2005, but one can assume that more recent figures are the same if not worse. The article went on to note, "A rise in suicides among soldiers serving in the military has alarmed Pentagon planners and members of Congress as the war in Iraq enters its sixth year." The military suicide rate increased 40 percent from normal with the onset of the Iraq War.

"The frequency and the length of deployments are stretching people to the limit and they can't tolerate it," Charles Figley, a psychologist who directs the Traumatology Institute at Florida State University, said in a telephone interview. "They're taking risks, taking alcohol and taking their own lives because they want to extinguish their pain." While 38 percent of the soldiers who took their own lives had a diagnosed mental health condition, only 27 percent were receiving mental health care, according to the Centers for Disease Control report. A separate study had found that combat veterans were twice as likely to take their own lives as people who hadn't been in battle.

The military has ensured that there are "enough" soldiers by increasing the frequency and length of deployments. The upshot has been substantial harm to those deployed, like increasing suicide rates. If one believes in a volunteer military and in the war being fought, it's hard to see what justification one could provide for not volunteering if one were eligible. Many prowar young people who have not volunteered are probably more fit than soldiers who are already serving and are suffering the effects of their experiences. This is the proper comparison since prowar youth who volunteered would be allowing those who are already serving to come home. One would think that this is the best way by which they could show their support for the troops.

Volunteerism and Alienated War

Does anyone really know what "volunteerism" means as a characterization of our approach to the military? Many have pointed out that soldiers are volunteers only in the sense that employees of General Motors are; that is, they have chosen the job rather than being coerced into it. But no one speaks of autoworkers as volunteers, so why characterize soldiers this way, except to obscure our departure from the citizen-soldier tradition? A volunteer system is not just one that people enter into freely. It is characterized by a structure of expectations. Consider the case of blood. If a community endorses procuring blood through a volunteer approach, this creates some expectation that average citizens will step forward and give blood if needed. No such expectation is created by the choice to procure blood through market mechanisms. To speak of "expectations" does not mean that everyone must actually give blood (or fight a war). It means that they must have good reasons for not doing so if they are needed.

I have suggested that other people's volunteering is not a good reason for not volunteering. In fact, other people's volunteering heightens the responsibility on me to volunteer if I have not done so. Their act is a form of a gift to me that obliges me to reciprocate in some way. I noted Hitchens's remark that he "expected" policemen, firemen, and soldiers to accept "gruesome death" on "his behalf." To "expect" such things is to feel no *gratitude* when they occur; it speaks from a position of entitlement. To feel no gratitude is to feel no responsibility for reciprocating those acts by volunteering oneself, for example. This sense of entitlement pervades society generally, but it's particularly problematic in children of leaders. By contrast, many children of the less advantaged do feel gratitude. A *New York Times* article of February 16, 2006 ("Army Effort to Enlist Hispanics Draws Recruits, and Criticism") explained the high rates of enlistment of Latinos by the fact that many Latinos in the military are immigrants or the children of immigrants, and this typically engenders a sense of gratitude for the United States and its opportunities, something recruiters stress in their pitch. It quoted seventeen-year-old high school student Edgar Santana, "I get the freedoms, and I can enjoy them, so I believe I have to pay back that debt."

Suppose the Bush twins attended a high school that their father ran. Suppose their father began a volunteer blood drive that they heartily endorsed. Yet neither they nor their father gave the slightest thought to *their* giving blood. Suppose not enough students stepped forward to give blood, and still the twins and their father did not think of doing so. Instead, the father looked for more imaginative ways to prompt other students to step forward. At some point we would not only view them as clueless to the point of hypocritical. We would suspect that the whole point of having a "volunteer" system was to spare the twins the burden of giving blood.

We don't have a draft, and we don't have a true volunteer system. Do we have a mercenary system?

The chickee-hawk orientation makes perfect sense on the mercenary model. When I meet a need of mine by hiring someone to do it, his doing it does not in any way heighten my responsibility to think about doing it myself. Paying people to give blood creates no responsibility to give blood myself. To this extent, Milton Friedman was right in calling it a mercenary approach. But in other ways it does not work by pure market principles. We do not offer financial incentives for soldiers to undertake especially risky ventures. Saddam Hussein reimbursed families of suicide bombers. We do not pay bonuses to families of those who give their lives in battle. We employ a market approach to generating soldiers, but it is not (yet) a pure fight-for-pay system.

This points to the transitional nature of alienated war. The question of what kind of military we have is not a theoretical one. Our ideology of wartime remains very much that of the citizen-soldier tradition and its ethic of shared sacrifice. Supporters of the Iraq War evoke this ideology in arguing for why we must stay the course. We must honor those who gave their lives for us. But if fighting and dying are increasingly activities that are paid labor, just like any other job, it is hard to see why its sacrifices should be honored more than any other job. If a bridge leads to nowhere, we do not continue to build it to honor those who have died in construction accidents. Soldiers deserve honor because they have given their lives, not sold their lives. Yet our approach to acquiring their services is increasingly one of buying and selling.

PARENTS AND CHILDREN

> If most Americans are unwilling to send their children to fight in Iraq, it must mean that most Americans do not feel that winning the war is absolutely essential.
>
> —Bob Herbert, "Sharing the Sacrifice, or Ending It,"
> *New York Times*, December 8, 2005[13]

What is the responsibility of prowar parents to encourage their children or loved ones to volunteer? This was the question raised by the fact that no top Bush administration official had a relative who served in Iraq or Afghanistan. It is raised by the absence from conflict of children or loved ones of leaders from both political parties who support the War on Terror. The response of prowar pundits to this challenge has been nothing short of vitriolic. They have charged that it is totally lacking in logic, yet few say where precisely its lack of logic lies. The most extensive discussion I have found is by Christopher Hitchens in a piece titled "Don't 'Son' Me—End This Silly Talk about Sacrificing Children." I will use it as the reference point for our discussion.

When Is a War Worth It?

Hitchens's piece was prompted by two earlier articles, one by *Washington Post* editorialist Richard Cohen and another by *The New Yorker*'s George

Packer. Cohen's article recounted how he came to take seriously the chickee-hawk issue.[14] It described an exchange with the late novelist John Gregory Dunne before the first Gulf War.[15] Cohen informed Dunne that he supported ousting Hussein from Kuwait. "But when Dunne asked me if I wanted these things badly enough that I would want my own son to fight in the upcoming war, I said no—I would leave that to others." Dunne responded by calling him a hypocrite. Cohen acknowledged that he did not know what to make of Dunne's criticism at first. He sensed that Dunne had a point, yet he regarded the Gulf War as akin to a police action or firefighting. We ask policeman and firemen to risk their lives "to do what we are not willing or able to do ourselves," so why not soldiers?

The invasion of Iraq and the recognition that it had been initiated on false premises prompted Cohen to reconsider his views. This time, the occasion was an article by prowar author Robert Kagan that asked, "Was it not worth at least some sacrifice to remove such a man from power?" On reading this, Cohen was struck by the abstractness of the talk of "sacrifice."

> When Kagan and others talk about "sacrifice," what do they mean? They mean the other guy. This is not actually something new under the sun—older men have forever sent younger men to war—but this war is a category unto itself. It's not only that there is no draft—and none contemplated—but also that taxes have not been raised, and we're not even asked to save paper or aluminum foil or something like that for the war effort. The war is being conducted out there, on television, and although U.S. fatalities are creeping toward 2,000, they are nothing like the numbers from Vietnam (58,000). The sacrificing can continue for years before most of us are asked to sacrifice a thing.

The next to enter the discussion was *New Yorker* writer George Packer with a piece, "The Home Front" (July 4, 2005). The article began by recounting the death of Kurt Frosheiser in November 2003 south of Baghdad. Kurt, twenty-two years old from Des Moines, Iowa, was a Lynyrd Skynyrd fan who enlisted "to be part of something bigger than myself." Packer's article explored the ambiguities of Kurt's father's response to his son's death. Near the end of the article, Kurt's father, Chris Frosheiser, said this about Iraq:

> We need to see the coffins, the flag-draped coffins. The hawks need to see it. They need to know there's a big price to pay. If they don't have skin in the game, they need to see it. And the doves need to see the dignity of the sacrifice. They don't always see that.

Packer continued,

> He wanted to collect Kurt's posthumous medals, his folded funeral flag, his autopsy report, and a photo of the head wound, and take them on the road,

making fifteen-minute presentations around the country. He would tell those who supported the war, "Suit up and show up." He would tell war opponents about the nobility of a soldier's duty. Or he wouldn't say anything at all. He simply wanted people to see.

Packer's article did not take sides pro or con on the Iraq conflict. Nor was Kurt's father obviously pro or con after his son's death. The focus was rather on the sacrifice that war involved. If believing in war means believing in its sacrifices, those sacrifices should not be hidden from us—by hiding the flag-draped coffins.

Hitchens saw all this as rank sentimentality. His reaction was one of rage.

Hitchens had been relentless from the start in attacking those who doubted the Iraq invasion. In July 2003, after returning from Iraq, he spoke to Fox News about such naysayers. Asked how things were "really" going, he ridiculed those who said that the conflict would become a "quagmire." "The press is still investing itself, it seems to me, in a sort of cynicism. It comes out better for them if they can predict hard times, bogging down, sniping, attrition." None of this was happening, he assured Fox:

> It's going a lot better. . . . It's quite extraordinary to see the way that American soldiers are welcomed. To see the work that they're doing and not just rolling up these filthy networks of Baathists and Jihaddists, but building schools, opening soccer stadiums, helping people connect to the Internet, there is a really intelligent political program as well as a very tough military one.

Indeed, he was distressed that not everyone knew this. "I felt a sense of annoyance that I had to go there myself to find any of that out."[16]

Hitchens has been a consistent critic of the chickenhawk charge. It figured prominently in a short book published in 2003 soon after the Iraq invasion, *A Long Short War: The Postponed Liberation of Iraq*. The book was dedicated to Ahmad Chalabi, described in the preface as Hitchens's "comrade in a just struggle" in the ten-year campaign to convince the United States to bring about regime change in Iraq. Chalabi was later identified as the source of much of the misinformation of the United States about Iraqi weapons of mass destruction. (He boasted to the British *Sunday Telegraph* about misleading the United States.) In 2004 he was investigated for fraud, grand theft of both national and private assets, and other criminal charges in Iraq, leading to a raid of his home by Iraqi police and American soldiers. He has since been accused of providing Iraqi state secrets to Iran. Hitchens argued that intervening would "rescue Iraq from mere anarchy and revenge."[17] An entire chapter was devoted to dismissing the chickenhawk issue as "ugly," "stupid," a "silly smear," and "McCarthyism."[18]

Two years later, Hitchens published "Don't 'Son' Me . . ." in response to the articles by Cohen and Packer. He began,

> Oh, Jesus, another barrage of emotional tripe about sons. From every quarter, one hears that the willingness to donate a male child is the only test of integrity. It's as if some primitive Spartan or Roman ritual had been reconstituted, though this time without the patriotism or the physical bravery. Worse, it has a gruesome echo of the human sacrifice that underpins Christian fundamentalism.

Hitchens addressed the Cohen piece first, starting with a summary. "Dunne had said that he wouldn't break bread with a man who favored war but was not willing to sacrifice his own son." Hitchens proceeded to flail away at those who said that "sacrificing" one's child was a condition of having an opinion at all on the war.

> The fathering of a grown male child does not entitle you to exclude from the argument anybody who is not thus favored. A childless person is not prevented from speaking in time of war. Nor is a person whose children are too young to serve. Nor are those of enlistment age, who are unlikely to have sons of their own. Nor is a person who has disabled children. One could easily extend the list of citizens who have exactly the same right to opine on their country's right to fight—or not to fight.

But the issue between Cohen and Dunne had absolutely nothing to do with Cohen's "right" to have an opinion at all. The issue was whether he was a hypocrite—whether he stood by the position that he held.

Hitchens went on to argue that the entire question of whether parents should encourage their children to serve misconstrued the nature of volunteerism:

> When it comes to the confrontation in Iraq, the whole notion of grown-ups volunteering is dismissed or lampooned. Instead, it's people's children getting "sent." Recall Michael Moore asking congressmen whether they would "send" one of their offspring, as if they had the power to do so, or the right? Nobody has to join the armed forces, and those who do are old enough to vote, get married, and do almost everything legal except buy themselves a drink. Why infantilize young people who are entitled to every presumption of adulthood?

Michael Moore asked Congressmen if they would provide their children with enlistment materials and urge them to sign up. This had nothing to do with forcing anyone to act against his or her will. Cohen was presumably aware, as was Dunne, that parents could not compel their children to fight in a war; it's difficult to see why Hitchens would construe them as debating this possibility. Indeed, if Hitchens were concerned that people not be coerced, one would think he would have spoken up against the "stop-loss" policy that has forced young men and women to remain in Iraq against their wishes.

Proceeding to Packer's article, Hitchens continued to bemoan those who say that you can't have an opinion on the war unless you had sent a child to serve. In a subsequent response to Hitchens, Packer noted that he had never said anything of the sort:

> I didn't say that people who don't put on a uniform have no moral standing to an opinion about the Iraq War. Hitchens is welcome to continue having his, and sometimes I'll agree with them. I didn't say that the father in the piece "sent" his son to war and thereby earned atavistic authority for his "sacrifice"; the son enlisted against his father's wishes.

Indeed, no one has advanced the position that Hitchens attacks. Hitchens considered a remark of Andrew Bacevich, cited in the Packer piece: "If this is such a great cause, let us see one of the Bush daughters in uniform." (Bacevich has subsequently lost a son in Iraq.) Hitchens responded by asking, "Can you imagine what would be said about such a cheap emotional stunt?" "Emotional stunt"? Military recruiters have attested to the positive impact such a "stunt" would have. Hitchens then proceeded to rant against those who would see the children of leaders serving as confirming the justice of the war. Again, no one has advanced such a view.

Hitchens seemed upset by the whole notion of sacrifice. The idea that lives are given in sacrifice in war evoked for him the most barbarian pagan rituals. He chastised antiwar activists for endorsing this pagan practice. I share his worries about celebrating sacrifice. But the single greatest champion of such sacrifice was George W. Bush, who claimed that a main reason for staying in Iraq is to "honor" the sacrifices already made. In prowar contexts, Hitchens seemed perfectly happy with such talk. He approvingly quoted the mother of the fallen soldier, Kurt Frosheiser, that "it's an honor to give my son to preserve our way of life." He commended her for being a "Gold Star Mother"—that is, a mother of the fallen whose organization identifies as its aim to "perpetuate the memory of those whose lives were sacrificed in our wars." Then he ridiculed talk of sacrifice when it came from the left.

The strangest of Hitchens's claims was that the issue here threatened civil control of the military. His article concluded,

> Much more important than this, however, is the implied assault on civilian control of the military. In this republic, elected civilians give crisp orders to soldiers and expect these orders to be obeyed. No back chat can even be imagined, let alone allowed. Do liberals really want the Joint Chiefs to say:

"Mr. President, I'll respect that order when you have a son or daughter in uniform"?

This is a startling description of the Iraq fiasco: Bush gives "crisp" orders, and his generals obey. Actually, Bush consistently maintained that he followed the advice of his generals. Since the military consistently questioned Bush policies, I personally would see nothing wrong in a general's asking Bush why his own children were not in uniform. Hitchens was unaware that our citizen-soldier tradition of shared sacrifice, even by the privileged, was a chief backbone of our civil control tradition. In the name of civil control, Hitchens championed arrangements that were leading to a mercenary military.

You Can Count Me Out

At the end of the Bush presidency, the mainstream media finally began raising questions about the children of figures like Bush. None of these were addressed to Bush himself or his wife, who might have commented on the question of parents' urging their children to serve. They were addressed to the children themselves and only in response to the relentless challenges of celebrity figures like Matt Damon on the issue. In an age of alienated war, we rely on movie stars to pose the sharp political questions. Damon first raised the issue on *Hardball* with Chris Matthews, remarking, "I don't think that it's fair . . . that it seems like we have a fighting class in our country that's comprised of people who have to go for either financial reasons or, I don't think that that is fair." He added, "And if you're gonna send people to war . . . then that needs to be shared by everybody, you know, and if the president has daughters who are of age then maybe they should go too."

Subsequently, reporters like Diane Sawyer were compelled to raise the issue with the Bush daughters themselves.[19] By then, the War on Terror was well into its fifth year, yet no Bush relative had thought to serve. Bush's niece Lauren was a runway model, and a nephew, Billy, reported on the lives of celebrities for *Access Hollywood*. Ashley Bush, the youngest daughter of Bush's brother Neil, was presented at the Fifty-Second Annual International Debutantes Ball at the Waldorf Astoria. The proceeds from this gala event went to support the "Soldiers,' Sailors,' Marines' and Airmen's Club" on Lexington Avenue, a residence facility to provide "Service to Those Who Have Served Their Country" (according to the club's slogan). Ashley Bush was accompanied on one arm by Cadet Michael Wolk, of West Point, in full dress uniform and on the other arm by her older brother, Pierce Bush, a student at the University of Texas after a brief attendance at Georgetown University and someone who has spoken forcefully of his support for "my uncle's values."

Responding on ABC's *20-20* to Diane Sawyer's query, Bush twin Jenna replied, "Obviously I understand that question and see what the point of that question is for sure." This was progress, as she apparently disagreed with Christopher Hitchens and others who were offended by the question of children's service. She went on to say, "I think there are many ways to serve your country." But to the direct question—"If the war in Iraq is so noble, why aren't you and your sister serving our country there?"[20]—she replied, "I don't think it's a practical question. I think if people really thought about it, they know that we would put many people in danger." This was an issue raised of Prince Harry and his service in Iraq as well. The British military solved the problem by not informing the public where Prince Harry was serving. They removed him from Iraq when the news was divulged by the American media. The argument that the children of leaders serving puts other soldiers in danger always strikes me as curious. Until recently, it was not considered grounds for keeping the children of prominent figures out of the military (like Lincoln's son or the Roosevelts). Aren't soldiers in Iraq in danger *already*? Having the children of the elite serve alongside the children of ordinary families might compel the military to greater caution, making circumstances less dangerous for the average soldier. In the fall of 2007, the government admitted that thousands of soldiers returning from Iraq and Afghanistan were disabled by posttraumatic stress disorder. A Boston television station reported that the military was shipping many of them back to the front lines in violation of its own policies. Dr. Judith Herman, a psychiatrist who specialized in posttraumatic stress disorder, was quoted, "I don't think it's safe for the individual soldier. I don't think it's safe for his unit either to send someone who is so impaired back into a situation of danger."[21] Perhaps the military would be more diligent in these matters if it knew that the soldiers being redeployed might include the Bush twins.

WAGING WAR: METHODS AND CONTRADICTIONS

From the start, I have referred to the ideals of shared sacrifice of the nation's founders. But this is not the eighteenth century. War and society are different. Many of the factors that made the early citizen-soldier model practicable are no longer present. We can no more return to the founding vision of how wars should be fought than we can return to the New England town meeting. Is all this talk of citizen-soldiers and shared sacrifice anachronistic?

Alternatives

The fact that we cannot realize an ideal in its purity is not grounds for forgetting about it entirely. It is certainly not grounds for forgetting that the ideal ever existed or forgetting the larger thinking behind it. But it is difficult to imagine how a sense of shared responsibility could be revived absent a draft. Specific proposals seem inadequate to the task or highly improbable given today's political culture. Many of them seem fanciful to the point of ludicrous, given the detachment of people from the military endeavors of their government. The behavior of leaders is a persistent theme in the popular media because many people feel that, if leaders were held to higher standards, this might impact the society generally. Consider, then, some of the suggestions I have made along the way.

1. *A "Just Say Yes!" campaign*: Everything about the idea should recommend itself to social conservatives. Such a campaign could enlist politicians, celebrities, and other civic leaders to encourage the nation's youth, especially the children of the privileged, to offer themselves for military service. Young people often explain their failure to volunteer by appealing to their unsuitability for service. A "Just Say Yes!" campaign would encourage every prowar young person to submit his or her name and background information to the military and let the military decide which best fits its needs. Social conservatives believe that private initiative rather than government action best suits our collective needs. They believe in cultivating a sense of personal responsibility as part of this. As noted at the start, they believe that personal responsibility is powerful enough to convince young people to swear off drugs and sex. Surely, it will compel them to enlist in the global War on Terror should they support it.

A "Just Say Yes!" campaign could take the proabstinence campaign model. One of the many websites promoting abstinence is run by the Abstinence Clearinghouse, an organization devoted to promoting the appreciation for and practice of sexual abstinence through various materials. It sponsors regional and national conferences, including events like "Abstinence Idol" modeled on television's *American Idol*. It maintains an Abstinence Network linking together those who seek to inform and educate young people on the importance of abstaining from intercourse before marriage. It provides technical assistance to schools and other societal institutions in helping young people at risk for sexual diseases or unintended pregnancy. Under President Bush, the federal government vigorously threw itself behind the abstinence cause. It invested millions of dollars promoting abstinence to teenagers, 90 percent of whom are having sex by their figures. In the fall of 2006, the federal government announced a new initiative to promote the abstinence message among unmarried people in their late twenties.

Accordingly, patriotic conservatives could develop websites promoting military service among the privileged. They could maintain a military service network providing materials and encouragement to affluent youth to volunteer for war service. Money could be invested targeting elite colleges and other elite institutions promoting a special ethic of military service among the privileged. Contests could be held, modeled on *American Idol*, in which contestants compete in their ardor to serve their country.

None of this will ever happen, of course. A political candidate who proposed such things as part of his or her platform would be seen as eccentric if not mentally unstable. What does it say about today's social conservatives that they so aggressively promote abstinence but shy away from promoting military service? The one is not easier than the other. Given the choice between no sex for two years and military service for two years, many might choose the latter. A problem promoting abstinence is that you don't know if you're succeeding. People can so easily lie about it. This is not a problem with military service. Doesn't this make it all the more attractive as a social project?

2. *Adopt a form of "conscription lite"*: This would make military service more like jury service. It would be a social obligation that society enforces; hence, it would impinge on personal liberty in the same way that jury service does. But its impact on personal liberty would be mitigated by softening the sanctions for refusing to serve. Those who did not wish to serve could submit an explanation that would include whether they supported the military conflict at hand and, if so, why they believed that others should do the fighting but not them. Those who did not wish to serve might then be given a number of alternatives. One could be modeled on European practices. If you did not want to serve two years in the military, you could be obliged to spend four years doing some other form of national service. Or you could pay a fine that would be proportional to your income status or your family's, with lower-income people paying very little and upper-income people paying much more.

There are two major problems with conscription lite as I see it. Throughout this book, I have insisted that if society wages war and if you endorse that action, then you should be willing to share in its sacrifices—specifically, you should be willing to fight in it if you are able. Conscription lite does not ensure this. At best, all it would do is ensure that if you are *not* willing to share in the sacrifices of a war you endorse, then you would not be let off scot-free—you would have to sign a form to that effect to begin with. Persons with no shame might be perfectly happy to do this, however; conscription lite does nothing to address the shameless chickenhawk.

A second problem is that some will see it as still coercive. Many on both the left and the right regard the decision to fight in war as a purely personal matter. I have questioned this view of things on the grounds that the decision is a political one that lends itself to public appraisal. But not every decision of this sort is one for which we are institutionally accountable, and conscription lite makes us accountable in ways that many may find intrusive. Donating to presidential campaigns is a personal decision but also a political one insofar as it engages questions of civic responsibility. But I wouldn't want the government requiring me to account for my decisions on this matter, perhaps by filing written explanations. By the same logic, many will feel that the government's requiring young men and women to account for themselves in matters of military service makes them answerable to the state in ways that are offensive.

War and Liberal Values

Military service poses a problem for a liberal democratic culture such as our own. We cherish both liberty and fairness. We cherish liberty in holding that individuals should be free to do what they want to do, especially in matters involving life and death. Hence, we reject the notion that anyone can be forced to become a soldier; for this reason, we reject the draft. But we also believe in fairness, which in matters of war and peace means everyone doing their fair share. The one expresses the value of individuality, the other the value of community. Especially in matters of war and peace, our political traditions have insisted that the community's defense means that everyone must pitch in. But how do we ensure that everyone does their fair share without employing mechanisms that coerce the individual?

Many assume that there *must* be a way to fight wars that squares with our basic values. There is little discussion in political philosophy of how liberal democratic society fights wars. The discussion that there is proceeds on the assumption that war is a legitimate endeavor, and hence that there must be a way for a liberal democratic society to fight it that does not contradict its core principles. The type of reasoning here is what John Kenneth Galbraith called in another context the principle of "ceremonial adequacy." We assume that things must be all right, so we search for a logic that makes them so. Earlier political philosophers, like Hobbes, Locke, or Kant, did not share this benign view of the war-making endeavor. All of them had serious doubts about whether the military institution, with its hierarchal relations, could be squared with the libertarian and egalitarian commitments of modern society.[22] I share these doubts. The enterprise of war making inevitably creates a contradiction between the values of liberty and fairness, two of the values that we hold most dear. If I had to diagnose the surreal thinking that has come to surround the entire issue of military service, I would probably say that it's a denial mechanism for a contradiction that our political culture cannot solve. Or, rather, the only solution lies in abolishing the enterprise that places them in contradiction—war.

NOTES

1. This phrase has been attributed to numerous figures in the Civil War speaking of that day's chickenhawks.

2. Andrew J. Bacevich, *The New American Militarism: How Americans Are Seduced by War* (Oxford: Oxford University Press, 2006), cited in George Packer, "The Home Front," *New Yorker*, July 4, 2005.

3. Charles Moscos, "Our Will to Fight Depends on Who Is Willing to Die," *Wall Street Journal*, March 20, 2002.

4. Donald M. Kington, "The Plattsburg Movement and Its Legacy," *Relevance: The Quarterly Journal of the Great War Society* 6, no. 4 (Autumn 1997), http://www.worldwar1.com/tgws/rel011.htm (accessed November 10, 2007). See also his book *Forgotten Summers: The Story of the Citizens' Military Training Camps, 1921–1940* (San Francisco: Two Decades Publishing, 1995).

5. Adam Smeltz, "Young Republicans Support Iraq War, but Not Willing to Join the Fight," *Knight Ridder*, September 1, 2004.

6. Kirsten Searer, "Young Republican Meeting Target of Military Question," *Las Vegas Sun*, July 8, 2005.

7. Max Blumenthal, "Generation Chickenhawk," *The Nation*, June 28, 2005.

8. The importance of war bonds was dramatized in Clint Eastwood's excellent World War II film *Flag of Our Fathers*.

9. Tucker Carlson, "Hired Guns," *Esquire*, March 2004.

10. William Kristol, "What Obama Left Out," *New York Times*, June 2, 2008.

11. Andrew Cline, "Challenging the Chickenhawk Epithet," *American Spectator*, September 1, 2005.

12. Tom Randall and Rob Waters, "Military Personnel Account for 20% of U.S. Suicides," *Bloomberg.com*, April 10, 2008.

13. See also Herbert's editorial of August 18, 2005, "Blood Runs Red, Not Blue."

14. Richard Cohen, "The Other Guy's Sacrifice," *Washington Post*, June 24, 2005.

15. Dunne wrote eloquently on the chickenhawk issue and the ethics of military service. See, for example, John Gregory Dunne, "The Horror Is Seductive," *New York Review of Books*, May 29, 2003.

16. "Vanity Fair's Christopher Hitchens on What It's Really Like in Iraq," *FoxNews.com*, July 25, 2003.

17. Christopher Hitchens, *A Long Short War: The Postponed Liberation of Iraq* (New York: Plume, 2003), 18.

18. Hitchens, *A Long Short War*, 20–22.

19. Diane Sawyer, *20-20*, September 28, 2007.

20. See, for example, *Time*, October 11, 2007 (question posed by Donald Pence of San Francisco).

21. "Mentally Ill Veterans Sent Back to War," *TheBostonChannel.com*, November 11, 2007.

22. I have discussed some of these objections in my essay "The State and War Making," in *For and Against the State*, ed. Jan Narveson and Jack Sanders (Lanham, MD: Rowman & Littlefield, 1996).

Conclusion:
The Face in the Mirror

The first war memorials were monuments to great leaders and their victories. Remembering the dead was a secondary concern. The Arc de Triomphe commemorated Napoleon but contained no names of his dead soldiers. They had been shoveled into mass graves and forgotten. World War I saw the first memorials to fallen soldiers, starting with the memorials that local communities created for their members who had gone to war and not returned. They were modest but moving testimonies to those who believed in ideals worth giving their lives for. The modern war memorial is a product of the age of the citizen-soldier, symbolizing the huge losses born by ordinary men and women. After World War I, many countries, including the United States, created tombs of the unknown soldier. They symbolized the belief that when the nation goes to war, the fallen soldier could be anyone. War does not discriminate on class, racial, or gender grounds.

The most renowned American war memorial is the Vietnam Memorial. The idea for it originated with Jan Scruggs, who served in Vietnam from 1969 to 1970 as an infantry corporal and wanted to recognize the sacrifice of all who served and fell. The competition to determine its design garnered 1,421 entries. The winner was Maya Ying Lin, then still an undergraduate at Yale University. The design she submitted centered on walls of polished granite whose mirrorlike surface would reflect the images of surrounding trees, lawns, and other monuments. It would stretch into the distance directing the eye toward the Washington Monument in the east and the Lincoln Memorial to the west. Today, the wall contains 58,256 names of the killed and still missing in Vietnam.

The charge to the design competition listed four aims. First, the memorial should be reflective and contemplative in character. Vietnam was a war that should prompt ongoing reflection about its meaning and the meaning of war generally for the national culture. Second, the memorial should harmonize with its surroundings. Visiting it, one does not get the impression of garish celebration created by other monuments that ostentatiously draw attention to themselves. The Vietnam Memorial seems to engender a sense of humility, of the kind so absent in the Vietnam venture itself. Third, the memorial should contain the names of those who died or were still missing. Finally, it should make no political statement about the war.

The latter was impossible, though. Maya Lin's design clearly makes a statement through its simple, stark character, absent martial fanfare. War has lost its heroism. It is no longer an enterprise for gallant individuals, if it ever was; instead, it is masses of troops slogging through the black mud of the jungle or the blinding sand of the desert—unclear about where they're going or how they got there in the first place.

But another striking feature of the memorial has been little noted. Its shiny black marble surface is such that when you stand up close, to read the names of the dead, you see the reflection of your *own* face. The memorial captures the fact that the dead on that wall are *our* dead. We are responsible for the decisions that sent them there. We bear the burden of the mistakes that were made in doing so. The reflection of our face is a ghostly one. Those who died in Vietnam are not the only ghosts left by that war. The living are haunted as well—or should be. Our wars are a mirror to the kind of country we are. Are the mechanisms of alienated war a means to escaping those ghosts?

In the fall of 2006, *New York Times* columnist Bob Herbert editorialized about "The Stranger in the Mirror." He asked if Americans still recognized themselves now that their government had launched an unprovoked invasion of a small country half a world away and was publicly claiming the right to engage in torture. "We could benefit from looking in a mirror, and absorbing the shock of not recognizing what we've become." But alienated war is all about taking *away* that mirror, blunting the sense that military actions in faraway lands are something that all of us bear the responsibility for. Tombs of the Unknown Soldier symbolized the fact that war was something that everyone should be ready to fight. Today's soldiers are just as unknown as ever, but now it's because we turn our eyes from the reality of who is doing our fighting.

What would a memorial for alienated war look like? It is hard not to be cynical about this. An alienated war memorial would have prominent corporate sponsors, perhaps with phone numbers to call for those interested in fighting the next war. The section of the monument devoted to corporate warriors would be plusher and better appointed than that devoted to members of the U.S. military itself, befitting the higher pay and privileges that mercenaries enjoy. A separate "Lou Dobbs Wing" might contain the names of all those noncitizens and illegal aliens who died to defend the legitimate citizens of the United States. Finally, there would be no mention of the fact that the names on the monument signified those who had died—since this would admit the fact that war involved death.

THE TWILIGHT OF MARTIAL LIBERALISM

Throughout this book, I have regarded military service as a central part of the political culture. The citizen-soldier model, as embodied in the draft, was not just an instrument for generating soldiers. It defined a form of politics that dominated much of the twentieth century but began to disappear with the Vietnam War.

My name for this politics is *martial liberalism*. Let me explain this term. When political philosophers speak of "liberalism," they mean something broader than what it means in ordinary discourse. They have in mind the liberal tradition, one that originates in English politics in thinkers like John Locke and is taken up by the founding fathers as a central part of the American political ideology. Liberalism in this sense names not a partisan point of view but an outlook shared by most Americans throughout their history. It is characterized by its stress on individual rights of the kind found in the Declaration of Independence and other national documents. Many of these rights cluster around the notion of liberty (freedom of speech, freedom of conscience, and so on), and they also include the rights of citizenship, like the right to participate in the political process. Jefferson's insistence that all men are created equal shows that liberalism as a tradition contains a strong commitment to equality. Initially, though, the rights of liberalism were enjoyed by a precious few. All men were equal, but not women; property owners could vote, but not others; and so on. Over time, and especially in the twentieth century, more and more people came to enjoy these rights. And the rights were expanded to include *welfare* rights, rights to things like public education and social security that were seen as the entitlements of citizenship.

What explains this extension and expansion of rights? A key factor was war. We think of war and democracy as opposed. But starting with the ancient Greeks, there has often been a strange link between war and the expansion of individual and social rights.[1] In the age of mass wars, governments could not rely on coercion alone to generate soldiers and mobilize people back on the home front. So they instituted a trade-off where citizens served in war in return for individual and social rights. I touched on this briefly in chapter 1 in speaking of how war in the past had been a mobilizing factor for social change. War's role in creating the modern liberal welfare state is one that historians and sociologists have amply documented. There is a "direct connection," writes Anthony Giddens of the modern nation-state, between war and "the early development of both democracy and the welfare state; citizenship rights were forged in the context of mass mobilization for war."[2] To capture this fact for twentieth-century America, I call its dominant politics martial liberalism. It was a liberal politics in the rights it perceived as precious. It was a *martial* politics in the degree to which the extent and expansiveness of those rights was driven by considerations of war.[3]

By happy coincidence, the term "martial liberalism" evokes the name of George C. Marshall. Marshall oversaw the American military during World War II, but before the war began, he was instrumental in framing and gathering support for the Selective Service Act of 1940. He did so from the conviction that the nation's military institutions must be shaped by its political ideals of citizenship.[4] After the war, he was associated with programs like the GI Bill and, of course, the Marshall Plan, vast social programs that rewarded the citizenry's sacrifices in war and sought to extend the democratic spirit of those sacrifices.

The citizen-soldier ideal stood at the heart of martial liberalism. Indeed, martial liberalism can be understood as built on two principles:

1. *All citizens are soldiers*: Not every citizen was a member of the armed forces. Every young male was a potential soldier who could be required to fight. But when war began, every adult citizen was expected to contribute to the war effort in some way. This was crucial to the Greatest Generation ideology. World War II did not simply engage young men on the battlefield; it engaged the rest of the society at home in manifold acts of shared sacrifice, from growing their own food to saving tin to buying war bonds. Martial liberalism reached its apogee in World War II but was vibrant throughout the 1950s and 1960s, when the nation's martial orientation reached into all areas of domestic life. As a young man in the 1950s and early 1960s, I received a public education funded by defense concerns to keep up with the Russians, I was required to take a yearly physical fitness test instituted by the president to ensure that young Americans were in fighting shape, I was driven to school on public highways built by defense dollars, and if my family had been less well off, we might have lived in public housing that, with the GI Bill, was a reward for returning veterans. And, of course, every Friday we huddled under our desks in preparation for nuclear attack.

All of which explains why none of us found it strange that we would be expected to spend two years or more in the armed forces. As citizens we were already soldiers.

But the reverse holds true as well:

2. *All soldiers are citizens*: Basically, being a soldier meant being a citizen—which got you two sorts of benefits. One was the traditional rights of liberalism. Voting was the clearest example. There were three major expansions of voting rights in the twentieth century: the enfranchisement of women, the guarantee of voting rights for African Americans, and the lowering of the voting age to eighteen years. The first and the third were direct results of wars. Women received the vote after World War I in return for their efforts, and eighteen-year-olds received it after Vietnam for the same reason. The enfranchisement of African Americans was more the result of organized political effort. Yet a key factor was the legacy of World War II and the contradiction in blacks being required to serve yet still denied their full rights.[5] Throughout the century, the notion grew that those asked to serve should be given formal rights. When John F. Kennedy was asked about religious bigotry, his response was that "no one asked me my religion in the South Pacific."

In his 1960 inaugural, a key text of martial liberalism, Kennedy also stressed the link between war concerns and economic ones, like abolishing poverty. This points to the second sort of benefit citizens as soldiers were guaranteed: material, or economic, ones. Average citizens came to expect that the government would not only guarantee their formal rights but provide them with tangible goods as well. The best example was the GI Bill, one of the largest social benefit programs in American history. It was instrumental in the expansion of public education after the war, especially in higher education. War has always played a crucial role in the economic development of the country. World War II completely transformed the West Coast, integrating it more fully into the rest of the nation's economy. Both world wars were responsible for massive migrations of African Americans out of the South in ways that transformed the political culture of the society. The best example of a war-inspired public works project benefiting everyone was the federal interstate highway system, built by President Eisenhower as a Cold War measure. It remains the largest public works project in American history. Even the modern welfare system had martial origins. It originated in the later nineteenth century in the system of pensions for Civil War veterans and their widows.

To speak of how war enabled liberal democracy is not to deny that there were countervailing trends. Throughout the twentieth century and into the twenty-first, the greatest threats to the right to free speech have come from war-related national security paranoia. More generally, while war has extended the rights of citizenship, it has often reduced the meaning of citizenship to support for the state in times of war. Being a good American meant doing what you're told. The upshot can be put in terms of a paradox: as formal rights (of citizenship especially) became more and more extensive, they became less and less meaningful. Raymond Aron perceived this dialectic at work in the twentieth century generally. "In the 20th century, the soldier and the citizen have become interchangeable," he wrote in *The Century of Total War*. The citizen achieves a certain equality in virtue of that fact. "But the citizen soldier is integrated into an immense machine over which he loses all control. Group autonomy, freedom of judgment, the expression of opinion become luxuries which the country in peril finds difficult to safeguard."[6]

Aspects of martial liberalism were present from the start of the republic. The Civil War extended the warfare–welfare link. But martial liberalism came into its own in the twentieth century with the dramatic expansion of the federal government in the two world wars and the Cold War. Its demise began with the Vietnam War. Indeed, I think we can date the beginning of its end specifically: January 30, 1968—the beginning of the Tet offensive in Vietnam. That was the turning point of the war itself, and it initiated a long-term cultural transformation in the culture as a whole. It was just a matter of time before the nation's elites concluded that war was no longer something their own children would be expected to fight. This was part of the larger disengagement of the society from war generally, leading to the situation of today, when citizens no longer think of themselves as soldiers and are increasingly open to the idea that their soldiers will not even be citizens.

CITIZENS WITHOUT SOLDIERS?

> By the end of the 20th-century death was no longer seen as being part of the social contract. War, or the ever-present possibility of war, no longer provided the cohesive force that held society together, and nothing comparable has emerged to take its place.[7]
>
> —Michael Howard

My focus in this book has been alienated war. The larger question we are left with is the alienation from the political realm generally if war is no longer what binds citizens to society.

Oliver Wendell Holmes was once one of the most admired men in America. He is revered as one of twentieth-century liberalism's great heroes. He is the only Supreme Court justice to be the subject of a major Hollywood film. Here are some words from one of his most famous speeches, delivered at Harvard University:

> I do not know what is true. I do not know the meaning of the universe. But in the midst of doubt, in the collapse of creeds, there is one thing I do not

doubt, that no man who lives in the same world with most of us can doubt, and that is that the faith is true and adorable which leads a soldier to throw away his life in obedience to a blindly accepted duty, in a cause which he little understands, in a plan of campaign of which he has little notion, under tactics of which he does not see the use.

The "faith" that Holmes speaks of here is patriotism, the belief in giving one's life for one's country. This is the speech that helped convince Theodore Roosevelt to elevate Holmes to the Supreme Court, so moved was he by the patriotic sentiments expressed. To the average American today, such sentiments will seem like lunacy. These words might as well be spoken by a Martian. They certainly wouldn't elevate anyone to the Supreme Court.

But that is just to say that we live in the twilight of martial liberalism. Americans used to believe that loving their country meant a willingness to die for it. Hardly anyone believes this anymore, least of all those who benefit from the country most. This is an overwhelmingly positive development in my view. The experiences of the twentieth century succeeded where pacifist propaganda failed. It convinced people that war was not a heroic adventure and that the faiths inspiring it were anything but adorable. We are right in wanting to avoid it. We should only be consistent in not asking others to do what we abhor. Our task is to draw the full implications of the end of patriotism in its traditional form. This means fashioning a politics in which the option of war has been taken off the table.

This leaves us with the question of how to understand community. Martial liberalism coupled citizenship with soldiering. Now that these are uncoupled, it is no longer clear what citizenship means or why it should be important. This is reflected in the decline of civic involvement bemoaned by social theorists like Robert Putnam and Theda Skocpol. It is the unacknowledged background to the anxieties about community and its meaning that have been prominent in political philosophy since the 1970s. As Michael Howard writes, war no longer binds society together, and nothing comparable has taken its place. The older ideal held that patriotism found its purest expression in war. Our task is to fashion a new kind of patriotism that finds its purest expression in peace and its promotion.

NOTES

1. John Keegan, *A History of Warfare* (New York: Vintage Books, 1994), 231 ff.

2. Anthony Giddens, *Beyond Left and Right: The Future of Radical Politics* (Stanford, CA: Stanford University Press, 1994), 233. See also Anthony Giddens, *The Nation-State and Violence*, vol. 2 of *A Contemporary Critique of Historical Materialism*

(Berkeley: University of California Press, 1987). He writes, "The military involvements of states also strongly influenced the development of citizenship rights and their connections to other features of societal organization, in ways that can be fairly readily traced out, even if they are missing from most sociological discussions of these phenomena" (233). See also Ronald R. Krebs, *Fighting for Rights: Military Service and the Politics of Citizenship* (Ithaca, NY: Cornell University Press, 2006).

3. On the United States, see Michael S. Sherry, *In the Shadow of War: The U.S. since the 1930s* (Darby, PA: Diane Publishing, 1995).

4. Eric Larrabee, *Commander in Chief* (New York: Harper & Row, 1987), 114.

5. Ronald Takaki, *A Different Mirror: A History of Multicultural America* (Boston: Back Bay Books, 1994). He writes, "World War Two was the transition to the civil rights revolution. The defense of democracy abroad stirred demands for racial justice at home; with peace came new challenges against discrimination and inequality" (399).

6. Raymond Aron, *The Century of Total War* (Boston: Beacon Press, 1954), 9, 88.

7. Michael Howard, *The Invention of Peace* (New Haven, CT: Yale University Press, 2000), 100.

Bibliography

Appy, Christian G. *Working-Class War*. Chapel Hill: University of North Carolina Press, 1993.

Aron, Raymond. *The Century of Total War*. Boston: Beacon Press, 1954.

Avant, Deborah D. *The Market for Force: The Consequences of Privatizing Security*. Cambridge: Cambridge University Press, 2005.

Bacevich, Andrew J. *American Empire: The Realities and Consequences of U.S. Diplomacy*. Cambridge, MA: Harvard University Press, 2004.

———. *The New American Militarism: How Americans Are Seduced by War*. Oxford: Oxford University Press, 2006.

———. *The Limits of Power: The End of American Exceptionalism*. New York: Metropolitan Books, 2008.

Bailyn, Bernard. *The Ideological Origins of the American Revolution*. Cambridge, MA: Belknap Press, 1992.

Bank, Steven A., Kirk J. Stark, and Joseph J. Thorndike. *War and Taxes*. Washington, DC: Urban Institute Press, 2008.

Baskir, Lawrence, and William Strauss. *Chance and Circumstance: The Draft, The War, and the Vietnam Generation*. New York: Alfred A. Knopf, 1978.

Bates, David Homer. *Lincoln in the Telegraph Office: Recollections of the United States Military Telegraph Corps during the Civil War*. Whitefish, MT: Kessinger Publishing, 2008.

Benjamin, Martin. *Splitting the Difference: Compromise and Integrity in Ethics and Politics*. Lawrence: University Press of Kansas, 1990.

Blackburn, Simon. *Ruling Passions*. Oxford: Clarendon Press, 1998.

Blum, John Morton. *V Was for Victory: Politics and American Culture during World War II*. San Diego, CA: Harvest/HBJ Book, 1977.

Bourne, Randolph. *War and the Intellectuals*, edited by Carl Resek. New York: Harper & Row, 1964.

Brewer, John. *The Sinews of Power: War, Money and the English State, 1688–1783.* Cambridge, MA: Harvard University Press, 1990.

Brokaw, Tom. *The Greatest Generation.* New York: Random House, 2004.

Bruce, W. Cabell. *John Randolph of Roanoke 1773–1833: A Biography Based Largely on New Material.* Whitefish, MT: Kessinger Publishing, 1922.

Byrd, Robert C. *Losing America: Confronting a Reckless and Arrogant Presidency.* New York: Norton, 2004.

Carroll, James. *House of War: The Pentagon and the Disastrous Rise of American Power.* Boston: Mariner Books, 2007.

Carter, Stephen L. *Integrity.* New York: HarperPerennial, 1996.

Chambers John Whiteclay, II. *To Raise an Army: The Draft Comes to Modern America.* New York: Free Press, 1987.

Crenson, Matthew A., and Benjamin Ginsberg. *Downsizing Democracy: How America Sidelined Its Citizens and Privatized Its Public.* Baltimore: Johns Hopkins University Press, 2004.

Cress, Lawrence. *Citizens in Arms: The Army and the Militia in American Society to the War of 1812.* Chapel Hill: University of North Carolina Press, 1982.

Deigh, John. "Shame and Self-Esteem: A Critique." *Ethics* 93 (1983): 225–45.

Deudney, Daniel. "Publius before Kant: Federal-Republican Security and Democratic Peace." *European Journal of International Relations* 10, no. 3 (2004): 315–56.

———. *Bounding Power: Republican Security Theory from the Polis to the Global Village.* Princeton, NJ: Princeton University Press, 2006.

Dewey, John. *The Political Writings,* edited by Debra Morris and Ian Shapiro. Indianapolis: Hackett, 1993.

Dionne, E. J., Kayla Drogosz, and Robert Litan, eds. *United We Serve: National Service in the Future of Citizenship.* Washington, DC: Brookings Institution Press, 2003.

Donald, David Herbert. *Lincoln.* New York: Simon & Schuster, 1995.

Doyle, M. W. "Kant, Liberal Legacies, and Foreign Affairs." *Philosophy and Public Affairs* 12 (1983): 205–35, 323–53.

Ely, John Hart. *War and Responsibility.* Princeton, NJ: Princeton University Press, 1995.

Fallows, James. *National Defense.* New York: Vintage Books, 1981.

Farrand, Max, ed. *The Records of the Federal Convention of 1787.* New Haven, CT: Yale University Press, 1911.

Feaver, Peter. *Armed Servants: Agency, Oversight, and Civil-Military Relations.* Cambridge, MA: Harvard University Press, 2005.

Feaver, Peter D., and Richard H. Kohn, eds. *Soldiers and Civilians: The Civil-Military Gap and American National Security.* Cambridge, MA: MIT Press, 2001.

Ferguson, Niall. *The Cash Nexus: Money and Power in the Modern World, 1700–2000.* New York: Basic Books, 2002.

———. *Colossus: The Rise and Fall of the American Empire.* New York: Penguin, 2005.

Flynn, George Q. *The Draft, 1940–1973.* Lawrence: University Press of Kansas, 1993.

———. *Conscription and Democracy: The Draft in France, Great Britain, and the United States.* Westport, CT: Greenwood Press, 2001.

Frankfurt, Harry. *The Importance of What We Care About: Philosophical Essays.* Cambridge: Cambridge University Press, 1988.

Franks, Thomas. *What's the Matter with Kansas?* New York: Holt Paperbacks, 2005.

Freer, Iam. *The Complete Spielberg.* London: Virgin Publishing, 2001.

Friedberg, Aaron L. *In the Shadow of the Garrison State: America's Anti-Statism and Its Cold War Grand Strategy.* Princeton, NJ: Princeton University Press, 2000.

Friedman, Leon. "Conscription and the Constitution: The Original Understanding." *Michigan Law Review* 67, no. 7 (1968).

Friedman, Milton. "Fair versus Free." In *Bright Promises, Dismal Performances: An Economist's Protest.* San Diego, CA: Thomas Horton and Daughters, 1983.

Fullinwider, Robert K., ed. *Conscripts and Volunteers: Military Requirements, Social Justice, and the All-Volunteer Force.* Totowa, NJ: Rowman & Allenheld, 1983.

Fussell, Paul. *Wartime: Understanding and Behavior in the Second World War.* Oxford: Oxford University Press, 1990.

Giddens, Anthony. *The Nation-State and Violence.* Vol. 2, *A Contemporary Critique of Historical Materialism.* Berkeley: University of California Press, 1987.

———. *Beyond Left and Right: The Future of Radical Politics.* Stanford, CA: Stanford University Press, 1994.

Guralnick, Peter. *Last Train to Memphis: The Rise of Elvis Presley.* Boston: Back Bay Books, 1995.

Gutmann, Amy, and Dennis Thompson. *Democracy and Disagreement.* Cambridge, MA: Belknap Press, 1998.

Halberstam, David. *War in a Time of Peace: Bush, Clinton, and the Generals.* New York: Scribner, 2002.

Hannity, Sean. *Deliver Us from Evil—Defeating Terrorism, Despotism, and Liberalism.* New York: HarperCollins, 2004.

Hardy, David T. "The Second Amendment and the Historiography of the Bill of Rights." *Journal of Law and Politics* 4 (1987): 1–62.

Harpham, E. J. "Liberalism, Civic Humanism, and the Case of Adam Smith." *American Political Science Review* 80 (1984): 764–74.

Hitchens, Christopher. *A Long Short War: The Postponed Liberation of Iraq.* New York: Plume, 2003.

Holmes, Richard. *Acts of War: Behavior of Men in Battle.* New York: Free Press, 1989.

Howard, Michael. *The Invention of Peace.* New Haven, CT: Yale University Press, 2000.

Ivins, Molly. *Shrub: The Short but Happy Political Life of George W. Bush.* New York: Vintage Books, 2000.

Johnson, Chalmers. *Nemesis: The Last Days of the American Republic.* New York: Metropolitan Books, 2006.

Kaldor, Mary. "Cosmopolitanism and Organized Violence." Paper presented at the "Conceiving Cosmopolitanism" conference, Warwick, United Kingdom, April 27–29, 2000.

———. *New and Old Wars: Organized Violence in a Global Era.* Stanford, CA: Stanford University Press, 2007.

Kant, Immanuel. *Perpetual Peace and Other Essays,* translated by Ted Humphrey. Indianapolis: Hackett, 1983.

Kateb, George. *The Inner Ocean: Individualism and Democratic Culture.* Ithaca, NY: Cornell University Press, 1994.

Keegan, John. *A History of Warfare.* New York: Vintage Books, 1994.

Kennedy, Paul. *The Rise and Fall of the Great Powers.* New York: Vintage Books, 1989.

Kington, Donald M. *Forgotten Summers: The Story of the Citizens' Military Training Camps, 1921–1940.* San Francisco: Two Decades Publishing, 1995.

———. "The Plattsburg Movement and Its Legacy." *Relevance: The Quarterly Journal of the Great War Society* 6, no. 4 (Autumn 1997), http://www.worldwar1 .com/tgws/rel011.htm (accessed November 10, 2007).

Kohn, Richard H. *Eagle and Sword: The Federalists and the Creation of the Military Establishment in America, 1783–1802.* New York: Free Press, 1975.

Krebs, Ronald R. *Fighting for Rights: Military Service and the Politics of Citizenship.* Ithaca, NY: Cornell University Press, 2006.

Larrabee, Eric. *Commander in Chief.* New York: Harper & Row, 1987.

Lembke, Jerry. *The Spitting Image: Myth, Memory, and the Legacy of Vietnam.* New York: New York University Press, 2000.

Levinson, Sanford. "The Embarrassing Second Amendment." *Yale Law Journal* 99 (1989): 637–59.

Lifton, Robert Jay. *Home from the War: Vietnam Veterans Neither Victims nor Executioners.* New York: Simon & Schuster, 1973.

MacPherson, Myra. *Long Time Passing: Vietnam and the Haunted Generation.* Garden City, NY: Anchor/Doubleday, 1984.

Mann, James. *Rise of the Vulcans: The History of Bush's War Cabinet.* New York: Viking Adult, 2004.

McCloskey, Paul N., Jr. *The Taking of Hill 610 and Other Essays on Friendship.* Woodside, CA: Eaglet Books, 1992.

McMaster, H. R. *Dereliction of Duty: Johnson, McNamara, the Joint Chiefs of Staff, and the Lies That Led to Vietnam.* New York: HarperPerennial, 1998.

Mead, Walter Russell. *Special Providence: American Foreign Policy and How It Changed the World.* New York: Alfred A. Knopf, 2001.

Millet, Allan, and Peter Maslowski. *For the Common Defense.* New York: Free Press, 1994.

Millis, Walter. *Arms and Men: A Study in America Military History.* New Brunswick, NJ: Rutgers University Press, 1981.

Moscod, Charles, and Frank Wood, eds. *The Military: More Than Just a Job?* McLean, VA: International Defense Publishers, 1988.

Münkler, Herfried. *The New Wars.* Cambridge: Polity Press, 2004.

Nash, Gary B. *The Unknown American Revolution.* New York: Viking, 2005.

Parrish, Thomas. *Roosevelt and Marshall: Partners in Politics and War.* New York: Quill, 1991.

Percy, Sarah. *Mercenaries: The History of a Norm in International Relations.* New York: Oxford University Press, 2007.

Pettit, Phillip. *Republicanism: A Theory of Freedom and Government.* Oxford: Oxford University Press, 2000.

Pocock, John Greville Agard. *The Machiavellian Moment: Florentine Political Thought and the Atlantic Republican Tradition*. Princeton, NJ: Princeton University Press, 2003.

Powell, Colin L., and Joseph Persico. *My American Journey*. New York: Ballantine Books, 1996.

Putnam, Robert. *Bowling Alone: The Collapse and Revival of American Community*. New York: Simon & Schuster, 2000.

Rawls, John. *A Theory of Justice*. Cambridge, MA: Harvard University Press, 1971.

Reynolds, Glenn Harlan. "A Critical Guide to the Second Amendment." *Tennessee Law Review* 62 (1995): 461–511.

Ricks, Thomas E. *Fiasco: The American Military Adventure in Iraq, 2003 to 2005*. New York: Penguin, 2007.

Rossiter, Clinton. *Seedtime of the Republic*. New York: Harcourt, 1953.

Roth-Douquet, Kathy, and Frank Schaeffer. *AWOL: The Unexcused Absence of America's Upper Classes from Military Service—and How It Hurts Our Country*. New York: Collins, 2007.

Royster, Charles. *A Revolutionary People at War: The Continental Army and American Character, 1775–1783*. Chapel Hill: University of North Carolina Press, 1996.

Ryan, Cheyney. "The State and War Making." In *For and Against the State*, edited by Jan Narveson and Jack Sanders. Lanham, MD: Rowman & Littlefield, 1996.

Sandel, Michael J. *Democracy's Discontent: America in Search of a Public Philosophy*. Cambridge, MA: Belknap Press, 1998.

———. "What Money Can't Buy: The Moral Limits of Markets." *The Tanner Lectures on Human Values*. Brasenose College, Oxford (1998), 89–122.

Scahill, Jeremy. *Blackwater: The Rise of the World's Most Powerful Mercenary Army*. New York: Nation Books, 2008.

Scarry, Elaine. "War and the Social Contract: Nuclear Policy, Distribution, and the Right to Bear Arms." *University of Pennsylvania Law Review* 139 (May 1991): 1257–316.

Schlesinger, Arthur M. Jr. *The Cycles of American History*. Boston: Houghton Mifflin, 1999.

———. *The Imperial Presidency*. Boston: Mariner Books, 2004.

Schwoerer, Lois G. *"No Standing Armies!" The Antiarmy Ideology in Seventeenth-Century England*. Baltimore: Johns Hopkins University Press, 1974.

Sechser, Todd S. "Are Soldiers Less War-Prone Than Statesmen?" *Journal of Conflict Resolution* 48, no. 5 (2004): 746–74.

Shaw, Martin. *The New Western Way of War: Risk-Transfer War and Its Crisis in Iraq*. Cambridge: Polity Press, 2005.

Sher, R. B. "Adam Ferguson, Adam Smith, and the Problem of National Defense." *Journal of Modern History* 61 (1989): 240–68.

Sherry, Michael S. *In the Shadow of War: The U.S. since the 1930s*. Darby, PA: Diane Publishing, 1995.

Singer, P. W. *Corporate Warriors: The Rise of the Privatized Military Industry*. Ithaca, NY: Cornell University Press, 2007.

Skocpol, Theda. *Diminished Democracy: From Membership to Management in American Civic Life*. Norman: University of Oklahoma Press, 2004.

Slotkin, Richard. *Gunfighter Nation: The Myth of the Frontier in Twentieth-Century America*. Norman: University of Oklahoma Press, 1998.

Snyder, Clare. *Citizen-Soldiers and Manly Warriors: Military Service and Gender in the Civic Republican Tradition*. Lanham, MD: Rowman & Littlefield, 1999.

Takaki, Ronald. *A Different Mirror: A History of Multicultural America*. Boston: Back Bay Books, 1994.

Tax, Sol, ed. *The Draft: A Handbook of Facts and Alternatives*. Chicago: University of Chicago Press, 1967.

Taylor, Gabrielle. *Pride, Shame, and Guilt: Emotions of Self-Assessment*. Oxford: Clarendon Press, 1985.

Useem, Michael. *Conscription, Protest and Social Conflict*. New York: Wiley, 1973.

Velleman, James David. "The Genesis of Shame." *Philosophy & Public Affairs* 30, no. 1 (Winter 2001): 27–52.

Walker, Thomas C. "The Forgotten Prophet: Tom Paine's Cosmopolitanism and International Relations." *International Studies Quarterly* 44 (2000): 219–38.

Wallis, Jim. *The Soul of Politics: Beyond "Religious Right" and "Secular Left."* San Diego, CA: Harvest Books, 1995.

Walzer, Michael. *Obligations: Essays on Disobedience, War, and Citizenship*. Cambridge, MA: Harvard University Press, 2005.

Watts, Steven. *The Republic Reborn: War and the Making of Liberal America, 1790–1820*. Baltimore: Johns Hopkins University Press, 1989.

Weatherup, Roy G. "Standing Armies and Armed Citizens: An Historical Analysis of the Second Amendment." *Hastings Constitutional Law Quarterly* 2, no. 4 (1975): 961–1001.

Weisman, Steven R. *The Great Tax Wars: Lincoln—Teddy Roosevelt—Wilson: How the Income Tax Transformed America*. New York: Simon & Schuster, 2004.

Winch, Peter. *Ethics and Action*. London: Routledge and Kegan Paul, 1972.

Wollheim, Richard. *On the Emotions*. New Haven, CT: Yale University Press, 1999.

Woodward, Bob. *Bush at War*. New York: Simon & Schuster, 2003.

———. *Plan of Attack*. New York: Simon & Schuster, 2004.

Index

About the Author

Cheyney Ryan is professor of philosophy at the University of Oregon, where he also teaches in the law school's graduate program in conflict resolution. He has been a law and humanities fellow at Harvard Law School and a senior visiting fellow at Merton College, Oxford, where he worked with Oxford's changing-character-of-war program. He has published widely in both political philosophy and the philosophy of law, with a special focus on war, peace, and nonviolence. He has received numerous awards for his scholarship, including the Joseph J. Blau Prize from the Society for Advancement of American Philosophy for the most significant contribution to history of American philosophy in 2003.